THE NEGRO ARTISAN

——:——

Report of a Social Study made under the direction of Atlanta University; together with the Proceedings of the Seventh Conference for the study of the Negro Problems, held at Atlanta University, on May 27th, 1902.

——:——

EDITED BY
W. E. BURGHARDT Du BOIS,
Corresponding Secretary of the Conference.

——:——

Atlanta University Press,
ATLANTA, GA.,
1902.

"THE work with the Negro must affect also our work with the brown man and the yellow man. The object is not to train him only to become useful or innocuous, to be a helot of toil, to be a producer,—but under and over all is the fact that the Negro, however unfit he may be now or for some time to come to exercise the political franchise, must be educated so that in time he may become worthy to be in full sense a citizen. We can not endure as a republic if we have classes among us not educated to assume the duties of citizenship. As moral human beings we cannot afford to treat another human being as if he were less than human."

DR. FELIX ADLER.

January 9, 1903.

"WHEN I speak of industrial education I do not mean to disparage higher education, which will provide teachers. The important thing is to give the best education which it is possible for the recipient to use, which will bring out the best in the student."

W. H. BALDWIN, JR.,
President General Educational Board.

January 9, 1903.

Printing Statement:

Due to the very old age and scarcity of this book, many of the pages may be hard to read due to the blurring of the original text, possible missing pages, missing text, dark backgrounds and other issues beyond our control.

Because this is such an important and rare work, we believe it is best to reproduce this book regardless of its original condition.

Thank you for your understanding.

"THE whole country should be grateful to this institution for the painstaking and systematic manner with which it has developed from year to year a series of facts which are proving most vital and helpful to the interests of our nation."

Booker T. Washington, speech at the Seventh Atlanta Conference.

CONTENTS.

A Bibliography of the Negro Artisan and the Industrial Training of Negroes.

African Laborers, Importation of, DeBow's Review, 24:421.

American Missionary, 46 vol., 1856–1902.

America's Race Problems, N.Y., McClure, Phillips & Co., 1901, 8 o. pp. 187.

Awakening of the Negro, Atlantic, 78:322.

Benjamin C. Bacon, Statistics of the colored people of Philadelphia, taken by and published by order of the board of education of the Pennsylvania Society for the promotion of the abolition of slavery, 2d ed. Phila. 1859, 8 o. pamphlet, 24 pp.

Samuel J. Barrows, What the Southern Negro is Doing for Himself, Atlantic, 67:805.

John S. Bassett, Slavery and Servitude in the Colony of South Carolina, Johns Hopkins Press, Baltimore, 1896.

John S. Bassett, Slavery in the State of North Carolina, Johns Hopkins Press, Baltimore, 1899.

Bibliography of Negro Education in Report U. S. Bureau of Education, 1893–94, pp. 1038–61.

The Black North (Studies of Negroes in Northern Cities), N.Y. Times, 1901.

Jeffrey R. Brackett, Notes on the progress of the colored people of Maryland since the war; a supplement to the "Negro in Maryland: a study of the institution of slavery." Johns Hopkins Press, Baltimore, 1890, 8 o. pp. 96.

Jeffrey R. Brackett, The Negro in Maryland: a study of the institution of slavery. Johns Hopkins Press, Baltimore, 1889, 8 o. 268 pp.

A Brief Sketch of the schools for black people and their descendants, established by the Society of Friends, etc., Phila. 1857, 8 o. pamph. 32 pp.

P. A. Bruce, Economic History of Virginia in the 17th century, 2 vol., New York.

U. S. Bureau of Education, Annual Reports, 1870–1901.

U. S. Census Bureau, Censuses of 1850, 1860, 1870, 1880, 1890, and 1900.

Cincinnati Convention of Colored Freedmen of Ohio, Proceedings, Jan. 14–19, 1852; Cincinnati, 1852, 8 o.

Coleman Cotton Mill, Gunton's Magazine, Sept. 1902.

Colored Help for Textile Mills, Manufacturers' Record, (Baltimore, Md.) Sept. 22, 1893.

Condition of the Negro. What he is doing for himself and what is being done for him. Testimony from both races, (a symposium), Independ. 43:477.

J. L. M. Curry, Difficulties, complications and limitations connected with the education of the Negro. (Trustees of the John F. Slater Fund—occasional papers, No. 5), Baltimore, 1895, pp. 23, 8 o.

J. E. Rankin, Industrial Education for the African, Independ., April 2, 1891, vol. 43, p. 3., Educ. 5:636.

E Deloney, The South Demands More Negro Labor, De Bow, 25:491.

W. E. B. DuBois, The Philadelphia Negro, 520 pp., Ginn & Co., 1896.

Education of Negroes, New World, 9:625.

R T. Ely, The Labor Movement in America, Crowell, 1890.

T. Thomas Fortune, Black and White, New York, 1884, 6 o., pp. 311, Fords & Co.

Freedmen and Free Labor at the South, Christian Examiner, 76:344.

Freedmen and Southern Labor Problems, N. Ecclesiastical Review, 3:257.

Freedmen's Bureau, Annual Reports of the Bureau for Refugees, Freedmen, and Abandoned Lands, 1866–1872.

Henry Gannett, Occupations of the Negroes, (Trustees of the John F. Slater Fund—occasional papers, No. 6), Baltimore, 1895, 8 o. pp. 16.

Hampton Negro Conference, Reports, 1897–1901.

Attitus G. Haygood, Our Brother in Black: his Freedom and his Future; New York, 1881, 12 o.

Richard Humphreys, Founder of institute for colored youth, Barnard's Am. Jour. Ed., 19:379.

Index to acts and resolutions of Congress, and to proclamations and executive orders of the President, from 1861–1867, relating to the refugees, freedmen, etc., Washington.

Industrial Capacity of Negroes, Edinburg Review, 45:383.

Industrial Education of Negroes, Andover Review, 14:254.

Industrial Question, Lippincott, 59:266.

Industrial Training of Negroes, Our Day, 16:79,343.

Edward Ingle, The Negro in the District of Columbia, Baltimore, Johns Hopkins Press, 1893, 8 o. pp. 110.

Wm. H. Johnson, Institute for colored youth, Philadelphia, 1857, Pa. Sch. Jour. 5:387.

Wm. Preston Johnson, Industrial Education of the Negroes, Educ. 5:636.

U. S. Department of Labor, Bulletins:
Negroes in Cities, No. 10.
Negroes of Farmville, Va., No. 14.
Negroes of the Black Belt, No. 22.
Negroes of Sandy Spring, Md., No. 32.
Negro Land-holder of Georgia, No. 35.
The Negroes of Litwalton, Va., No. 37.
The Sugar Plantation Negro, No. 38.

Labor and Capital: Investigation of Senate Committee (Blair committee) 5 vol., Washington, 1885.

E. Levasseur, The American Workman, translated by T. S. Adams, edited by T. Marburg, Baltimore, Johns Hopkins Press, 1900, 517 pp.

T. B. Macaulay, Social and Industrial Capacities of Negroes, critical and misc. essays, 6:361-404.

G. E. McNeill, The Labor Movement, the Problem of Today; Boston and New York, 1887, 670 pp.

S. C. Mitchell, Higher Education and the Negro, (in Report of U. S. Bureau of Education, 1895, pt. 2, p. 1360.)

Mohonk Conference on the Negro Question. First conference held at Lake Mohonk, N. Y., June 4–6, 1890, Boston, 1890, 8 o. pp. 144. Second conference held at Lake Mohonk, N. Y., June 3–5, 1891, Boston, 1891, 8 o. pp. 125.

Negro as an Industrial Factor, Outlook, 62:31.
Negro as an Industrial Factor, International Monthly, 2:672.
Negro as a Mechanic, North American Review, 156:472.
Negro as He Really Is, World's Work, 2:848.
Negro Exodus. Report and Testimony of the Select Committee of the U. S. Senate, etc., 3 vol., Washington.
Negro Exodus (1879) Atlantic, 44:222; Amer. Journal of Social Sci., 11:1,22; International Review, 7:373, N. Y. Nation, 28:242,386; Methodist Quarterly, 39:722; Bankers' Monthly, 33:933.
Negro and Knights of Labor, Public Opinion, 2:1.
Negroes of the South Under Free Labor, Scribners, 21:830.
Negro in Southern Manufactures, Nation, 53:208.
Negro Labor, Tradesman (Chattanooga, Tenn.) July 15, 1889.
Negro Labor, Tradesman (Chattanooga, Tenn.) July 20, 1891.
Negro Manual Training Experiment in Texas, Independ., 47:5552.
Negro School at New Haven, Niles Register, 41:74, 85.
The Negro Skilled Laborer in the South, Tradesman (Chattanooga, Tenn.) Oct. 15, 1902.
Frederick Law Olmstead, A Journey in the Back Country, N. Y., 1856.
Frederick Law Olmstead, A Journey in the Seaboard Slave States, N. Y., 1856.
Frederick Law Olmstead, A Journey Through Texas, N. Y., 1857.
Edward L. Pierce, The Freedmen at Port Royal, Atlantic, 12:291.
T. V. Powderly, Thirty Years of Labor, 1889, 693 pp.
Publications of Atlanta University, 7 numbers, Atlanta, 1896–1902.
Report of the Industrial Commission on the Relations and Conditions of Capital and Labor, etc., 19 volumes, Washington, 1901. (Consult especially Volumes VII, VIII, XII, XIV and XVII.)
Report of the Condition of the Colored People of Cincinnati, 1835.
Albert Shaw, Negro Progress on the Tuskegee Plan, Rev. of Revs., 9:436.
Social Condition of Negroes Before the War, Conservative Review, 3:211.
Southern Workman, 31 volumes, 1871–1902.
Henry Talbot, Manual Training, Art and the Negro, An Experiment. (Reprinted from the Pub. Sch. Journal, 1894.) 16 o. pp. 34.
Trade Schools for Negroes, American, 19:353.
Of the Training of Black Men, Atlantic, 90:289.
Trustees of the John F. Slater Fund, Occasional Papers, 10 numbers, Baltimore, 1891–1897. (Nos. 1–6, partly reprinted in Report U. S. Bureau of Education, 1894–95, chapter 32.)
Twenty-two Years' Work of the Hampton Normal and Agricultural Institute, etc., Hampton, 1891, 8 o. pp. 57.
Booker T. Washington, Address delivered at the opening of Atlanta Exposition, Sept. 18, 1895, "Atlanta Constitution," Sept. 19, 1895.
Booker T. Washington, Future of the American Negro, Boston, 1897.
Booker T. Washington, Up From Slavery, N. Y., 1901.
Carroll D. Wright, The Industrial Evolution of the United States, Chatauqua, 1897, 362 pp.
R. R. Wright, The Negro as an Inventor, A. M. E. Ch. Review, 2:397.
G. W. Williams, History of the Negro Race in America, 2 vol. in one, 481–611 pp. Putnam's, 1882.

TO THE READER.

This study is intended for the general reader, the student of social questions and the special student of the Negro problems.

The *general reader* will find the most interesting material in sections 2, 3, 5, 11, 14, 15, 21, 29, 30, 52, 53, 59, 61, 63 and 64. The chief conclusions of the study may be found by a hurried reader in sections 14, 15, 52, 53, 59, and 63.

The *student* of social questions will find food for thought in nearly all but the purely statistical parts; he is recommended to sections 2, 3, 5, 7, 9, 11, 13, 14, 15, 16, 17, 19, 20, 21, 22, 23, 26, 27, 28, 29, 30, 36, 38, 40, 44, 48, 49, 51, 52, 53, 54, 55, 56, 57, 58, 59, 61, 62, 63, and 64.

The *special student* of the Negro problems will find that the whole study has been arranged primarily for his needs, and by aid of the table of contents, index, and bibliography his use of the results has been made as easy as possible. Errors will undoubtedly be found and in such case the editor would be very thankful for specific information.

Introduction.

THE ATLANTA CONFERENCE.

FOR the past six years Atlanta University has conducted through its annual Negro Conferences a series of studies into certain aspects of the Negro problems. The results of these conferences put into pamphlet form and distributed at a nominal price have been widely quoted and used. Certainly the wisdom of President Horace Bumstead and Mr. George G. Bradford in establishing the conferences, and the co-operation of graduates of Atlanta, Fisk, Howard, Lincoln, Hampton, Tuskegee, Meharry, and other institutions, has been amply vindicated and rewarded by the collection and publication of much valuable material relating to the health of Negroes, their social condition, their efforts at social reform, their business enterprises, their institutions for higher training, and their common schools.

Notwithstanding this success the further prosecution of these important studies is greatly hampered by the lack of funds. With meagre appropriations for expenses, lack of clerical help and necessary apparatus, the Conference cannot cope properly with the vast field of work before it.

Studies of this kind do not naturally appeal to the general public, but rather to the interested few and to students. Nevertheless there ought to be growing in this land a general conviction that a careful study of the condition and needs of the Negro population—a study conducted with scientific calm and accuracy, and removed so far as possible from prejudice or partisan bias—that such a study is necessary and worthy of liberal support. The twelfth census has, let us hope, set at rest silly predictions of the dying out of the Negro in any reasonably near future. The nine million Negroes here in the land, increasing steadily at the rate of over 150,000 a year, are destined to be part and parcel of the Nation for many a day if not forever. We must no longer guess at their condition, we must know it. We must not experiment blindly and wildly, trusting to our proverbial good luck, but like rational, civilized, philanthropic men, spend time and money in finding what can be done before we attempt to do it. Americans must learn that in social reform as well as in other rational endeavors, wish and prejudice must be sternly guided by knowledge, else it is bound to blunder, if not to fail.

We appeal therefore to those who think it worth while to study this, the greatest group of social problems that has ever faced the Nation, for substantial aid and encouragement in the further prosecution of the work of the Atlanta Conference.

SOCIOLOGICAL WORK AT ATLANTA UNIVERSITY.

The work of social study at Atlanta University falls under six heads:

A. *Sociological Laboratory.*

The work in the department of Economics and History aims not only at mental discipline but also at familiarizing students with the great economic and social problems of the day. It is hoped that thus they may be able to apply broad and careful knowledge to the solution of the many intricate social questions affecting the Negro in the South. The department aims, therefore, at training in good, intelligent citizenship; at a thorough comprehension of the chief problems of wealth, work and wages; at a fair knowledge of the objects and methods of social reform; and with the more advanced students, at special research work in the great laboratory of social phenomena, which surrounds this institution.

The more advanced courses of study now offered include:

Modern European History (1 year).

Economics (2 terms).

Political Science (1 term).

Sociology, with special reference to the Negro (1 year).

Instruction is given by means of a special class room library with reference books and the leading text books, the arranging of charts and tabular work, the presentation at regular intervals of special reports and theses, and field work in and about the city of Atlanta for the observation of economic and social conditions. The aim is gradually to equip a library and laboratory of sociology which will be of the highest value for instruction and training. Contributions to the laboratory for general or specific objects are greatly needed.

B. *General Publications.*

Members of the Department of Sociology of this Institution have, from time to time, published the following studies and essays on various phases of the Negro problem:

Suppression of the Slave Trade, 335 pp., Longmans, 1896.

The Philadelphia Negro, 520 pp., Ginn & Co., 1899.

The Negroes of Farmville, Va., 38 pp., Bulletin U. S. Department of Labor, January, 1898.

Condition of the Negro in Various Cities, 112 pp., Bulletin U. S. Department of Labor, May, 1897.

The Negro in the Black Belt, 17 pp., Bulletin U. S. Department of Labor, May, 1899.

The Study of the Negro Problems, 21 pp., Publications of the American Academy of Political and Social Science, No. 219.

Strivings of the Negro People, *Atlantic Monthly,* August, 1896.

A Negro Schoolmaster in the New South, *Atlantic Monthly,* January, 1899.

The Negro and Crime, *Independent,* May 18, 1896.

The Conservation of Races, 16 pp., Publications of the American Negro Academy, No. 2.

The American Negro at Paris, *Review of Reviews*, November, 1900.

Careers Open to College-bred Negroes, 14 pp., Nashville, 1899.

The Suffrage Fight in Georgia, *Independent*, November 30, 1899.

The Twelfth Census and the Negro Problems, *Southern Workman*, May, 1900.

The Evolution of Negro Leadership, (a review of Washington's "Up from Slavery,") *Dial*, July 16, 1901.

The Storm and Stress in the Black World, (a review of Thomas' "American Negro,") *Dial*, April 16, 1901.

The Savings of Black Georgia, *Outlook*, September 14, 1901.

The Relation of the Negroes to the Whites in the South, Publications of American Academy of Social and Political Science, No. 311. (Reprinted in America's Race Problems, McClure, Phillips & Co., 1901.)

The Negro Land-holder in Georgia, 130 pp., Bulletin of U. S. Department of Labor, No. 35.

The Negro as He Really Is, *World's Work*, June, 1901.

The Freedmen's Bureau, *Atlantic Monthly*, March, 1801.

The Spawn of Slavery, *Missionary Review*, October, 1901.

The Religion of the American Negro, *New World*, December, 1900.

Results of Ten Tuskegee Conferences, *Harper's Weekly*, June 22, 1901.

The Burden of Negro Schooling, *Independent*, July 18, 1901.

The Housing of the Negro, *Southern Workman*, July, September, October, November, December, 1901, and February, 1902.

The Opening of the Library, *Independent*, April 3, 1902.

Of the Training of Black Men, *Atlantic Monthly*, September, 1902.

Hopeful Signs for the Negro, *Advance*, October 4, 1902.

C. University Publications.

The regular University publications are as follows:

Annual Catalogue, 1870–1902.

Bulletin of Atlanta University, 4 pp., monthly; 25 cents per year.

No. 1. Mortality of Negroes, 51 pp., 1896, (out of print.)

No. 2. Social and Physical Condition of Negroes, 86 pp., 1897; 50 cents.

No. 3. Some Efforts of American Negroes for Social Betterment, 66 pp., 1898; 50 cents.

No. 4. The Negro in Business, 78 pp., 1899; 50 cents.

No. 5. The College-Bred Negro, 115 pp., 1900, (out of print;) 2nd edition, abridged, 1902, 32 pp., 25 cents.

No. 6. The Negro Common School, 120 pp., 1901; 25 cents.

No. 7. The Negro Artisan, 1902; 25 cents.

Select Bibliography of the American Negro, for general readers, second revised edition, 1901; 10 cents.

Atlanta University Leaflets, 15 numbers; free.

D. Bureau of Information.

The Corresponding Secretary of the Atlanta Conference undertakes, upon request, to furnish correspondents with information upon any phases of the Negro problem, so far as he is able; or he points out such sources as exist from which accurate data may be obtained. No charge is made for this work except for actual expenses incurred. During the past years the United States Government, professors in several Northern and Southern institutions, students of sociology, philanthropic societies and workers, and many private persons, have taken advantage of this bureau. A column of "Notes and Queries" is published monthly in the *Bulletin*.

E. The Lecture Bureau.

The department has for some time furnished lectures on various subjects connected with the history and condition of the American Negro, and upon other sociological and historical subjects. School duties do not admit of the acceptance of all invitations, but so far as possible we are glad to extend this part of the work. Expenses must in all cases be paid and usually a small honorarium in addition, although this latter is often contributed to any worthy cause. During the past few years lectures have been given before the

Twentieth Century Club of Boston.
The Unitarian Club of New York.
The American Academy of Political and Social Science.
The American Society for the Extension of University Teaching.
The American Negro Academy.
Hampton Institute.
Fisk University.
Cooper Union, New York City, etc., etc.

F. The Annual Meeting of the Conference.

The results of each annual investigation are first reported in May of each year to a meeting of the Negro conference which assembles at the University. It is then discussed and afterward edited and printed the following fall. The attendance at these conferences is largely made up of local city Negroes, although Southern whites are always on the programme and visitors from abroad are usually present. An attempt is made here especially to encourage practical movements for social betterment, and many such enterprises have had their inception here.

Proceedings of the Seventh Atlanta Conference.

TUESDAY, May 27, at 10:00 a. m.

SYMPOSIUM: "The Condition of Negro Artisans."

Texas—Mr. Elijah H. Holmes, of Prairie View State Normal School, Texas.

Memphis, Tenn.—Mr. H. N. Lee, of LeMoyne Institute, Tennessee.

Atlanta, Ga.—Mr. Alexander Hamilton, Jr., of the firm of Hamilton & Son, building contractors.

At 3:30 p. m.

Miss Lucy C. Laney, of Haines Institute, Ga., presiding.

SUBJECT: "Boy and Girl Artisans in the Home."

Music by Orphans from the Carrie Steele Orphanage.

1. Music.
2. Opening Remarks, by the Chairman.
3. Symposium of Five-minute Speeches.
   Mrs. M. A. Ford, of Morris Brown College.
   Miss E. O. Werden, of Spelman Seminary.
   Miss R. L. Wolfe, of the Atlanta Kindergarten.
   Mrs. J. R. Porter, President of the Woman's Club.
4. Music.
5. Symposium of Five-minute Speeches.
   Mrs. Isabella W. Parks, of South Atlanta.
   Mrs. S. S. Butler, of Atlanta.
   Mrs. Geo. W. White, of Atlanta.
   Miss Anna E. Hall, Deaconess, M. E. Church.
6. Artisans in the Homes: Answers from 600 school children.
   By the Secretary.
7. Music.

At 8:00 p. m.

SUBJECT: "The Negro Artisan."

Opening Remarks—President Horace Bumstead.

The Industrial Settlement—Mr. William E. Benson, of the Dixie Industrial Company, Kowaliga, Ala.

The Trades School—Major R. R. Moton, of Hampton Institute, Va.

The Higher Education and the Industries—President J. G. Merrill, of Fisk University, Tenn.

The Trades Union Movement—Hon. C. C. Houston, Secretary of the State Federation of Labor and member of the Legislature of Georgia.

Closing Remarks—Mr. Booker T. Washington, of Tuskegee Institute, Ala.

Among other things Mr. Washington said:

"For several years I have watched with keen interest and appreciation the work of these annual conferences, and the whole country should be grateful to this institution for the painstaking and systematic manner with which it has developed from year to year a series of facts which are proving most vital and helpful to the interests of our nation. The work that Dr. DuBois is doing will stand for years as a monument to his ability, wisdom and faithfulness.

* * * * * * * * * *

"I hope you will excuse me if, for a few moments, I seek to discuss the occupation of our people in a broader way than the narrower one suggested by the subject under discussion at this conference. I want to say as a foundation for my remarks that my belief is that the proper way to begin in the development of a race would be the same as with an individual. The proper place to begin to develop an individual is just where the individual is. We can begin in no wiser way to develop any race than by beginning just where that race finds itself at the moment of beginning.

"I think you will agree with me when I assert that by far the largest proportion of our people are engaged in some form of agriculture, are engaged in the cultivation of the soil. Since the bulk of our people are to live out of the soil, are accustomed to agricultural life, it is my opinion that agriculture should be made the chief industry for our people, at least for a long period of years. The Negro should be encouraged to own and cultivate the soil; in a word, as a rule, should be encouraged to remain in the country districts. The Negro is at his best in most cases when in agricultural life; in too many cases he is at his worst in contact with city life. Of course, out of agriculture, the fundamental industry, will grow most, if not all, of the most skilled occupations with which, I understand, this conference is now specifically dealing.

"In order that the Negro may be induced to remain in the country districts, we should see to it that life is made not only bearable and safe but attractive and comfortable. We cannot expect our people to remain in the country when they can send their children to school but four months in a year, when by moving to a city they can keep their children in school eight or nine months. Nor can we expect them to remain in the country districts unless they are are assured of the same protection of life and property that is guaranteed to them in the cities. Nor can we expect them to remain upon the soil if we are to let them understand that by agriculture is meant simply drudgery, ignorance and unskilled methods of labor. From the beginning of time agriculture has constituted the main foundation upon which all races have grown strong and useful.

"Our knowledge must be harnessed to the things of real life. I want to see more of our educated young men and women take hold in a downright, earnest, practical manner of the fundamental, primary, wealth-producing occupations that constitute the prosperity of every people. I would much rather see a young colored man graduate from college and go out and start a truck garden, a dairy farm, or conduct a cotton plantation, and thus become a first-hand producer of wealth, rather than a parasite living upon the wealth originally produced by others, seeking uncertain and unsatisfactory livelihood in temporary and questionable positions. I repeat, do not seek positions but create positions. All people who gained wealth and recognition have come up through the soil and have given attention to these fundamental wealth-producing industries. The young man who goes out into the forest, fells a tree and produces a wagon is the one who has added something to the wealth of the community in which he lives.

"I emphasize the ownership and cultivation of the soil, because land is cheaper in the South than it will ever be again, and if we do not get hold of a portion of the soil and use it in laying a foundation for our civilization now, I fear we will not get hold of it in the future. In the country the Negro and his children are free, as a rule, from the temptations which drag so many down in the large cities. The Negro is there always free, too, from the severe competition which, in so many cases, discourages and overmasters him.

"The fundamental industry of agriculture will enable us to lay the foundation upon which will grow wealth, habits of thrift, economy, and will enable us in the end to give our children the best education and development.

* * * * * * * * * *

"In the case of the Negro artisan we should be careful to follow the same course as in regard to agriculture. We should find out the kind of skilled labor in which the Negro is most likely to find employment; the kind of skilled labor in greatest demand. After we find out the kind for which the Negro is best fitted, and the kind which offers the greatest encouragements, I should say emphasize in that direction. If the greatest demand is in the direction of wood work, emphasize wood work. If the greatest demand is in the direction of iron work, emphasize iron work. If in some form of leather, emphasize leather work. If in brickmasonry or plastering, emphasize these.

"Many of the trades which were formerly in our hands have in too large a degree slipped from us, not that there was a special feeling against our working at these trades on the part of the native Southern white man, but because, I fear, we failed to fit ourselves to perform the service in the very best manner. We must not only have carpenters but architects; we must not only have persons who can do the work with the hand, but persons at the same time who can plan the work with the brain.

"I have great faith in the value of all the industries to which I have referred, not only because of their economic value, but because of their mental and moral value.

"Go into the North or South and ask to have pointed out to you the most prosperous and reliable colored man in that community, and in the majority of cases, I believe, you will have pointed out to you a Negro who has learned a trade; and, in many cases, you will find that this trade was learned during the days of slavery.

* * * * * * * * * *

"Later on, I hope that this conference will find it in its way to take up the question of domestic service. This is one which we should no longer blink at, but should face squarely. We should do the propér thing regardless of criticism, which will enable our people to hold on to all forms of domestic service in the South.

* * * * * * * * * *

"If we are wise and patient, we can use all forms of service in a way, not only to lift ourselves up, but to bind us eternally in fellowship and good will to the Southern white man by whose side we must live for all time."

After adopting the following resolutions the Conference adjourned:

The Seventh Atlanta Conference, in considering the situation of Negro artisans, has come to the following conclusions:

1. While the Negro artisans are still losing strength in many communities, they are beginning to gain in others, and it would seem as if the tide against them was turning and that concerted action and intelligent preparation would before long restore and increase the prestige of skilled Negro working men.

2. To realize this hope it is necessary, first, to preserve what skill we have, and, secondly, to enter new fields. From keeping our present efficiency we are hindered by the lack of a proper apprentice system, and from entering new trades we are stopped by the opposition of organized labor in trades unions. The South has never had a careful apprentice system, and it must build it. Skilled Negro workmen must never rest satisfied until they have imparted their skill to other and younger men, and parents must remember that an excellent career for a child may be found by apprenticing him to a good carpenter or a first-class mason.

3. In trades or places where Negro workmen are numerous and efficient, trades unions admit and defend them. Where they are few in number they are proscribed and barred by these same unions, no matter what their skill or individual desert. This is unjust and wrong. Negroes should sympathize with and aid the labor movement where it is fair and honest with all men, and should publish to the world all cases of proscription and injustice.

4. We especially commend Trades Schools as a means of imparting skill to Negroes, and manual training as a means of general education. We believe the movements in this line, especially in the last ten years, have been of inestimable benefit to the freedmen's sons.

5. We believe that, in the future, industrial settlements of Negroes properly guided, financiered and controlled, offer peculiarly promising fields of enterprise for a philanthropy based on solid business principles.

6. Finally, we insist that no permanent advance in industrial or other lines can be made without three great indirect helps: Public Schools, Agencies for Social Betterment, and Colleges for Higher Training: illiteracy must be wiped out, savings banks, libraries and rescue agencies established, and, above all, black men of light and leading, College-bred men, must be trained to guide and lead the millions of this struggling race along paths of intelligent and helpful co-operation.

L. M. HERSHAW,
W. A. HUNT,
W. E. B. DUBOIS, } Committee on Resolutions.

The Negro Artisan.

1. *Scope and Method of the Inquiry.* The present study is at once a continuation of the investigations of Atlanta University, in both economic and educational lines, and is a study of skilled work and the training of black boys for it. The peculiar difficulty of most social studies is the fact that the available information must usually come from interested persons. This has been felt in former Atlanta studies: Negroes had to be asked about their own social condition, business men about their business and college-bred men about their work. To some extent, to be sure, this testimony has been corroborated by observation and the testimony of third parties, but the general fact remains that men and women with prejudices and mixed motives must give us the information used, not only in

these but in all social inquiries. In this investigation there are, however, some peculiar advantages, owing chiefly to the fact that it has been possible to get concurrent testimony from three entirely distinct sources on practically the same points. The condition of a modern workingman is best known by himself, his fellow-workmen, and his employer. If to this is added the testimony of the community surrounding him, and a study of his social history and education, we have as complete a picture as one could expect. In this study, the following schedule of questions has been answered by about 1,300 Negro skilled laborers, living for the most part in the State of Georgia:

1. Name..
2. Address..
3. Age: U. 20.......... 20 to 30.......... 30 to 40.......... 40 or over..........
4. Sex: M.................. F..................
5. Conjugal condition: S.......... M.......... W.......... Sep..........
6. Trade..

   Works { For himself........ Owns tools........ Hires others........
   Works { For wages...... Invests other capital...... Foreman........

   Years engaged ....

   How learned..

   Attended trade school....... How long.............. Where..............
7. Wages, per........................ Time unoccupied per year......................
8. Relation to whites:

   Wages of whites in same work....................................

   Works with whites...

   Works primarily for whites..

   Works primarily for Negroes..
9. Trades Union: Belongs to what Union?...

   Do whites belong?..

   Can you join with whites?..
10. Education: Read............ Write............ Higher training..............
11. Own real estate: Yes........ No........
12. Facts..

....

Besides this, the following schedule was placed in the hands of correspondents of this Conference—mostly College-bred Negroes and professional men—and they were asked to study their particular communities. Reports were thus received from 32 states, besides Ontario, Costa Rica and Porto Rica:

THE ARTISAN.

An *Artisan* is a skilled laborer—a person who works with his hands but has attained a degree of skill and efficiency above that of an ordinary manual laborer—as. for instance, carpenters, masons, engineers, blacksmiths, etc. *Omit* barbers, ordinary laborers in factories, who do no skilled work, etc.

1. Name of Place..State ....
2. Are there many Negro skilled laborers here!

3. What trades do they follow chiefly?
4. What trades did they follow chiefly 20 years ago?
5. Write here the names, addresses and trades of the leading Negro Artisans.
6. Is the Negro gaining or losing in skilled work?
7. If he is losing, is this due to his inefficiency or to the great growth of the South in industrial lines?
8. What results can you see of the industrial school training? Are young men entering the trades?
9. What are the chief obstacles which the Negro meets in entering the trades?
10. Is there any discrimination in wages?
11. Can Negroes join the trades unions? Do they join?
12. Write here a short history of Negro artisans in your community—the number and condition before the war, noted cases since the war, etc.

Every trades union affiliated with the American Federation of Labor, and all others that could be reached, were asked to answer the following questions. Ninety-seven answered; eleven made no replies after repeated inquiries:

1. Name of Union.
2. May Negroes join this Union ?
3. If not, how is their membership prevented ?
4. If they may join, how many Negro members have you at present ?
5. How many had you in 1890?
6. How many Negro applicants have been refused admission to your knowledge ?
7. Can local Unions refuse to admit a Negro if he is otherwise qualified ?
8. Can local Unions refuse to recognize the travelling card of a Negro Union man?
9. Do Negroes make good workmen?
10. What are the chief objections to admitting them to membership in your Union ?
11. Are these objections likely to be overcome in time ?
12. General observations (add here any facts or opinions you may wish. They will be held as strictly confidental, if you so desire).

The central labor bodies in every city and town of the Union were sent the following schedule of questions. Two hundred of these, representing 30 states, answered:

1. Name of Council or Assembly.
2. Are there any Unions affiliated with you which are composed of Negro members ?
3. If so, how many, and what is their membership ?
4. Are there any Negro members in any of the local Unions ?
5. If so, how many, and in which Unions ?
6. Do any of the local Unions bar Negroes from membership ?

7. Have Negro applicants ever been refused admission to any of the Unions?
8. Do local Unions ever refuse to recognize the travelling card of a Negro mechanic?
9. Do Negroes make good workmen in any of the trades? In which trades are they the best?
10. What are the chief objections usually raised against admitting them to Trades Unions?
11. Are these objections likely to disapper in time?
12. General observations (add here any facts or opinions you may wish. They will be held as strictly confidental, if you so desire.)

To the state federations a letter was sent asking for whatever general information was available on the subject. Most of them answered these requests.

To the industrial schools the following schedule was sent. Many of the schools were not able to answer definitely, and some returned no answer at all. The principal schools reported:

1. Name of institution.
2. Address.
3. How many of your graduates or former students are earning a living entirely as artisans?
4. How many of the above mentioned are:

Carpenters,	Dressmakers,	Tailors.
Blacksmiths,	Iron and steel workers,	....
Brickmakers,	Shoemakers,	....
Masons,	Painters,	....
Engineers,	Plasterers,	....
Firemen,	Coopers,	....

5. Where are most of these artisans located at present?
6. How many of the rest of your graduates or former students are earning a living partially as artisans?
7. What trades and other work do they usually combine?
8. What difficulties do your graduates meet in obtaining work as artisans?
9. Do they usually join Trades Unions?
10. How many of them teach industries in schools?
11. Can you furnish us with a list of your graduates from industrial courses, with occupations and addresses?

In 1889 and 1891, the *Chattanooga Tradesman* made interesting and exhaustive studies of skilled Negro labor in the South. The Corresponding Secretary of the Conference invited the Editors of the *Tradesman* to cooperate with Atlanta University in a third investigation, in 1902, each bearing half the expense. The Department of Sociology of the University prepared the following schedule, which was distributed by the *Tradesman* and answered by business establishments all over the Southern States:

THE NEGRO SKILLED LABORER.

An Inquiry conducted by THE TRADESMAN (Chattanooga, Tenn.,) in conjunction with the Sociological Department of Atlanta University.

1. Name of firm..
2. Address (street, city and state)..
3. Kind of business..
4. Total number of employees of all kinds.......................................
5. Total number of Negro employees..
6. How many of the Negroes are skilled or semi-skilled workmen?
7. What kinds of skilled work do the Negroes do?
8. What wages do the Negroes receive?
9. How do they compare in efficiency with white workmen?
10. Are the Negro workmen improving in efficiency?
11. How much education have your Negro workmen received?
12. What effect has this education had?
13. Shall you continue to employ skilled Negro workmen?

The Superintendents of Education in all the Southern States were consulted as to manual training in the schools, and most of them answered the inquiries.

Six hundred children in the public schools of Atlanta, Ga., were asked to write out answers to the following questions:

1. What kinds of work do you do at home?
   Do you sew? Do you sweep?
   Do you cook? Do you tend chickens?
   Do you wash? Do you work in the garden?
   Do you iron? Do you keep flowers?
2. Have you got a hammer and saw at home?
   Do you use them?
   Have you any other tools at home?
3. Do you ever make little ornaments to hang on the walls, or to put anywhere in the house?
4. What do you like to do best?
5. What are you going to do when you grow up?
6. How old are you?
7. What is your name?
8. Where do you live?

Finally such available information was collected as could be found in the United States' census, the reports of the Bureau of Education, and other sources as indicated in the bibliography. On the whole the collected information on which this study is based is probably more complete than in the case of any of the previous studies.

2. *The Ante-bellum Artisan.* Before the civil war both slaves and free Negroes were artisans to some extent. It is difficult to-day, however, to determine just what proportion could do skilled work and how their work would compare with that of artisans of to-day. We are told that in Virginia*:

"The county records of the seventeenth century reveal the presence of many Negro mechanics in the colony during that period, this being especially the case with carpenters and coopers. This was what might be expected. The slave was inferior in skill, but the ordinary mechanical needs of the plantation did not demand the highest aptitude. The fact that the African was a servant for life was an advantage covering many deficiencies; nevertheless, it is significant that large slaveholders like Colonel Byrd and Colonel Fitzhugh should have gone to the inconvenience and expense of importing English handicraftsmen who were skilled in the very trades in which it is certain that several of the Negroes belonging to these planters had been specially trained. It shows the low estimate in which the planters held the knowledge of their slaves regarding the higher branches of mechanical work."

As examples of slave mechanics it is stated that among the slaves of the first Robert Beverly was a carpenter valued at £30, and that Ralph Wormeley, of Middlesex county, owned a cooper and a carpenter each valued at £35. Colonel William Byrd mentions the use of Negroes in iron mining in 1732.† In New Jersey slaves were employed as miners, iron-workers, saw-mill hands, house and ship-carpenters, wheelwrights, coopers, tanners, shoemakers, millers and bakers, among other employments,** before the Revolutionary war. As early as 1708 there were enough slave mechanics in Pennsylvania to make the freemen feel their competition severely.‡ In Massachusetts and other states we hear of an occasional artisan.

During the early part of the 19th century the Negro artisans increased. In the District of Columbia many "were superior mechanics . . . . Benjamin Banneker, the Negro Astronomer, assisting in surveying the District in 1791"†† Olmsted, in his journeys through the slave states, just before the civil war, found slave artisans in all the states:††† In Virginia they worked in tobacco factories, ran steamboats, made barrels, etc. On a South Carolina plantation he was told by the master that the Negro mechanics "exercised as much skill and ingenuity as the ordinary mechanics that he was used to employ in New England." In Charleston and some other places they were employed in cotton factories. In Alabama he saw a black carpenter—a careful and accurate calculator and excellent work-

*Bruce: Economic History of Virginia in the 17th century, ii. pp. 405-6.

†Writings, edited by Bassett, pp. 345, 349, 360.

**Cooley: Slavery in New Jersey.

‡Philadelphia Negro, p. 141 ff.

††Ingle: Negro in District of Columbia.

†††Olmsted: Seaboard Slaves States, Journey Through Texas, and Journey in the Back Country.

man; he was bought for $2,000. In Louisiana he was told that master mechanics often bought up slave mechanics and acted as contractors. In Kentucky the slaves worked in factories for hemp-bagging, and in iron works on the Cumberland river,† and also in tobacco factories. In the newspapers advertisements for runaway mechanics were often seen, as, for instance a blacksmith in Texas, "very smart," a mason in Virginia, etc. In Mobile an advertisement read "good blacksmiths and horse-shoers for sale on reasonable terms."

An ex-governor of Mississippi says:*

"Prior to the war there were a large number of Negro mechanics in the Southern States; many of them were expert blacksmiths, wheelwrights, wagon-makers, brick-masons, carpenters, plasterers, painters and shoemakers. They became masters of their respective trades by reason of sufficiently long service under the control and direction of expert white mechanics. During the existence of slavery the contract for qualifying the Negro as a mechanic was made between his owner and the master workman."

Such slaves were especially valuable and formed usually a privileged class, with a large degree of freedom. They were very often hired out by their masters and sometimes hired their own time although this latter practice was frowned upon as giving slaves too much freedom and nearly all states forbade it by law; although some, like Georgia, permitted the custom in certain cities. In all cases the slave mechanic was encouraged to do good work by extra wages which went into his own pocket. For instance, in the semi-skilled work of the Tobacco-factories, the Virginia master received from $150–$200 annually for his slave and the employer fed him; but the slave, by extra work, could earn for himself $5 or more a month. So carpenters sometimes received as much as $2 a day for their masters, and then were given the chance to earn more for themselves. In Texas nine slaves, some of them carpenters, were leased at an average of $280.22 a year and probably earned something over this. If the mechanic was a good workman and honest the master was tempted to allow him to do as he pleased so long as he paid the master a certain yearly income. In this way there arose in nearly all Southern cities a class of Negro clients free in everything but name; they owned property, reared families and often lived in comfort. In earlier times such mechanics often bought themselves and families and became free, but as the laws began to bear hard on free Negroes they preferred to remain under the patronage and nominal ownership of their white masters. In other cases they migrated North and there worked out their freedom, sending back stipulated sums. Many if not most of the noted leaders of the Negro in earlier times belonged to this slave mechanic class, such as Vesey, Nat Turner, Richard Allen and Absalom Jones. They were exposed neither

†Note the attempt to conduct the Baltimore Iron Works by slaves contributed by the shareholders, Cf. N. Y. *Nation* Sept. 1, 1891, p. 171.

*Ex-Gov. Lowry in North American Review, 156 : 472.

to the corrupting privileges of the house servants nor to the blighting tyranny of field work and had large opportunity for self development.

Usually the laws did not hinder the slaves from learning trades. On the other hand the laws against teaching slaves really hindered the mechanics from attaining very great efficiency save in rare cases—they must work by rule of thumb usually. North Carolina allowed slaves to learn mathematical calculations, but not reading and writing; Georgia in 1833 decreed that no one should permit a Negro "to transact business for him in writing." Gradually such laws became more severe: Mississippi in 1830 debarred slaves from printing offices and Georgia in 1845 declared that slaves and free Negroes could not take contracts for building and repairing houses, as mechanics or masons.† Restrictions, however, were not always enforced, especially in the building trades, and the slave mechanic flourished.

One obstacle he did encounter however from first to last and that was the opposition of white mechanics. In 1708 the white mechanics of Pennsylvania protested against the hiring out of Negro mechanics and were successful in gettiug acts passed to restrict the further importation of slaves †† but they were disallowed in England. In 1722 they protested again and the Legislative Assembly declared that the hiring of black mechanics was "dangerous and injurious to the republic and not to be sanctioned."‡ Especially in border states was opposition fierce. In Maryland the legislature was urged in 1837 to forbid free Negroes entirely from being artisans; in 1840 a bill was reported to keep Negro labor out of tobacco ware-houses; in 1844 petitions came to the legislature urging the prohibition of free black carpenters and taxing free black mechanics; and finally in 1860 white mechanics urged a law barring free blacks "from pursuing any mechanical branch of trade."§ Mississippi mechanics told Olmsted that they resented the competition of slaves and that one refused the free services of three Negroes for six years as apprentices to his trade. In Wilmington, N. C., 1857, a number of persons destroyed the frame work of a new building erected by Negro carpenters and threatened to destroy all edifices erected by Negro carpenters or mechanics. A public meeting was called to denounce the act and offer a reward. The deed was charged upon an organized association of 150 white workingmen. There were similar disturbances in Virginia, and in South Carolina white mechanics about this time were severely condemned by the newspapers as "enemies to our peculiar institutions and formidable barriers to the success of our own native mechanics."‖

In Ohio about 1820 to 1830 and thereafter, the white Mechanics' Societies combined against Negroes. One master mechanic, President of the Me-

---

†Stroud's Laws, p. 107.

††Cf. the Philadelphia Negro.

‡Cf. the Philadelphia Negro.

§Brackett: Negro in Maryland, pp. 106, 210.

‖Olmstead: Seabord Slave States and Journey in the Back Country.

chanical Association of Cincinnati, was publicly tried by the Society for assisting a young Negro to learn a train. Such was the feeling that no colored boy could find entrance as apprentice, and few workmen were allowed to pursue their calling. One Negro cabinet-maker purchased his freedom in Kentucky and came to Cincinnati; for a long time he could get no work; one Englishman employed him but the white workmen struck. The black man was compelled to become a laborer until by saving he could take small contracts and hire black mechanics to help him.† In Philadelphia the series of fearful riots against Negroes was due in large part to the jealousy of white working men, and in Washington, D. C., New York and other cities, riots and disorder on the part of white mechanics, aimed against Negroes, occurred several times.

There were, no doubt, many very efficient slave mechanics. One who learned his trade from a slave†† writes us an interesting and enthusiastic account of the work of these men:

"During the days of slavery the Negro mechanic was a man of importance. He was a most valuable slave to his master. He would always sell for from two to three times as much in the market as the unskilled slaveman. When a fine Negro mechanic was to be sold at public auction, or private sale, the wealthy slave owners would vie with each other for the prize and run tne bidding often up into high figures.

"The slave owners early saw the aptitude of the Negro to learn handicraft, and fully appreciating what vast importance and value this would be to them (the masters) selected their brightest young slavemen and had them taught in the different kinds of trades. Hence on every large plantation you could find the Negro carpenter, blacksmith, brick and stone mason. These trades comprehended and included much more in their scope in those days than they do now. Carpentry was in its glory then. What is done now by varied and complicated machinery was wrought then by hand. The invention of the planing machine is an event within the knowledge of many persons living to-day. Most of our 'wood working' machinery has come into use long since the days of slavery. The same work done now with the machine, was done then by hand. The carpenter's chest of tools in slavery times was a very elaborate and expensive outfit. His 'kit' not only included all the tools that the average carpenter carries now, but also the tools for performing all the work done by the various kinds of 'wood-working' machines. There is little opportunity for the carpenter of to-day to acquire, or display, genius and skill in his trade as could the artisan of old.

"One only needs to go down South and examine hundreds of old Southern mansions, and splendid old church edifices, still intact, to be convinced of the fact of the cleverness of the Negro artisan, who constructed nine-tenths of them, and many of them still provoke the admiration of all who see them, and are not to be despised by the men of our day.

---

†Condition of People of Color, &c.

††Mr. J. D. Smith, Stationary Engineer, Chicago, Ill.

"There are few, if any, of the carpenters of to-day who, if they had the hand tools, could get out the 'stuff' and make one of those old style massive panel doors,—who could work out by hand the mouldings, the stiles, the mullions, etc., and build one of those windows, which are to be found to-day in many of the churches and public buildings of the South; all of which testify to the cleverness of the Negro's skill as artisan in the broadest sense of the term. For the carpenter in those days was also the 'cabinet maker,' the wood turner, coffin maker, generally the pattern maker, and the maker of most things made of wood. The Negro blacksmith held almost absolute sway in his line, which included the many branches of forgery, and other trades which are now classified under different heads from that of the regular blacksmith. The blacksmith in the days of slavery was expected to make any and everything wrought of iron. He was to all intents and purposes the 'machine blacksmith,' 'horseshoer,' 'carriage and wagon ironer and trimmer,' 'gunsmith,' 'wheelwright'; and often whittled out and ironed the hames, the plowstocks, and the 'single trees' for the farmers, and did a hundred other things too numerous to mention. They were experts at tempering edge tools, by what is generally known as the water process. But many of them had secret processes of their own for tempering tools which they guarded with zealous care.

"It was the good fortune of your humble servant to have served his time as an apprentice in a general blacksmithing shop, or shop of all work, presided over by an ex-slave genius known throughout the state as a 'master mechanic.' In slavery times this man hired his own time—paying his master a certain stipulated amount of money each year, and all he made over and above that amount was his own.

"The Negro machinists were also becoming numerous before the downfall of slavery. The slave owners were generally the owners of all the factories, machine shops, flour-mills, saw-mills, gin houses and threshing machines. They owned all the railroads and the shops connected with them. In all of these the white laborer and mechanic had been supplanted almost entirely by the slave mechanics at the time of the breaking out of the civil war. Many of the railroads in the South had their entire train crews, except the conductors, made up of the slaves—including engineers and firemen. The 'Georgia Central' had inaugrated just such a movement, and had many Negro engineers on its locomotives and Negro machinists in its shops. So it will be seen at once that the liberation of the slaves was also the salvation of the poor white man of the South. It saved him from being completely ousted, as a laborer and a mechanic, by the masters, to make place for the slaves whom they were having trained for those positions. Yet, strange as it may seem to us now, the great mass of poor white men in the South who were directly and indirectly affected by the slave mechanic—being literally forced out of the business, took up arms and fought against the abolition of slavery!

"While the poor whites and the masters were fighting, these same black men were at home working to support those fighting for their slavery. The Negro mechanic could be found, during the conflict, in the machine shops, building engines and railroad cars; in the gun factories making arms of all kinds for the soldiers; in the various shops building wagons, and making harness, bridles and saddles, for the armies of the South. Negro engineers handled the throttle in many cases to haul the soldiers to the front, whose success, in the struggle going on, meant continued slavery to themselves and their people. All of the flour mills, and most of every other kind of mill, of the South, was largely in charge of black men.

"Much has been said of the new Negro for the new century, but with all his training he will have to take a long stride in mechanical skill before he reaches the point of practical efficiency where the old Negro of the old century left off. It was the good fortune of the writer once to fall into the hands of an uncle who was master of what would now be half a dozen distinct trades. He was generally known as a mill-wright, or mill builder. A mill-wright now, is only a man who merely sets up the machinery, and his work is now confined mostly to the hanging of shafting, pulleys and belting. In the days of slavery the mill-wright had to know how to construct everything about the mill, from foundation to roofs. This uncle could take his men with their 'cross cut saws' and 'broad axes' and go into the forests, hew the timbers with which to build the dams across the rivers and streams of water, to erect the 'mill house' frames, get out all the necessary timber and lumber at the saw mill. Then he would, without a sign of a drawing on paper, lay out and cut every piece, every mortise and tenon, every brace and rafter with their proper angles, &c., with perfect precision before they put the whole together. I have seen my uncle go into the forest, fell a great tree, hew out of it an immense stick or shaft from four feet to five feet in diameter, and from twenty to thirty feet long, having as many as sixteen to twenty faces on its surface, or as they termed it, 'sixteen' and 'twenty square.' He would then take it to the mill seat and mortise it, make the arms, and all the intricate parts for a great "overshot" water wheel to drive the huge mill machinery. This is a feat most difficult even for modern mechanics who have a thorough knowledge of mathematics and the laws of mechanics.

"It is difficult for us to understand how those men with little or no knowledge of mathematics, or mechanical rules, could take a crude stick of timber, shape it, and then go to work and cut out a huge screw and the 'Tap blocks' for those old style cotton presses."

To the above testimony we may append reports from various localities. From *Alabama* we have a report from an artisan at Tuskegee who was 14 or 15 years old at the breaking out of the civil war. The Principal of the Academic Department writes: "He is one of the most remarkable men you ever saw. He is a fine tinner, shoemaker and harness maker, and until the school grew so large held all these trades under his instruction. He is an all-round tinker and can do anything from the repairing of a watch to the mending of an umbrella." This man names 25 Negro carpenters, 11 blacksmiths, 3 painters, 2 wheelwrights, 3 tinsmiths, 2 tanners, 5 masons, and 14 shoemakers in Tuskegee and the surrounding districts before the war. "Tuskegee was a small place" he writes "and you will wonder why such a number of mechanics were there. The answer is this: there were a large number of wealthy white people who lived in the county, owning large numbers of slaves, and there was thus a lot of work all through the country districts; so they were sent out to do the work." Of them in general he says: "The mechanics as a rule lived more comfortably than any other class of the Negroes. A number of them hired their time and made money; they wore good clothes and ate better food than the other classes of colored people. In other words they stood higher in the estimation of the white people than any of the others. A very small number of them were allowed to live by themselves in out of the way houses. All the master wanted of them was to stay on his place and pay over their wages promptly. As a rule a white man contracted for the jobs and overlooked the work. These white men often did not know anything about the trade but had Negro foremen under them who really carried on the work." From *Georgia* there are two reports: in Albany, "Before the civil war all of the artisans in this section of the state were colored men. Their masters compelled some of their slaves to learn these trades so that they could do the necessary work around the plantations." In Marshalville, on the other hand, "There were only two Negro artisans here before the war." From *West Virginia* comes a report: there were "but two skilled laborers" previous to the war in Bluefield. In Chester, *South Carolina*, "Before the war there were practically no Negro artisans." Charleston reports: "We have no accurate data to work on, except experiences of ex-slaves, who seem to agree that though the anti-bellum artisan was very proficient, yet he could not be compared in point of intelligent service with the artisan of to-day." From Greenville we learn: "The Negro since the war has entered trades more largely and in more varied lines. He is now in trades not open to him before freedom." In *Mississippi* one town reports that "Before the war Negroes were not artisans from choice, but many large planters would train some of their slaves in carpentry or blacksmithing for plantation use. Then the Negro did not have to ask, Does this trade pay? Now he does." Another locality says: "Before the war the principal trades were carpentry and blacksmithing and were done by trained slaves." In *Louisiana* "Before and since the war Negroes have built some of the best structures" in New Orleans and Baton Rouge. Olmsted noted many Negro mechanics here. In *Texas* there were "few if any" Negro mechanics in Georgetown before the war, while in Dallas they did "most of the skilled labor." In *Arkansas* artisans were few. In *Tennessee* there were relatively more artisans before the war than now in Nashville, fewer in Murfreesboro and McMinnville and about the same number in Maryville. In the *District of Columbia* there were many Negro artisans in ante-bellum times, as shown by the directories:

Negro Artisans in Washington, D. C.*

	1827	1830	1850	1855	1860
Carpenters	2	2	2	1	25
Blacksmiths	2	2	2	2	11
Brickmasons	1		2	2	20
Tailors	1	1			
Shoemakers	3	3	7	1	13
Pasterers	1	1	3		12
Tanners	1	1			2
Pump-borers		1			
Caulkers		1			2
Masons		1			1
Coppersmiths			1		
Bakers				1	2
Coopers				2	1
Cabinet-makers					1
Slaters					1
Machinists					1
Wheelwrights					2
Whitesmiths					1
Painters					4
Bookbinders					1
Tinners					2

It is not altogether clear from such incomplete reports as to just what the status or efficiency of the ante-bellum artisan was. It is clear that there were some very efficient workmen and a large number who knew something of the various trades. Still, we must remember that it would be easy to exaggerate the ability and importance of the mass of these workmen.

"The South was lacking in manufactures, and used little machinery. Its demand for skilled labor was not large, but what demand existed was supplied mainly by Negroes. Negro carpenters, plasterers, bricklayers, blacksmiths, wheelwrights, painters, harnessmakers, tanners, millers, weavers, barrelmakers, basketmakers, shoemakers, chairmakers, coachmen, spinners, seamstresses, housekeepers, gardeners, cooks, laundresses, embroiderers, maids of all work, were found in every community, and frequently on a single plantation. Skilled labor was more profitable than unskilled, and therefore every slave was made as skillful as possible under a slave system."†

Here we have, perhaps, the best key to the situation in the South before the war; there was little demand for skilled labor in the rather rude economy of the average slave plantation and the Negro did the most of this. The slave artisan, however, was rather a jack-of-all-trades than a mechanic in the modern sense of the term—he could build a barn, make a barrel, mend an umbrella or shoe a horse. Exceptional slaves did the work exceptionally well, but the average workman was poor, careless and

*Taken from the directories of these years and apt to be incomplete. Mr. L. M. Hershaw kindly did this work.

†G. T. Winston in Annals of the American Academy, July, 1901, p. 111.

ill-trained, and could not have earned living wages under modern competitive conditions. While then it is perfectly true to say that the slave was the artisan of the South before the war it is probably also true that the average of workmanship was low and suited only to rough plantation life. This does not, of course, gainsay for a moment the fact that on some of the better plantations and in cities like Richmond, Savannah, Charleston, and New Orleans, there were really first-class Negro workmen who did good work.

3. *Economics of Emancipation.* Slaves and the lowest freemen were the ordinary artisans of Greece and Rome, save only as the great artists now and then descended from above as sculptors and architects. In mediaeval times mechanics were largely bondsmen and serfs and were purchased and imported just as black carpenters formed a part of the expenses of a Texas emigrant in 1850. While exceptional mechanics in the middle ages acquired a degree of practical freedom just as the Negro mechanics of the South did, yet they were in earlier times serfs. Gradually in free communities there arose a class of free mechanics, but in the rural districts and in the households of the lords they still, for many generations, remained serfs. The rise and development of cities gave the freed artisan his chance; there, by defensive and offensive organization, he became the leading factor in the economic and political development of the new city-states. His development was rapid, and about the 14th century a distinction between laborers and masters arose which has gradually grown and changed into our modern problem of labor and capital.

A very interesting comparison between this development and the situation of the Southern freedmen might be drawn at some length. Even before the war a movement of slaves to the cities took place: first of house-servants with the masters' families and then of slave artisans: if the slave was a good artisan he was worth more hired out in the city than on the country plantation. Moreover, the Negro greatly preferred to be in town—he had more liberty, more associates, and more excitement. Probably in time there would have been evolved in the South a class of city serf-artisans and servants considerably removed from the mass of field-hands. It is significant that the Georgia law prohibiting slaves from hiring their time specifically excepted certain of the larger towns.

After emancipation came suddenly, in the midst of war and social upheaval, the first real economic question was the self-protection of freed working men. There were three chief classes of them: the agricultural laborers chiefly in the country districts, the house-servants in town and country and the artisans who were rapidly migrating to town. The Freedman's Bureau undertook the temporary guardianship of the first class, the second class easily passed from half-free service to half-servile freedom. The third class, the artisans, however, met peculiar conditions. They had always been used to working under the guardianship of a master and even though that guardianship in some cases was but nominal yet it was of the greatest value for protection. This soon became clear as the Negro freed artisan set up business for himself: if there was a creditor to be sued he could no longer bring suit in the name of an influential white master; if there was a contract to be had, there was no responsible white patron to answer for the good performance of the work. Nevertheless, these differences were not strongly felt at first—the friendly patronage of the former master was often voluntarily given the freedman and for some years following the war the Negro mechanic still held undisputed sway. Three occurrences, however, soon disturbed the situation:

(*a*). The competition of white mechanics.

(*b*). The efforts of the Negro for self-protection.

(*c*). The new industrial development of the South.

These changes were spread over a series of years and are not yet complete, but they are the real explanation of certain facts which have hitherto been explained in false and inadequate ways. It has, for instance, been said repeatedly that the Negro mechanic carelessly threw away his monopoly of the Southern labor market and allowed the white mechanic to supplant him. This is only partially true. To be sure, the ex-slave was not alert, quick and ready to meet competition. His business hitherto had been to *do* work but not to *get* work, save in exceptional cases. The whole slave system of labor saved him from certain sorts of competition, and when he was suddenly called to face the competition of white mechanics he was at a loss. His especial weakness was the lack of a hiring contractor. His master or a white contractor had usually taken jobs and hired him. The white contractor still hired him but there was no one now to see that the contractor gave him fair wages. Indeed, as the white mechanics pressed forward the only refuge of the Negro mechanic was lower wages. There were a few Negro contractors here and there but they again could only hope to maintain themselves by markedly underbidding all competitors and attaining a certain standing in the community.

What the Negro mechanic needed then was social protection—the protection of law and order, perfectly fair judicial processes and that personal power which is in the hands of all modern laboring classes in civilized lands, viz., the right of suffrage. It has often been said that the freedman throwing away his industrial opportunities after the war gave his energies to politics and succeeded in alienating his friends and exasperating his enemies, and proving his inability to rule. It is doubtless true that the freedman laid too much stress on the efficacy of political power in making a straight road to real freedom. And undoubtedly, too, a bad class of politicians, white and black, took advantage of this and made the reconstruction Negro voter a hissing in the ears of the South. Notwithstanding this the Negro was fundamentally right. If the whole class of mechanics here, as in the Middle Age, had been without the suffrage and half-free, the Negro would have had an equal chance with the white mechanic, and could have afforded to wait. But he saw himself coming more and more into competition with men who had the right to vote, the prestige of race and blood, the advantage of intimate relations with those acquainted with the market and the demand. The Negro saw clearly that his industrial rise depended, to an important degree, upon his political power and he therefore sought that power. In this seeking he failed primarily because of his own poor training, the uncompromising enmity and apprehensions of his white neighbors and the selfishness and half-hearted measures of his emancipators. The result was that the black artisan entered the race heavily handicapped—the member of a proscribed class, with restricted rights and privileges, without political and social power. The result was of course that he was enabled to maintain himself only by accepting low wages and keeping at all hazards the good-will of the community.

Even here however he could not wholly succeed. The industrial conditions in the country were rapidly changing. Slowly but surely the new industrial South began to arise and with it came new demands on the mechanic. Now the Negro mechanic could not in the very nature of the case meet these demands; he knew how to do a few things by rule of thumb—he could build one of the rambling old-fashioned southern mansions, he could build a slave shanty; he could construct a rough sugar hogshead and resole a shoe; in exceptional cases he could do even careful and ingenious work in certain lines; but as a rule he knew little of the niceties of modern carpentry or iron-working, he knew practically nothing of mills and machinery, very little about railroads—in fact he was especially ignorant in those very lines of mechanical and industrial development in which the South has taken the longest strides in the last thirty years. And if he was ignorant, who was to teach him? Certainly not his white fellow workmen, for they were his bitterest opponents because of strong race-prejudice and because of the fact that the Negro works for low wages. Apprenticeship to the older Negro mechanics was but partially successful for they could not teach what they had never learned. In fact it was only through the lever of low wages that the Negro secured any share in the new industries. By that means he was enabled to replace white laborers in many branches, but he thereby increased the enmity of trades-unions and labor-leaders. Such in brief was the complicated effort of emancipation on the Negro artisan and one could not well imagine a situation more difficult to remedy.

4. *Occupations and Home-training.* Manifestly it is necessary that any constituent group of a great nation should first of all earn a living; that is, they must have the ability and will to labor effectively and must receive enough for that labor to live decently and rear their children. Since emancipation the Negro has had greater success in earning a living as a free workingman than the nation had a right to expect. Nevertheless, the situation to-day is not satisfactory. If we compare the occupations of Negroes and native and foreign whites, we have:

Occupations of American Negroes, 1890:

1. Agriculture, Fishing and Mining, 1,757,403, or 57%
2. Domestic and Personal Service, 963,080, or 31%
3. Manf. and Mechanical Industries, 172,970, or 6%
4. Trade and Transportation, 145,717, or 5%
5. Professional service, 33,994, or 1%

Occupations of Native Whites,* 1890:

1. Agriculture, Fishing and Mining, 5,122,613, or 47%
3. Manf. and Mechanical Industries, 2,067,135, or 19%
4. Trade and Transportation, 1,722,462, or 16%
2. Domestic and Personal Service, 1,342,028, or 12%
5. Professional Service, 640,785, or 6%

Occupations of Foreign Whites, 1890:

3. Manf. and Mechanical Industries, 1,597,118, or 31%
2. Domestic and Personal Service, 1,375,067, or 27%
1. Agriculture, Fishing and Mining, 1,305,901, or 26%
4. Trade and Transportation, 712,558, or 14%
5. Professional Service, 114,113, or 2%

Dividing the Negro wage earners by sex we have:

	Male	Female	Total
Professions	1.2%	0.9	1.1
Agriculture	63.4	44.0	57.2
Trade and Transportation	6.8	0.2	4.7
Manf. and Mechanical Industries	7.0	2.8	5.6
Domestic and Personal Service	21.6	52.1	31.4
	100.0	100.0	100.0

There is manifestly here a strikingly small proportion of this race engaged in trade, transportation, manufactures and the mechanical industries—about one-tenth, as compared with 45% of the foreign-born, and 40% of all the native born.† If we take all the States of the Union we have the following figures for 1890:

*Native whites, with native parents.

†With native and foreign parents.

NEGRO WAGE-EARNERS, 1890.

	All Occupations.		Trade and Transportation.		Manufacturing and Mechanical Industries.	
	Males.	Females.	Males.	Females.	Males.	Females.
The United States.	2,101,233	971,890	143,350	2,399	146,126	26,929
1. Alabama..	192,322	101,085	9,147	140	9,917	951
2. Alaska..............	....	....	....	....	....	....
3. Arizona.......	1,091	71	13	....	12	4
4. Arkansas..........	86,861	30,115	2,787	27	3,403	275
5. California..........	4,301	1,041	457	3	358	106
6. Colorado...	2,765	792	406	5	402	55
7. Connecticut.......	4,064	1,964	634	7	565	165
8. Delaware..........	9,334	3,016	633	21	816	51
9. Dis. of Columbia	21,238	18,770	4,776	195	2,839	1,490
10. Florida..	46,302	19,071	4,106	52	4,501	746
11. Georgia..............	246,913	122,352	16,397	372	16,604	1,924
12. Idaho........	83	23	8	....	2	1
13. Illinois..........	19,270	4,713	1,994	41	1,602	361
14. Indiana..............	14,648	4,210	1,426	23	1,669	175
15. Iowa...................	3,615	730	289	1	309	35
16. Kansas	13,889	3,400	1,148	20	1,315	124
17. Kentucky..........	76,411	31,255	7,381	66	6,519	840
18. Louisiana	159,180	83,978	6,045	129	8,455	2,774
19. Maine................	409	145	68	2	55	11
20. Maryland.........	63,166	32,642	7,538	144	4,458	1,074
21. Massachusetts...	7,593	3,435	1,402	34	1,132	426
22. Michigan..........	5,065	1,329	448	6	549	137
23. Minnesota.........	1,719	383	216	5	88	48
24. Mississippi	198,531	105,306	5,671	74	5,686	803
25. Missouri	43,940	16,715	4,862	44	3,525	396
26. Montana............	971	140	45	1	45	13
27. Nebraska...........	3,741	959	323	4	370	64
28. Nevada.	130	22	17	1	5	2
29. New Hampshire	242	107	24	....	72	23
30. New Jersey........	16,143	7,738	2,111	25	1,864	263
31. New Mexico.......	888	156	40	....	24	3
32. New York.	23,272	13,664	4,231	54	2,288	1,005
33. North Carolina..	148,370	68,220	7,564	106	12,114	2,360
34. North Dakota...	146	23	10	....	4	1
35. Ohio	28,085	7,791	3,027	40	3,426	442
36. Oklahoma	958	125	28	1	42	2
37. Oregon	536	99	42	1	37	10
38. Pennsylvania. ...	37,534	15,704	5,213	104	4,630	1,077
39. Rhode Island.....	2,337	1,362	546	3	322	170
40. South Carolina...	186,714	102,836	6,860	188	9,842	2,341
41. South Dakota....	284	43	121	1	14	4
42. Tennessee..........	121,016	44,701	10,954	125	10,404	1,141
43. Texas...	123,395	46,691	6,386	69	5,794	461
44. Utah..................	298	51	14	1	14	2
45. Vermont...	322	109	33	....	31	6
46. Virginia	169,343	71,752	15,655	253	18,864	4,483
47. Washington	902	153	69	....	87	15
48. West Virginia...	11,478	2,623	2,080	7	927	41
49. Wisconsin	855	205	74	1	105	28
50. Wyoming..........	563	75	31	3	20	....

There is but one way of remedying such a distribution of occupations, and that is by training children and youth into new callings. This is a difficult matter. The children get their ideals of life from home life primarily, and among a people largely servants and farmers they would not naturally turn to trades or merchandizing. Still, the city groups of Negroes are changing rapidly and eagerly grasping after new ideals. To test the trend of thinking among the growing children of a city group the Conference questioned 600 of the Negro school children of Atlanta in such way as to bring out the influence of home-training in preparing them for artisans. There were 226 boys and 374 girls. Their ages were:

9 to 12 years	48
12 to 15 "	349
15 to 18 "	203

First they were asked what sort of work they were accustomed to do at home. They answered:

	BOYS.	GIRLS.
Sew†	59	350
Cook	64	304
Wash	64	323
Iron	51	348
Sweep	198	365
'Tend Chickens	134	159
Work in Garden	129	142
Keep Flowers	118	282

†Some did two or more of these sorts of work.

On being asked as to the tools they had in the home they answered as follows:

430 have hammer and saw at home.
121 have neither hammer nor saw.
11 have hammer.
1 has saw.
37 gave no answer.

---

322 use the hammer and saw.
108 do not use them.
420 have other tools besides the hammer and saw.
135 have no other kinds of tools.
45 gave no answer as to other kinds of tools.

---

294 of the girls and 114 of the boys were accustomed to making little ornaments or articles for the home; 82 of the girls and 110 of the boys never did this. When questioned as to what they liked to do best, and what they expected to be when grown up, they replied:

What do you like to do best?

BOYS.		GIRLS.	
To carpenter	37	To sew	193
To do garden-work	27	To cook	76
To "work"	25	To wash and iron	29
To 'tend chickens	24	To keep house	22
To sweep	16	To 'tend flowers	18
To do housework	13	To sweep	9
To play	11	To play music	6
To go to school	10	To 'tend chickens	5
To drive	8	To go to school	3
To draw	5	To read	3
To make ornaments	5	To make lace	1
To cook	5	To nurse	1
To wash and iron	4	To play	1
To play music	3	To sing	1
To sell goods	3		
To deliver goods	3	To "work"	5
To make money	1		
"Don't know"	8		

What are you going to do when grown?

BOYS.

Artisans, 58.

Carpenters	15	Wheelwrights	3
Masons	9	Carriage-makers	2
Blacksmiths	5	Boiler-maker	1
Machinists	5	Butcher	1
Railway Employees	5	Shoemaker	1
Firemen	4	Harnessmaker	1
Tailors	3	A "trade"	3

Professional Men, 41.

Physicians	20	Lawyers	3
Teachers	10	Dentist	1
Musicians and Music Teachers	6	Pharmacist	1

Servants and Laborers, 18.

Porters	10	Teamsters	2
Butlers	2	Waiter	1
Ice-cream-makers	2	Cook	1

Mercantile and Clerical Pursuits, 13.

Merchants	3	Book-keepers	2
Canvassers	2	Cotton-sampler	1
Commercial Men	2	Draughtsman	1
Typewriters	2		

Miscellaneous.

Farmer	1	"Gentleman"	1
"Help my race"	1	"President"	1
"Work"	14	"Don't know"	41

What are you going to do when grown?

GIRLS.

Professional Pursuits, 158.

Teachers	85	Physician	1
Musicians and Music Teachers	65	Elocutionist	1
Missionary	2	Singer	1
Students	2	Writer	1

Dressmakers and Seamstresses.....109.

Servants and Housework, 63.

Cooks	27	Housekeepers	5
Nurses	27	Laundresses	4

These answers reveal much of the home life and ideals of city Negroes: first there is no doubt but what the boys and girls naturally like to "do" something with the hands, the larger number of the boys wishing to be artisans of some sort despite the fact that not one in fourteen of their parents follow such callings. Outside of this they are of course attracted by the successes they see—the neat carriage of the black physician, the colored mail carrier, etc. At the same time it is clear they do not get at home much chance to exercise their mechanical ingenuity—even the simplest tools being unused in nearly half the homes. Here is the chance for kindergarten work and manual training. These children have actual contact with things less often than in the case of the average child. Much of the world about them is unknown in the concrete and consequently they have greater difficulty in grasping abstract ideas.

5. *The Rise of Industrial Training.* These facts have long been recognized in the training of children. In the case of the Negroes there were a number of mixed incentives to action which have not yet clearly worked themselves out to-day. *First* there was the idea of working one's own way through school which many consider an excellent moral tonic; *secondly* there was the idea of educating children in the main according to the rank in life which they will in all probability occupy. This is a wide-spread theory of education and can be especially traced in the European schools. *Thirdly* there was the scheme of using student labor to reduce the expenses of maintaining the school; *fourthly* there was the idea of training girls for house-work; *fifthly* there was the idea of having the youth learn trades for future self-support, and *sixthly* there was the idea of "learning by doing"—of using things to enforce ideas and physical exercises to aid mental processes. All these distinct aspects of education have been loosely lumped together in popular speech as "Industrial Education" with considerable resulting confusion of thought.

Among the Northern free Negroes "Industrial" training found early and earnest advocates. They meant by this some way of teaching black boys trades in order that they might earn a decent livelihood amid the economic proscription of the North.

As Mr. John W. Cromwell has lately said,† it is remarkable that in nearly every one of the dozen or more Negro conventions from 1831 to

†Southern Workman, July, 1902.

1860 there was developed strong advocacy of trade schools for Negro youths.

"In the convention of 1831, assembled at Philadelphia, it was decided to establish a college on the manual labor plan, as soon as twenty thousand dollars should be raised. Rev. Samuel E. Cornish, an educated colored Presbyterian clergyman, was appointed agent to secure funds. Within one year three thousand dollars had been secured for the purpose. Arthur Tappan, the philanthropist, bought several acres in the southern part of New Haven, Conn., and had completed arrangements for erecting thereon a building, fully equipped for the purpose, that would have done credit to the city, the state and the country. But the people of New Haven and of Connecticut were bitterly opposed to the location of such an institution in their midst. In a mass meeting of the citizens, the mayor, aldermen and councilmen leading, they declared this opposition in forcible and unmistakable language, even against the protest of so powerful a citizen as Roger S. Baldwin, who subsequently defended the Amistad captives, and became governor of the state and United States Senator. More than this, the commonwealth subsequently passed a law prohibiting the establishment of any institution of learning 'for the instruction of persons of color of other states.'

"Half a generation later, at the Colored National Convention of 1847, the demand for a colored college, led by so talented and able a controversialist as the late Alexander Crummell, noted even at that date for the same polished, incisive style and elegant diction which marked his later years, was offset by a firm and powerful constituency that successfully insisted on industrial training having the prior claim.

"But it was at Rochester, N. Y., in 1853, at the most influential of all the conventions in the history of the Negro race, that their approval of industrial education what most emphatically given. At a time when 'Uncle Tom's Cabin' and the name of its authoress, Harriet Beecher Stowe, were on every tongue, she, at the urgent request of friends in Great Britain, was planning a trip to Europe. The convention, following the lead of Frederick Douglass, commissioned her by an overwhelming voice to solicit funds in their name for the establishment of an industrial and agricultural institution. In England her reception was most enthusiastic,and her mission seems to have been favorably received. The enemies of the Negro in this country severely criticised her course, but after a defence by Frederick Douglas in his paper, 'The North Star,' copied in 'The Independent,' then edited by Rev. Henry Ward Beecher, the attacks ceased. When Mrs. Stowe returned to America she had changed her mind respecting the industrial education school, and the second attempt of the colored people to found in the North what has since succeeded so well in the South. came to naught.

"In the 'Autographs for Freedom,' published in 1854, Prof. Charles L. Reason, who writes the introductory article, says:

"The free colored man at the North . . . . in one department of reformatory exertion . . . . feels that he has been neglected. . . . . He has failed to see a corresponding earnestness, according to the influence of abolitionists in the business world, in opening the avenues of industrial labor to the proscribed youth of the land. This work, therefore, is evidently left for himself to do. And he has laid his powers to the task. The record of his conclusions was given at Rochester in July, and has become already a part of history.

" 'Though shut out from the workshops of the country, he is determined to make self-provision so as to triumph over the spirit of caste that would keep him degraded. The utility of the industrial institution he would erect must, he believes, commend itself to abolitionists.

" 'The usefulness, the self-respect and self-dependence—the combination of intelligence and handicraft—the accumulation of the materials of wealth, all referable to such an institution, present fair claims to the assistance of the entire American people.'

"Mr. Reason proves himself a prophet in forecasting conditions familiar to every observer. He adds:

" 'Whenever emancipation shall take place, immediate though it be, the subjects of it, like many who now make up the so-called free population, will be in what geologists call a transition state. The prejudice now felt against them for bearing on their persons the brand of slaves, cannot die out immediately. Severe trials will be their portion. The curse of a 'tainted race' must be expiated by almost miraculous proofs of advancement. . . . . To fight the battle on the bare ground of abstract principles will fail to give us complete victory. . . . . The last weak argument—that the Negro can never contribute anything to advance the national character, must be 'nailed to the counter as base coin.' . . . . Already he sees springing into growth from out his foster *work-school*, intelligent young laborers competent to enrich the world with necessary products—industrious citizens, contributing their proportion to aid on the advancing civilization of the country; self-providing artisans vindicating their people from the never-ceasing charge of a fitness for servile positions.' "

The Negroes who emigrated to Canada were more successful. In 1842 they held a convention to decide on the expenditure of $1,500 collected for them in England by a Quaker. They finally decided to start "a manual labor school where children could be taught the elements of knowledge which are usually the occupations of a grammar school; and where the boys could be taught in addition the practise of some mechanic art, and the girls could be instructed in those domestic arts which are the proper occupation and ornament of their sex."† Father Henson, the Negro who was chiefly instrumental in founding the school stated that the object was "to make it self-supporting by the employment of the students for certain portions of the time on the land." The school lasted some ten or fifteen years, but gradually decayed as the public schools were opened to Negro youth.

In many of the colored schools opened in the Northern states some industrial training was included. The Philadelphia "Institute for Colored

†Siebert: Underground Railroad, p. 206.

Youth" was founded by Richard Humphreys in 1837 for the education of Negroes "in school learning, in the various branches of the mechanic arts and trade, and in agriculture." For a while a farm and trade school was maintained from this fund in Bristol county, Penna., but the school is now in Philadelphia and is being reorganized as a technical and trade school.

When the civil war opened and the fall of slavery seemed imminent, some of the earliest suggestions for educating the blacks insisted on industrial training. The development, however, was slow and interesting. We may indicate the evolution of the Southern industrial school somewhat as follows:

1. Janitor work and chores performed by students.
2. Repair work and equipment by student labor.
3. Teaching of ordinary housework to girls.
4. Teaching of house-service for the training of servants.
5. The school of work; co-operative industry for gain, by use of student labor.
6. Teaching of trades.
7. The industrial settlement.
8. The social settlement.
9. Manual training.
10. Technological education.

A diagram will best illustrate the logical development of these successive ideas:

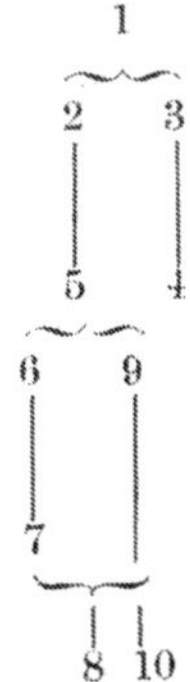

This diagram may be explained thus: at first nearly all the schools from necessity required their students to help in cleaning and arranging the school buildings and yards. Afterward this feature was kept as a part of the discipline and to this day in nearly all the boarding schools an hour or more of labor a day is required of each student regardless of his ability to pay for his schooling. From this situation (indicated by "1") two lines of training easily arose: first the boys by simple direction and oversight were enabled to make ordinary repairs about the school and even to make benches, tables and the like. This became a feature of many schools, both for its usefulness and discipline, (2). On the other hand the New England school teachers who came South found the Negro girls startlingly ignorant of matters of household economy, which are among the first things a properly-bred girl knows. These girls could not sew, they could not sweep, they could not make a bed properly or cook digestible food. Lessons in simple housework for the girls early became a part of the curriculum, (3). This was practically the extent of industrial training in nearly all schools, except Hampton, until about 1880. The new industrial movement then began to awaken the South and many began to see clearly that unless the Negro made especial effort he could gain no important place. The idea of a "School of Work" therefore arose. It was to furnish education practically free to those willing to work for it; it was to "do" things—i. e., become a center of productive industry, it was to be partially, if not wholly, self-supporting, and it was to teach trades, (5). Admirable as were some of the ideas underlying this scheme the whole thing simply would not work in practice: it was found that if you were to use time and material to teach trades thoroughly you could not at the same time keep the industries on a commercial basis and make them pay. Many schools started out to do this on a large scale and went into virtual bankruptcy. Moreover it was found also that it was possible to teach a boy a trade mechanically without giving him the full educative benefit of the process, and *vice versa,* that there was a distinct educative value in teaching a boy to use his hands and eyes in carrying out certain physical processes, even though he did not actually learn a trade. It has happened, therefore, in the last decade that a noticeable change has come over the industrial schools. In the first place the idea of commercially remunerative industry in a school is being pushed rapidly to the back-ground. There are still schools with shops and farms that bring an income, and schools that use student labor partially for the erection of buildings and the furnishing of equipment. It is coming to be seen, however, in the education of the Negro as clearly as it has been seen in the education of youths the world over that it is the *boy* and not the material product that is the true object of education, Consequently the object of the industrial school became to be the thorough training of boys regardless of the income derived from the process of training, and, indeed, regardless of the cost of the training as long as it was thoroughly well done.

Even at this point, however, the difficulties were not surmounted. In the first place modern industry has taken great strides since the war and the teaching of trades is no longer a simple matter. Machinery and long processes of work have greatly changed the work of the carpenter, the iron-worker and the shoemaker. A really efficient workman must be to-day an intelligent man who has had good technical training in addition to thorough common school and perhaps even higher training. To meet this situation the industrial schools began a further development; they established distinct Trade Schools for the thorough training of better class artisans and at the same time they sought to preserve for the purposes of general education such of the simpler processes of elementary trade learning as were best suited therefor. In this differentiation of the Trade School and manual training the best of the industrial schools simply followed the plain trend of the present educational epoch. A prominent educator tells us that, in Sweden, "In the beginning the economic conception was generally adopted and everywhere manual training was looked upon as a means of preparing the children of the common people to earn their living. But gradually it came to be recognized that manual training has a more elevated purpose and one indeed more useful in the deeper meaning of the term. It came to be considered as an educative process for the complete moral, physical and intellectual development of the child."*

This conception of the plan of physical training in the educative process is gradually making its way into all schools. It does not belong peculiarly to "Industrial" schools, although it was, so to speak, discovered there. It is rather a part of all true education. As Mr. A. G. Boyden has so well pointed out,† the modern "laboratory" methods are but part of this new educational movement: "The learner must handle the objects whose qualities he perceives through the senses." He must handle the objects whose *colors* he would know, place them together and form pleasing combinations and mix and apply colors with his own hands; he must handle bodies whose *forms* he would know, measure their dimensions, draw the forms and make them of clay, paper or wood. So too he must examine and analyze *minerals*, draw and examine *plants*, observe and dissect *animals*, apply *mathematics* to counters and measures and surfaces, perform actual experiments in *physics* and *chemistry* and take notes, mould land configurations and draw maps in *geography*; prepare written exercises in *grammar*, prepare outlines, charts and reports in *history* and *civics*. Finally the student must express frequently in writing what he thinks and studies.

Manual training as an integral part of general culture has but just begun to enter the Negro industrial schools. It was first established at Atlanta University in 1883 by Mr. Clarence C. Tucker. Here General Armstrong saw the system and induced Mr. Tucker to enter into the service of Hampton, where industrial training had been given from the first, and there introduce the distinct system of manual training. Hampton has since developed and perfected it in connection with Kindergarten and Sloyd work. In time from such manual training will probably develop higher technological and engineering schools, but this is the work of the future. On the other hand with the distinct Trade-school evolved also the idea of the Industrial settlement. The co-operative commercial organization, which was found impracticable in a school, has been, in one community at least, —Kowaliga—developed into a business organization. The school here has been definitely differentiated from business as such and the community organized for work. A slightly different development occurred at Calhoun, where a settlement of Northern people undertook not simply a school but social and economic work to lift the community to a higher social plane.

6. *The Industrial School.* There were in the United States in the scholastic year, 1899-1900, ninety-eight schools for Negroes which gave courses in industrial training. Their names and addresses are as follows:‡

*M. Gluys, quoted in Harris' Psychology of Manual Training.

†In Report of Conference on Manual Training, Boston, Mass.

‡Where dates are given after the name of the school the statistics are for that year and not for 1899-1900.

Name of School.	Address.	Total number of pupils receiving industrial training.	1899-1900. Students trained in industrial branches. Farm or garden work.	Carpentry.	Bricklaying.	Plastering.	Painting.	Tin or sheet-metalwork.	Forging.	Machine shop work.	Shoemaking.	Printing.	Sewing.	Cooking.	Other trades.
	Alabama.														
Kowaliga Academic and Industrial School	Kowaliga	205	5	3	0	0	2	0	3	5	0	0	125	10	2
Emerson Normal Institute	Mobile	100		40									60		
State Normal Institute	Montgomery	466	12	33					25			17	289	29	28
Agricultural and Mechanical College	Normal	499	22	17			17	1	15	25	20	25	76	34	227
Talladega College	Talladega	195	9	43								2	115	26	
Stillman Institute	Tuscaloosa	35	35												
Tuskegee Normal and Industrial School, '98 and '99	Tuskegee	1,180	149	57	36		10	13		32	13	13	90	61	
	Arkansas.														
Shorter University	Argenta	16										7		9	
Arkadelphia Acad. '98 & '99.	Arkadelphia	20	3										20	20	
Arkansas Baptist Col. "	Little Rock	56	50								2	12	50	2	
Philander Smith College	Little Rock	95										13	82	82	
Branch Normal College	Pine Bluff	109		32			2	5	15	10			45		
Southland College	Southland	120	40	2			2				1		60	20	40
State College for Colored Students	Dover	46	12	14			2		4			3	20	4	
	District of Columbia.														
Howard University	Washington	223		81				15				52	75		
Normal School, (col.)	Washington	38											38		
	Florida.														
Cookman Institute	Jacksonville	23	16										7	7	
Edward Waters College	Jacksonville	22											22		
Fessenden Academy	Martin	130	50	20									80	27	
Emerson Memorial Home and School	Ocala	76											76	19	21
Orange Park Normal and Manual Training School	Orange Park	79	36	36									43	43	
Florida State Normal and Industrial School	Tallahassee	100	30	16			6	16				2	48	48	
	Georgia.														
Jeruel Academy	Athens	80											80		
Knox Institute	Athens	114		22								15	94		
Atlanta University	Atlanta	233		32					20			10	167	51	34
Morris Brown College	Atlanta	83	6	2	9	1	2				1	4	44	44	
Spelman Seminary	Atlanta	450										32	402	50	63
Storrs School	Atlanta	93											93		
Haines Normal and Industrial Institute	Augusta	208										8	200	15	

Name of School.	Address.	Total number of pupils receiving industrial training.	1899-1900 Students trained in industrial branches.											
			Farm or garden work.	Carpentry.	Bricklaying.	Plastering.	Painting.	Tin or sheet-metal work.	Forging.	Machine shop work.	Shoemaking.	Printing.	Sewing.	Cooking.	Other trades.
	Georgia (Con.)														
Georgia State Industrial College, '98 and '99	College	140	12	8	8	8	10		8		8		40		
Fort Valley High and Industrial School	Fort Valley	75	26	30									50	36	
Dorchester Acad	McIntosh	209		85									124	21	
Ballard Nor. School	Macon	272											262	10	32
Central City College	Macon	91	35	26	5							11	15	10	
Beach Institute	Savannah	41											35	1	20
Clark University	South Atlanta	310		15					6		6	7	175	48	
Allen Nor. & Indus. Sch.	Thomasville	78											78	6	
	Kentucky.														
State Normal School for Colored Persons	Frankfort	170	72	50								18	70	70	
Chandler Nor. School	Lexington	111											111		
	Louisiana.														
Gilbert Academy and Indus. College	Baldwin	141	48					11	11						
Leland University	New Orleans	16											16		
Straight University	New Orleans	229		72								29	157		
	Maryland.														
St. Frances Academy	Baltimore	27											13	8	6
Industrial Home for Colored Girls, '98 & '99	Melvale	105											105	40	
Princess Anne Academy	Princess Anne	60	31	9					3		4	11	29	29	4
	Mississippi.														
Mount Hermon Female Seminary	Clinton	60											60	60	
Southern Christian Inst.	Edwards	43	18	14			3			5		5	15	10	2
Miss. State Nor. School	Holly Springs	80											80		
Rust University	Holly Springs	124	3	30			8				11		56	10	
Jackson College	Jackson	60											60		
Tougaloo University	Tougaloo	221	22	75					20				98	70	12
Alcorn Agricultural and Mechanical College	Westside	339	110	85			20				32				75
	Missouri.														
Lincoln Institute	Jefferson City	125		36					34	6		6	49		
Geo. R. Smith College	Sedalia	52										12	40		
	New Jersey.														
Manual Training and Industrial School	Bordentown	109		28									41	32	9

Name of School.	Address.	Total number of pupils receiving industrial training.	1899-1900 Students trained in industrial branches.											
			Farm or garden work.	Carpentry.	Bricklaying.	Plastering.	Painting.	Tin or sheet-metal work.	Forging.	Machine shop work.	Shoemaking.	Printing.	Sewing.	Cooking.	Other trades.
	North Carolina.														
Washburn Seminary....	Beaufort.......	118		48									70		
Biddle University.......	Charlotte.......	107		23	9	5					4	46	20		
Scotia Seminary.........	Concord.........	290											290	290	
Franklinton Christian College, '98 & '99.......	Franklinton....	10											10		
Agr. and Mechanical Col. for the Colored Race..	Greensboro.....	174	143	88					88	6			64	64	
High Point Normal and Industrial School......	High Point.....	60		12	8	3							60	15	
Lincoln Academy.......	Kings Mountain	155	6	5	2								110	85	13
Barrette Collegiate and Industrial School.....	Pee Dee........	75		5	10	5	2				5	5	20	20	
Plymouth State Nor. Sch.	Plymouth......	37											37		
St. Augustine's School...	Raleigh.........	100		6	8	8	3	1				12	50	50	
Shaw University........	Raleigh.........	190		70									120		
Livingstone College.....	Salisbury.......	9		4	3						9	9			
Gregory Nor. Sch., '97 & '98	Wilmington....	100											100		
Rankin-Richards Inst...	Windsor.........	16											16		
The Slater Indus. and State Nor. School......	Winston.........	118	5	22							3		38	37	
	Pennsylvania.														
Inst. for Colored Youth.	Philadelphia...	272		24	12						15	11		87	123
	South Carolina.														
Schofield Normal and Indus. School.........	Aiken.........	231	18	20							10	10	173	72	10
Browning Home School, '97 and '98............	Camden.........	136											100	36	
Avery Nor. Institute....	Charleston.......	75											75		
Brainerd Institute.......	Chester.........	205	57	24			2				2	3	117	40	40
Allen University........	Columbia.......	84											84	20	
Benedict College........	Columbia.......	213	10	8			9				4	25	109	20	
Penn. Nor. and Indus. School...............	Frogmore.......	179		98								12	91		
Brewer Nor. Sch. '98 & '99	Greenwood......	147											147		
Claflin University......	Orangeburg....	487	27	108	175	42	10		50	50		8	195	46	
	Tennessee.														
Warner Institute........	Jonesboro.......	78	76	3	2	1					2		52	84	30
Knoxville College.......	Knoxville.......	68	9	14								11	36	10	
Lemoyne Nor. Inst......	Memphis........	462		45								19	378	30	
Morristown Nor. Col....	Morristown.....	93											93	68	
Cen. Tenn. College......	Nashville........	70		10				4				41	9		12
Roger Williams Univ...	Nashville........	100										2	98		

Name of School.	Address.	Total number of pupils receiving industrial training.	1899-1900 Students trained in industrial branches. Farm or garden work.	Carpentry.	Bricklaying.	Plastering.	Painting.	Tin or sheet-metal work.	Forging.	Machine shop work.	Shoemaking.	Printing.	Sewing.	Cooking.	Other trades.
	Texas.														
Bishop College	Marshall	327							15	15		23	106	14	
Wiley University	Marshall	200			24		2				5	20	160	60	
Paul Quinn College	Waco	149	32	15								27	92		
	Virginia.														
Ingleside Seminary,'98-99	Burkeville	109	109	109									109	109	
Gloucester Agr. & Indus. College, '98 and '99	Cappahosic	97	30										20	27	20
Hampton Nor. & Agricultural Institute	Hampton	949	413	29	11	11	6		26	13	5	10	412		130
St. Paul Normal and Industrial School, '98-'99	Lawrenceville	230	18	10	4	5	2	1	6		10	8	72	22	72
Manassas Indus. School, '98 and '99	Manassas	65	3	27					23		1		38		
Norfolk Mission College	Norfolk	406										20	280	92	
Va. Nor. and Coll. Inst.	Petersburg	183											183	20	
Va. Union University	Richmond	12													
	W. Virginia.														
Storer College	Harper's Ferry	105		35									40	40	

The chief schools according to the number of students in industrial courses are:

Tuskegee, Ala	1,180	Alcorn, Miss	339
Hampton, Va	949	Bishop, Texas	327
A. & M. College, Normal, Ala	499	Clark, Ga	310
Claflin, S. C	487	Scotia, N. C	290
State N'mal, Montgomery, Ala	466	Institute, Penna	272
Spelman, Ga	450	Ballard, Ga	272
Norfolk, Va	406	Atlanta, Ga	233
LeMoyne, Tenn	402	St. Paul, Va	230
Straight, Va	229	Dorchester, Va	209
Howard, D. C	223	Haines, Ga	208
Tougaloo, Miss	221	Kowaliga, Ala	205

Wiley, Texas 200

These gross numbers, however, are of little value on account of the varying value and thoroughness of the courses given. The easiest course is that of sewing for girls, and this one item swells the returns unduly for it is often given in a desultory way. We can best compare the schools, therefore, by asking how many students are enrolled in the classes in carpentry, bricklaying, plastering, painting, iron and sheet metal work, forging and machine shop work.* The following schools have 50 or more thus enrolled:

Claflin, S. C	345	Dorchester, Ga	85
A. & M. College, Greensboro, N. C.	182	Lincoln, Mo	76
Tuskegee, Ala	161	Straight, Va	72
Alcorn, Miss	137	Shaw, N. C	70
A. & M. College, Normal, Ala.	117	Branch, Ark	64
Ingleside, Va	109	State Normal, Ky	59
Hampton, Va	101	State Normal, Montgomery, Ala.	58
Penn, S. C	98	Atlanta, Ga	52
Howard, D. C	96	Institute for Colored Youth, Pa.	51
Tougaloo, Miss	95	Manassas, Va	51
Ga. State College	50		

Here again difference in the time spent and the thoroughness of the work and its relation to the other work of the institution make comparison difficult. On the whole, however, we may designate the following as the chief Negro industrial schools:

Alabama: State Normal, Montgomery.
A. and M. College, Normal.
Tuskegee.

Arkansas: Branch Normal.

Florida: State Normal, Tallahassee.

Georgia: Spelman.
State Industrial College.

Kentucky: State Normal.

Louisiana: Straight.

Mississippi: Alcorn.
Tougaloo.

Missouri: Lincoln Institute.

North Carolina: Biddle.
Scotia.
A. and M. College, Greensboro.
High Point.
Shaw.
Slater I. and State N.

Pennsylvania: Institute for Colored Youth.

South Carolina: Scofield.
Brainerd.
Penn N. and I.
Claflin.
Colored N. I. A. and M.†

Tennessee: LeMoyne.

Texas: Prairie View.†
Bishop.

Virginia: Hampton.
Va. N. and C. I., Petersburg.
St. Paul.

*Printing and farming are omitted because often a job office and a truck farm are connected with a school for commercial purposes and are rated as casual "industrial courses."

†Not reported by Bureau of Education, 1899-1900.

Another criterion of the efficiency of Industrial Schools is the list of beneficiaries of the Slater fund, this fund being distributed especially among industrial schools after careful inspection of their work. In 1901-2 the following schools were aided, and may be regarded, therefore, as the best Negro Industrial Schools from the point of view of the Slater trustees:

Hampton, Va.	Shaw, N. C.
Spelman, Ga.	Montgomery, Ala.
Tuskegee, Ala.	Tougaloo, Miss.
Claflin, S. C.	Straight, La.
Bishop, Texas.	

7. *The Influence of the Slater Fund.* Perhaps the greatest single impulse toward the economic emancipation of the Negro has been the singularly wise administration of the gift of John F. Slater. Mr. Slater gave to a board of trustees in 1882, one million dollars for "the uplifting of the lately emancipated population of the Southern States and their posterity, by conferring upon them the blessings of Christian education."* Mr. Slater knew and sympathized with the efforts of the American Missionary Association and other agencies in the work of uplifting the Negroes. He said: "It is no small part of my satisfaction in taking this share in it, that I hereby associate myself with some of the noblest enterprises of charity and humanity, and may hope to encourage the prayers and toils of faithful men and women who have labored and are still laboring in this cause."* Mr. Slater did not particularly mention industrial training, although he had thought of it,** but he left the largest discretion to the trustees "only indicating, as lines of operation adapted to the present condition of things, the training of teachers from among the people requiring to be taught, if, in the opinion of the corporation, by such limited selection the purposes of the trust can be best accomplished; and the encouragement of such institutions as are most effectually useful in promoting this training of teachers."* The first plans adopted by the Slater fund Trustees looked toward "the encouragement and assistance of promising youth—a certain number of whom shall be annually chosen by the authorities of well-managed institutions approved by this Board of Trustees," but it was provided that "so far as practicable the scholars receiving the benefit of this foundation shall be trained in some manual occupation, simultaneously with their mental and moral instruction." The plan thus begun took clearer shape in 1883 when the board "*Resolved* that, for the present, this board confine its aid to such schools as are best fitted to prepare young colored men and women to become useful to their race; and that institutions which give instruction in trades and other manual occupations, that will enable colored youths to make a living, and to become useful citizens, be carefully sought out and preferred in appropriations from this Fund."

Dr. Haygood, the first general agent, in the fall of 1883 pointed out the especial recommendation of Mr. Slater as to the training of Negro teachers and recommended that "this Board should confine its operations to those institutions that are found to be most capable of training suitable teachers." He added, however, that "only a small number of the higher

*Letter of the Founder. **Proceedings, &c., 1891, p. 35.

grade schools for colored youth have made any experiments in connecting handicraft training with instruction in books." He added: "It is proper to say that some of the most experienced workers in this field are not convinced of the wisdom of making industrial training an important feature in their plans and efforts. Many equally experienced, entertain no doubts on this subject. They believe that industrial training is not only desirable as affording the means of making a more self-reliant and self-supporting population, but necessary as furnishing some of the conditions of the best intellectual and moral discipline of the colored people—especially of those who are to be the teachers and guides of their people."* The general agent made these recommendations of policy: 1st. Aid to students with exceptional gifts. 2nd. Aid for medical instruction, and 3rd, general appropriations as before indicated.

The first institutions aided were:

Clark University, Atlanta, Ga	$2,000
Lewis High School, Macon, Ga	200
Tuskegee Normal School, Tuskegee, Ala	100
Tougaloo University, Tougaloo, Miss	1,000
LeMoyne Institute, Memphis, Tenn	500
Claflin University, Orangeburg, S. C	2,000
Atlanta University, Atlanta, Ga	2,000
Talladega College, Talladega, Ala	2,000
Shaw University, Raleigh, N. C	2,000
Hampton Institute, Hampton, Va	2,000
Atlanta Baptist Female Seminary, Atlanta, Ga	2,000
Austin High School, Knoxville, Tenn	450

This list of schools increased rapidly in the next few years as the various schools added or enlarged their industrial departments. In 1886-7, the list of aided schools was as follows:

Atlanta University, Atlanta, Ga.
Beaufort Normal School, Beaufort, S. C.
Benedict Institute, Columbia, S. C.
Brainerd Institute, Chester, S. C.
Central Tenn. College, Nashville, Tenn.
Claflin Univ., Orangeburg, S. C.
Clark University, Atlanta, Ga.
Fisk University, Nashville, Tenn.
Gilbert Seminary, Baldwin, La.
Hampton Institute, Hampton, Va.
Hartshorn Memorial Female Institute, Richmond, Va.
Howard Univ., Washington, D. C.
Ky. Normal Univ., Louisville, Ky.
Jackson College, Jackson, Miss.
Leonard Medical School, Raleigh, N. C.
Leland Univ., New Orleans, La.
Moore St. Industrial School, Richmond, Va.
Mt. Albion State Normal School, Franklinton, N. C.
Mt. Herman Female Seminary, Clinton, Miss.
New Orleans Univ., New Orleans, La.
Paul Quinn College, Waco, Texas.
Paine Institute, Augusta, Ga.
Philander Smith College, Little Rock, Ark.
Roger Williams Univ., Nashville, Tenn.
Rust Univ., Holly Springs, Miss.
Scotia Seminary, Concord, N. C.
Shaw Univ., Raleigh, N. C.
Slater Industrial School, Knoxville, Tenn.
Spelman Female Seminary, Atlanta, Ga.

*Proceedings, &c., 1883.

LeMoyne Institute, Memphis, Tenn.
Lewis Normal Institute, Macon, Ga.
Lincoln Normal Univ., Marion, Ala.
Livingston College, Salisbury, N. C.
Meharry Medical College, Nashville, Tenn.
State Normal School, Huntsville, Ala.
State Normal School, Tuskegee, Ala.
Straight Univ., New Orleans, La.
Talladega College, Talladega, Ala.
Tillotson Institute, Austin, Texas.
Tougaloo University, Tougaloo, Miss.

General Agent Haygood reported in 1890:

"As to industrial training, so far as schools for Negroes are concerned, the discussion is now at an end. Men now consider only the question of method. Eight years ago industrial training was well under way at Hampton Institute; it was feebly attempted at three or four schools; not considered as possible at most of them; in not a few utterly condemned. Industrial departments are now recognized necessities everywhere. It is more than worth while to add that the results of industrial training in the schools aided by the Slater Fund have had much to do with the awakening throughout the South to the need of tool-craft for the white youth of these states.

"An important result of the Slater work in the South (and how important and far-reaching it were hard to say) is this: The industrial training introduced and fostered by the Slater fund has made the cause of Negro education more friends among Southern white men than all speeches and writings put together."*

The final report of Dr. Haygood in 1891 is a fit summing up of the work of the Slater fund for the first decade. He says in part:† "In his educational development the Negro is just now at the danger line—of which he most of all is unconscious. So far his education has developed wants faster than his ability to earn means to satisfy them. In the most of them the result is discontent; with many, unhappiness; in some, a sort of desperation; in not a few, dishonesty. On these points I have not the shadow of a doubt; this particular matter I have studied widely and minutely. A plow-boy earning from $100 to $150 a year—board and lodging 'thrown in'—has enough to satisfy his normal wants; this boy after six years at school, not only desires but needs from $300 to $500 a year to satisfy the wants that have been bred in him, while his earning capacity has not grown in proportion. This state of things grows out of a natural and universal law of humanity, and is peculiar to the American Negro because he is now, and by no fault or choice of his, in this crisis of development.

"The poorest people are not those who have little, but those who want more than they can readily earn. That many half-taught and unwisely-taught Negroes 'go to the bad' and seek money by 'short-cuts' is not surprising. In these matters the Negro's weakness illustrates his brotherhood to his white neighbors. The prisons show enough half-educated white people to prove that merely learning the rudiments does not secure virtue. In all races it is true that with new knowledge new temptations

*Proceedings, &c., 1890.

†Proceedings, &c., 1891, pp. 28, ff.

come; strength to resist comes after if at all. In all this a man of sense finds no argument against the education of the Negro, but a demonstration of the need, for him, and for the white race, of more and better education.

"'Better' is not the same as 'more'; the imminent need for the Negro is to find out what education is now fittest for him. Nothing in these statements means the exclusion of the Negro from the highest and widest studies of which some of them are capable; it does mean, as I see it, that the 'regulation college curriculum' is not what most Negro students need.'

No truer words have ever been spoken on the Negro problem and few groups of men have seen their efforts to turn the current of public opinion so successful as have the trustees of the Slater Fund. Dr. Haygood was able to say as he laid down his trust: "Every school in connection with the Slater Fund recognizes the utility and necessity of industrial training; so does every important school for the Negro race whether aided by the fund or not. In many of these institutions industrial training is well established and successfully carried on; in all of them enough is accomplished to do great good and encourage more effort. Everyone known to me earnestly desires to extend its work in this direction. At the beginning many doubted, some opposed, and not a few were indifferent. At this time no experienced teacher in Negro schools entertains so much as a doubt as to the desirableness and usefulness of this very important element of education."

With the advent of Dr. J. L. M. Curry as general agent, the Trustees of the Slater Fund have gradually adopted a policy of concentration of effort, giving something over one-half of their income of $60,000 to Hampton and Tuskegee, $10,000 to Spelman and Claflin and the rest to six other schools, including one medical school.

It is clear that the great movement for the industrial education of Negroes and the encouragement of Negro artisans is due primarily to the Trustees of the John F. Slater fund, and for this they deserve the thanks of the nation.

8. *Curricula of Industrial Schools.* We can best judge the work of Industrial Schools by asking: 1. What is the course of study? 2. How is it carried out? And how much time is given to it? Let us briefly ask this question of the chief schools, using the latest available catalogue for the answers.

Hampton Normal and Agricultural Institute, Va., (1901-2.)

The Hampton Institute consists of five departments:

1. Academic Department, (three year course.)
2. Normal Department with Model School, (two years, post-graduate.)
3. Agricultural Department.
4. Department of Productive Industries and Domestic Work.
5. Trades School.

In the Academic Department the following instruction in manual training and industries is given:

	BOYS.	GIRLS.	OTHER ACADEMIC WORK.
1ST YEAR.	Bench work, 100 hours.	Sloyd, 2 hrs-3 hrs per week. Sewing, 2 periods per week. Cooking, 2 periods per week.	Agriculture, Physics, (Chemistry), Hygiene, Geography, Arithmetic, English, Reading and Literature, Bible Study, Music, Drawing, Penmanship and Gymnastics.
2ND YEAR.	Wood-turning, 120 hours.	Sewing, 2 periods per week. Cooking, 2 lessons a week, 4 months.	Agriculture, Geography, Arithmetic, English, Reading and Literature, U. S. History, Bible Study, Music, Drawing and Gymnastics.
3RD YEAR.	Forging, 120 hours, or work in Trade School.	Dressmaking.	(Partially elective—3 or 4 courses to be chosen), Agriculture, Physics, Mathematics, English, Reading and Literature, Civics, History, Music, Drawing, and Gymnastics.

In the Whittier Model School, cooking is given in the fourth and fifth grades, and sewing in certain lower grades. There is also in the first five grades a regular course of manual training including work with scissors and knife, simple bench tools, sloyd, repairing, etc. There is also a kindergarten.

The Department of Productive Industries consists of industries which "are conducted as business enterprises and are open to the students who have passed a year in the Trade School or Training Department." They afford the opportunity of learning how productive industries are managed, of making a practical application of the principles learned in the Trade School, and incidentally of earning wages. They also furnish some opportunity for skilled labor to young men working for credit to enter the Day or Trade School." Finally there is a regular Trade School with courses in Carpentry, Painting, Wheelwrighting, Blacksmithing, Machinework, Tailoring, Bricklaying, Plastering, Shoemaking, Harnessmaking, Steam Engineering, and Tinsmithing. Every student in the trade school works 9 hours a day and spends two hours in the night school. They must be at least 16 years of age to enter, and each course requires three years for completion.

Hampton is especially noteworthy in the elaborate and careful attempt to correlate literary work and manual training: Agriculture is studied on the farm, physics and chemistry in laboratories, geography by field excursions, arithmetic with especial reference to shop work, etc. So important is this experiment in the history of education that it is worth while quoting verbatim the principal's account of the work*:

*33rd Annual Report, 1901.

"Our manual training department gives instruction to every student in the school. No boy graduates from Hampton without having worked in wood, iron and sheet metal, besides having taken a course in agriculture. No girl graduates from the school without having received instruction in wood work, enabling her to mend and make simple furniture, or without having been taught to cook and serve a meal, to make her own dresses and underclothing. She is also given a fair knowledge of plant and animal life. The course for boys consists of a year of joinery, then a half year each of wood turning and sheet metal work and in the Senior year a choice of work in one or more of the various trades departments.

In our Whittier school manual training begins with paper cutting and constructive work in wood, with clay modeling in the kindergarten. This is followed by sewing in Room 2 for both boys and girls, and the course ends in Room 6 with bench work for the boys and sewing and cooking for the girls. Our Normal Department is given practice in teaching manual training and already work similar to that in the Whittier School has been introduced into some of the public schools of the South. I should like to repeat what I have said before, and what is daily becoming more evident in the school life here, that this thorough systematic work in the training of the hand and the eye is doing much to develop truthfulness, patience, earnestness and a sense of responsibility in our young people.

"The academic work is broader and stronger and in closer touch with life and with the other departments of the school. In our study of language we are teaching our students to do something, then to talk and write about it, and finally to read about it. In the regular course, no books are used for the first three months except for reference. In the laboratories the young people make experiments in order to learn about water, air, the soil and plants. These are followed by conversations and written exercises upon what they have seen and done. The study of mathematics is of the same practical character. Each student keeps a cash book showing what the school owes him for work, what he owes the school for board, etc. Each month the student has an account rendered him by the treasurer's office. These two statements should agree; if they do not, means are taken to discover on which side the error lies. Articles are manufactured by students, and the cost in material, time, etc., is computed. Surveying operations are carried on. Bills and memoranda concerning transactions on the farm, in the work shops, in the commissary and kitchens, are sent in for the classes to put into proper shape. Figures are made to live.

"In our geography department we are emphasizing physiography and industries. A study of current events is still the basis of a large part of our geography course. Some of the most valuable and interesting work is done in connection with the daily news items.

"The cooking and sewing, agricultural and shop work are thus made to contribute to the understanding of geography and history. Our teaching of the natural sciences begins with direct observation of nature, the study of trees and animals, and the gathering and classifying of specimens. Much emphasis is placed upon the teaching of practical physics and chemistry, without which our agriculture, mechanical work and geography would be most superficial."

Tuskegee Normal and Industrial Institute, Ala., (1901-2).

Tuskegee offers a common school course of three years, and a grammar school course of four years. Each student in the day school attends school four days a week and works at some industry one day each week and alternate Saturdays. Night school students work at industries in the day and study in the evening. There is a model school with a course in manual training, and a kindergarten. The industries offered the boys include Carpentry, Blacksmithing, Printing, Wheelwrighting, Harnessmaking, Carriagetrimming, Painting, Machinery, Engineering and Founding, Shoemaking, Brickmasonry and Plastering, Brickmaking, Sawmilling, Tinsmithing, Tailoring, Mechanical Drawing, Architectural Drawing, Electrical Engineering and Canning. The industries for girls are Sewing, Dressmaking, Millinery, Cooking, Laundering, Mattress-making, Basketry, Nurse-training.

Spelman Seminary, Atlanta, Ga., (1901-2.)

This is a school for girls and is a good example of the older type of industrial school. The catalogue says:

"Our industrial department aims to fit the student for the practical duties of life by training the hands for skill in labor. It develops character by forming habits of regularity, punctuality, neatness, thoroughness, accuracy, and application.

"DOMESTIC ARTS."

"Our boarding students, through their share in the daily routine of life, receive practical instruction in the care of rooms, in washing dishes, table-work, cooking, and laundry work. Each pupil is expected to give one hour daily to house-work, some especial duty being assigned her.

"A new course in cooking has been introduced, which covers three years. The following is the outline:—First Year. The kitchen,—its furnishing, care of utensils, the fire, dish-washing; study of food principles; processes of food cookery; plain cooking. Second Year. The dining room,—furnishing, care of china and silver, serving; review of food principles with more elaborate methods of cooking; canning, preserving, and pickling. Third Year.—Home sanitation and economic ventilation, furnishing, cleaning; arranging bills of fare; packing lunches; cookery for invalids and children.

"SEWING."

"All classes in the grammar and intermediate departments are taught sewing. The course includes mending, darning, overhanding, stitching, hemming, basting, hem-turning, hem-stitching, button-hole making, and the cutting and making of undergarments.

"DRESS-MAKING."

"The full course in dress-making covers three years. The use of a chart for drafting is taught, and cutting and fitting and finishing. Dress-making is elective.

"PRINTING."

"We teach compositor's work in our printing classes. Our printing office contains a small printing press and all necessary equipments for printing. It issues monthly an eight-page school paper, the Spelman Messenger; it also prints our annual catalogue, besides the circulars, letter and bill heads, envelopes, programs and cards required for school use. This work insures instruction in a variety of typesetting. Printing is an elective."

There is also a course in nurse-training.

Claflin University, Orangeburg, S. C., (1901-02.)

Claflin offers the following courses:

In each of the eight primary and grammar grades:

Manual training, three weekly periods, 45 minutes each.

In each of the four years of the College Preparatory and Normal Courses; four times a week:

Boys: Wood-carving, forging, freehand and mechanical drawing.

Girls: Dress-making and domestic service.

"In the third year of either of these courses each student must select a trade." This trade is pursued the third and fourth years.

In the first two years of the college course: Architectural drawing.

The course of Manual Training includes:

Preliminary Sloyd.
High Swedish Sloyd.
Wood-carving.
Forging.
Freehand and mechanical drawing.
Mechanical drawing.
Architecture.

The trades to be chosen from are:

Carpentry, cabinet making and stair building.
Iron-working.
Brickmasonry and Plastering.
Wheelwrighting.
Painting.
Printing.
Tailoring.

These trades are pursued two years in the regular course and an elective third year is offered for those who wish to perfect themselves and "enter the work as a life business."

Shaw University, Raleigh, N. C., (1898-99.)

There is in this school four years of common school work, two years of preparatory work, a three years' Normal course and four years' College course. Manual training is a required study in every year except the last year of the Normal and the four years of the College course. The course is as follows:

1st year—Wood carpentry; freehand drawing.
2nd year—Forge work; mechanical drawing.
3rd year—Vise-work; mechanical drawing.
4th year—Designing; architectural work.

The catalogue says:

"We do not teach trades, and make no pretensions to doing it, for we have no desire to inaugurate a trade school, but we do pretend to carry on industrial work along educational lines, and this work will be extended more and more as fast as financial means are obtained.

"We purpose to do all our work in these departments, not only along educational lines, but up to the standard of the best educational thought on the subject.

"In the Manual Training Department we give a course in drawing and the use of tools. We follow Cross's system of freehand and Prang's system of mechanical drawing, and the plan of manual training as laid down by Professor Kilborn, of the Manual Training School in Springfield, Massachusetts. The course in drawing includes both geometrical and constructive. As the course becomes more extended and complete, greater attention will be given to mechanical drawing. Students in manua training and carpentry are taught the use and care of a great variety of tools and the principles that underlie their use.

"The Matron of Estey Seminary, who has had training in the best schools in the North, is following out a general system of housework and sewing that is of great educational value. Instead of work being done at haphazard, it is systematized in such a way that it is carried on in accordance with certain principles."

Tougaloo University, near Jackson, Miss., (1901-2.)

"Industrial work in some form is combined with all these courses," viz;

Kindergarten, Grammar School, Preparatory School and Teachers' Training Course.

"While it is true and understood that this work is valuable as a preparation for trades and an aid in obtaining a livelihood, the mental and physical development of students holds first place in the plan of instruction. Finished products are sought for as a mark of industry and skill, also for their commercial value. The regular course consists of four years' work in the wood-working, blacksmithing and brick-laying departments, in connection with which a thorough course in mechanical drawing is taught each year. For those who wish to thoroughly master carpentry, cabinet making, blacksmithing or bricklaying after completing the regular course, a special course will be given. This end should be accomplished by the average student in about three years, as he has already had one year's work in each of the above-named branches."

Wilberforce University, Wilberforce, O., (1901-2).

The industries offered are: Carpentry, 3 years' course; Sewing, 3 years' course; Printing, 3 years' course; Shoe-making, 2 years' course; Agriculture is about to be introduced, and also blacksmithing, brickmaking, and masonry. Usually about two hours a day is given to industries by students in the Normal Course.

Howard University, Washington, D. C., (1898-99.)

"Students of the preparatory and normal departments practice in the methods of certain trades at specified hours." The trades are: carpentry, printing, tin-smithing, bookbinding ("to bind and rebind for the library") and sewing.

Clark University, Atlanta, Ga., (1901-02).

Pupils in the common-school grades must take three years of industrial training. A regular trade course is also provided as follows:

1st year: Trade, 5 times a week, 14 hours a week in mathematics, biology, history and English.

2nd year: Trade, 5 times a week, 12 hours a week in drawing, mathematics, history, physics and English.

3rd year: Trade, 5 times a week, 11 hours a week in mathematics, chemistry and English.

The trades offered are Agriculture, Iron-working, Printing, Shoemaking, and Wood-working.

Berea College, Berea, Ky., (1899-1900).

This institution gives two-year courses in Farm economy and Home economy:

1ST YEAR.

FARM ECONOMY.	HOME ECONOMY.
Farming, 5 hours, 1 term.	Sewing, 5 hours, 1 term.
Woodwork, 5 hours, 1 term.	Cooking, 5 hours, 1 term.
Gardening, 5 hours, 1 term.	Gardening, 5 hours, 1 term.
Other studies, 13 hours, 3 terms.	Other studies, 13 hours, 3 terms.

2ND YEAR.

FARM ECONOMY.	HOME ECONOMY.
Horticulture, 5 hours, 2 terms.	Cooking, 5 hours, 1 term.
Farm Management, 5 hours, 1 term.	Household Economy, 5 hrs., 1 term.
Animal Husbandry, 5 hours, 1 term.	Dairying, 5 hours, 1 term.
Forestry, 5 hours, 1 term.	Other studies, 13 hours, 3 terms.
Farm Crops, 3 hours, 1 term.	
Other studies, 28 hours, 1 term.	

Short apprenticeships in farming, carpentry, printing, sewing and household economy are given to a limited number of students. They devote one-half their time to school studies and one-half to the trade.

Biddle University, Charlotte, N. C., (1897-98).

"Every student in the Preparatory and Normal School is required to take a trade in the School of Industries." Each student spends from one to two hours a day in the industrial department for four days each week during the three years' course. Six trades are taught: Carpentry, Printing, Bricklaying, Plastering, Tailoring and Shoemaking. About 1-6 of the student's time is given to the trade. One hundred and thirty-eight were enrolled in the five trades.

Walden University, (Central Tennessee College) Nashville, Tenn., (1899-1900).

Elective courses are offered in printing, carpentry, blacksmithing, tinwork, and sewing. Students will be paid for their labor as soon as it is valuable.

Alcorn A. and M. College, Westside, Miss., (1900-01).

An industrial course, beginning with the grammar grades, and covering five years is so arranged "that each student can take a trade in some one of the industries. All students in this course must enter upon the learning of some trade under the same requirements as class-room work." The trades offered are: Shoemaking, Agriculture, Carpentry, Blacksmithing and Printing.

Agricultural and Mechanical College of Alabama for Negroes, Normal, Ala., (1900-01).

The trade courses offered are: Carpentry. Iron-working, Shoemaking, Broom-making, Chairbottoming, Nurse-training, Millinery, Cooking, Laundering, Printing, Machine-shop, and Agriculture.

"All work, including building, repairing, blacksmithing, wheelwrighting, painting, broommaking, printing, shoemaking, mattress making, farming, cooking, dining room and general housework, is performed by the students. From four cents to fifteen cents per hour is allowed, according to the skill and faithfulness of the student. It can be easily seen that great advantages are offered by this institution to young men and women seeking an industrial and literary education. . . . . .

"Further, the aim is to turn all labor, and all articles produced by labor, to advantage and utility. Therefore, all of these industrial departments contribute in some way to the equipment of the Institution, and are, in most cases, a source of income to the student as well as a means of instruction."

The shop wages are:

"Work of the first-year class goes for lessons.

"Work of the second-year class goes for lessons.

"Work of the third-year class, one-half (½) net profit.

"Post-graduates and skilled labor, one-half (½) price of the work.

"All students becoming skilled workmen will receive a per cent of the profits of all articles manufactured or repaired by them while they are employed in the shops."

The Calhoun Colored School, Lowndes Co., Ala., (1901-02).

The report on manual training says:

"Upwards of a dozen school buildings have been kept in repair. There have been also the odd jobs of carpentry, painting, plumbing, etc., which might be classed under new work or improvements. Much of this work has been done by our larger boys of the day school, in classes, working one period of about an hour and three-quarters each week.

"The smaller boys have received instruction again this year in sloyd whittling during a corresponding period.

"The night-school boys have been six in number. These work all day. The variety of jobs which they learn to do in the course of a term is even greater than that of the day scholars. There has been this year an added interest on the part of the boys; and this, I believe, has been due to increasing ability to take hold of and do intelligently so many kinds of practical work, even if some sacrifice of the student to the work of the place was involved.

"But while the present system has been in the past of benefit to our boys educationally and to the school economically, Calhoun has grown to that stage where it seems advisable to separate the instruction and training for the day students from the repair work. The yearly increasing demands for repairs to the school plant have grown to such proportions that it is quite impracticable to carry the repairing with classes from the Academic Department, in a way that will be profitable alike to the student and the school.

"The bulk of the repair work, however, can still be carried with proper superintendence by night-school boys, needing such a chance to earn their way into day school; and this can still be so conducted that it will be of educational value to the student as well as a source of economy to the school."

Tillotson College, Austin, Texas, (1899-1900).

"Our course in Wood-working includes the 3rd, 4th, 5th, 6th and 7th grades. It gives the theory and use of all common wood-working tools and the elementary principles of wood-construction in carpentry and joinery.

"It begins with the simplest tools and exercises, developing gradually to the most complex and difficult.

"Working drawings are used constantly, so the student learns to understand and interpret all kinds of scale drawings.

"We give special attention to two things:

"First. The effect of this work in training the eye and mind to habits of accurate, intelligent and truthful observation, and the hand to the skilful and precise manipulation of tools.

"Second. To give, as far as possible, a knowledge of the principles involved in the use of wood-construction.

"Sewing, dress and garment-cutting and making are also taught."

Schofield Normal and Industrial School, Aiken, S. C., (1899-1900).

"It is growing more and more to be a necessity in the South, and all over the country, to teach youths how to use their hands as well as their heads. Hand training helps students to do better work in the school room. We teach how to do the best in all branches."

There are in operation a Printing department, Harness department, Carpentry shop, a shop for Iron-working, Farming, Shoemaking, Sewing and Dressmaking, House-keeping, Cooking and Laundry departments.

Good boys with recommendation, capable of doing general farm work, are allowed seven dollars and fifty cents ($7.50) a month with board, which goes toward paying expenses in the school boarding department when the engagement at the farm closes. No one is taken on the farm for less than four months and the time made cannot be sold to another: it must be taken out in board and schooling within one year or will be forfeited. Willing boys get one and a half months board and tuition for each month's work done on the farm.

Normal and Manual Training School, Orange Park, Fla., (1901-1902).

For Boys.—The course for boys, beginning with the most elementary work, embraces nearly every process and joint brought into general use in wood construction, and also the filing and polishing of finished articles, after the most approved methods.

Mechanical Drawing is taught in connection with shop work, with thorough drill in reading and making drawings for construction purposes, followed later by more general, complicated and finished work.

The students also receive experience in useful employment, such as repairing and caring for the school buildings, gardening, etc., and thus acquire order and thoroughness in their labor.

For Girls.—The course in sewing and dressmaking will include talks upon dress materials, suggestions in making over garments, and in choice of colors. The sewing room is a large, well-lighted room, equipped with sewing machine, drafting table, etc.

Prairie View State Normal School, Prairie View, Texas, (1898-1899).

"The great object of the mechanical department is to foster a high appreciation of the value and dignity of intelligent labor. A boy who sees nothing in manual labor but dull, brute force, looks with contempt upon the labor and the laborer; but, as soon as he acquires skill himself, the conditions are reversed, and hence-forth he appreciates the work and honors the workman.

"The work of this department is divided into three divisions: wood work, iron work, and drawing. Bench work in wood consists of exercises with the different wood-working tools, so arranged in a graded series as to embrace the use of all the tools in their various applications."

Virginia Union University, Richmond, Va., (1901-1902).

The course of industrial training is not intended to cover the entire work done in a regularly organized trade-school. Some, however, of the same work is undertaken, bnt not for the purpose of giving the student a definite trade. The aim is to give him such a mechanical training as will be of service to him in his chosen life work, whatever that may be.

"This general training will be of much greater value to the student than a course in which he would receive instruction and practice in a single trade. It will give him a good general knowledge of wood and iron materials used in building, and of the principles underlying the acquisition of all trades. It will give him right habits of work, and such training of the hand and eye as will enable him, with but little effort, and in a very short time, to master any trade to which he may choose to devote himself."

The Industrial Training Course includes mechanical and free-hand drawing, designing, the use of tools in wood and iron work, and blacksmithing, and printing, including typesetting and correcting proof. All students in the first year of the theological courses, and in the preparatory, academic, and ministers' courses, are required to do this work. It is, however, optional in the case of college students and students in the second and third year of the theological courses.

The industrial building is furnished with power from the electric and heating plant. It is also provided with the latest improved machinery for every line of work in which instruction is given. Students are, therefore, given instruction and practice in the use of machinery, as well as in the use of hand-tools.

Knox Institute and Industrial School, Athens, Ga., (1901-1902).

The following compulsory courses are given:

Primary Grades—1st, 2nd and 3rd: Clay modeling, 3 terms; drawing, 3 terms.

Intermediate Grades—4th and 5th: Drawing, 3 terms; clay modeling, 2 terms.
Sewing, carpentry and wood-carving, 3 terms.

Grammar Grades—6th and 7th: Sewing and carpentry, 3 terms.
Wood-carving, 1 term.
Handicraft, 2 terms.

"Handicraft" includes hat-making, mat-making, basket-making, picture-frame making, box-making, etc.

Benedict College, Columbia, S. C., (1902).

This institution offers to girls "thorough instruction in sewing, dressmaking and domestic work; and to young men thorough instruction in printing, and, so far as facilities allow, in carpentry, shoemaking, painting, horticulture and agriculture."

"All students are required to work one and one-half hours per day in some industrial work. Those who accept the reduced rates for ministers are required to work an additional half hour per day. The labor rendered is a part of the compensation and the charges are adjusted on that basis. The allowance for student labor is credited on the accounts. It is precisely the same, therefore, as if the college paid the student that amount in cash for his labor.

"Moreover, all labor required is instructive. Work in the dormitories and corridors, in dining room and kitchen, teaches the girls how such work should be done. Besides the domestic work all the young women work daily in sewing or dressmaking under the instruction of competent teachers.

'The work on the campus, the keeping of the premises clean, the pruning of trees, the laying out of walks, the culture of flower plants, and the work in the field, not only teach industry, and show how such work should be done, but cultivate the eye and the hand, and lead to refinement and the appreciation of the clean, the true, and the beautiful."

Rust University, Holly Springs, Miss., (1902).

"During the English Course one-fourth of the time is given to Industrial Training. Every young man is required, unless specially excused by the President, to enter a class in either Carpentry, Shoemaking, Agriculture, or some industrial work; and every young woman of the English Course is required to enter a class either in Dressmaking, General Sewing, Domestic Science, Mexican Drawn Work or Basket Making."

Ballard Normal School, Macon, Ga., (1896-1897).

The girls have, during the course, nine years work in the Sewing School under the constant supervision of their teachers.

In the Cooking Classes they are trained in the domestic arts of cooking and housekeeping. The boys of the higher grades are required to work five hours a week in the work shop, under the direction of a competent teacher.

Paul Quinn College. Waco, Tex., (1899-1900).

"Feeling that the need of the race is a large skilled labor class, Paul Quinn College has made the Industrial department co-ordinate with the other departments. Special effort is being made to broaden the scope of the work already represented and to add other trades.

"The Industrial Department is well organized and the grounds are well cultivated.

"The fruitfulness of the garden greatly reduces the current expenses of the boarding department. We manage to have vegetables of our own raising the whole year.

"Our system requires each student to work one hour each day. This gives needed exercise and training in useful employments."

Southern University, New Orleans, La., (1898-1899).

"A three years' Manual Training course, five hours per week, is required of all pupils who may have been assigned to this department for instruction.

"This shorter course is provided for the benefit of those pupils who are sufficiently advanced in their mathematical studies to take up the scientific or more advanced mechanical course which follows. It consists chiefly of manual training in the wood and metal working industries, and is designed to be thorough enough in its scope to give such pupils who have completed it, an intelligent understanding of the principles that underlie such trades as: Carpentry, Mill-Wrighting, Joining, Cabinet Making, Turning, Scroll, Sawing, Tinsmithing, Blacksmithing, Etc. The mastering of any of the above trades depends upon the individual skill acquired in their constant pursuit in after life.

"The mechanical or advanced course begins on the termination of the shorter course. It is most comprehensive in its scope, including such studies as Mechanical Drawing, Physics and Mechanics. Pattern making is taken up, and bench-work continued. The student is required to work from the measurements or drawings furnished or from his own designs. This course is pursued in conjunction with the Normal and regular Collegiate courses and extends over two years of instruction of 10 hours per week. The course at present confers no degree, but will be extended to the full length of the Collegiate course, as the future requirements of the university might suggest. The Mechanical course is elective, and is intended for students who wish to prepare themselves for some particular trade or line of industry."

Agricultural and Mechanical College for the Colored Race, Greensboro, N. C., (1902-3).

The department of mechanics offers a four years' course. The trustees "have decided that the first two years' work in this department shall be conducted as a trade school." The first and second year students, therefore, choose a single trade and work at it. After that time those who wish to graduate will receive instruction in other shops and in mathematics, science and drawing; the course is as follows:

FIRST YEAR.

FALL	WINTER	SPRING
Mathematics 5	Mathematics 5	Mathematics 5
Carpentry 3	Carpentry 3	Carpentry 15
Blacksmithing 3	Blacksmithing 3	Blacksmithing 15
Drawing 5	Drawing 5	Shoe & Harness Making
Free Hand Drawing 4	Free Hand Drawing 4	Technology 5
Tin Shop 3	Tin Work 15	
Shoe Making 3	Shoe Making 4	
	Material of Constr'tion 2	

SECOND YEAR.

FALL	WINTER	SPRING
Technology 5	Technology 5	Technology 5
Machine Design 4	Machine Design 3	Machine Design 4
Architecture 4	Architecture 4	Architecture 4
Algebra 5	Algebra 5	Algebra 5
Drawing 4	Drawing 4	Technical Drawing 4
Shop Work 15	Shop Work 15	Shop Work 15
Physics 4	Physics 4	Physics 4

THIRD YEAR.

FALL	WINTER	SPRING
Plane Geometry 5	Solid Geometry 5	Mathematics 5
Physics 4	Physics 4	Geology (General and Economic)
Technology 4	Technology 5	Physics 5
Reading and Essays 4	Technical Reading 4	Technology 5
Laboratory Work 4	Shop Work 15	Shop Work 15
Shop Work 4	Laboratory Work 4	Building Construction 4

FOURTH YEAR.

FALL	WINTER	SPRING
Trigonometry 5	Trigonometry 5	Surveying & Leveling 3
Mechanism 5	Mechanism 4	Photography
Plumbing and Heating 2	Lighting & V'ntil'ting 2	Thesis { Drawing 4
Power Transmission 2	Power Transmission 4	Thesis { Essay 2
Machine Design 4	Technology 5	Thesis { Model 6
Architecture 4	Shop Work	

There is a similar course in agriculture. Students receive from 5c to $12\frac{1}{2}$c an hour for work, credited to their school expenses. All students can thus "earn something each month, while the most industrious and energetic student will regularly earn more than his expenses."

Florida State Normal and Industrial School, Tallahassee, Fla., (1901-02).

The industrial department offers instruction in sixteen industries, and all students are required to take one or more of them. The instruction runs through the whole six years of the course. Manual training is the predominant feature in the first four years' work, and trade training in the last two years' work. The chief industries are: Mechanical and architectural drawing, printing, carpentry, painting, blacksmithing, wheelwrighting, tailoring, agriculture, sewing, cooking, millinery and dressmaking, laundering, etc.

Colored Normal, Industrial, Agricultural and Mechanical College of South Carolina, Orangeburg, (1896-97).

The industrial department aims "to give training in such industrial arts as may be suitable to men and women and conducive to self-reliance and usefulness. This Department teaches the following subjects: Sewing, Dress-making and Millinery, Cooking and Domestic Economy, Carpentry and Woodwork, Bricklaying and Plastering, Architecture, Mechanical Drawing and Painting, Ironworking and Machinery, Housekeeping, Farming, Upholstering and Cabinet-making, Saddlery, Harness-making and Shoe-making, Saw Milling and manufacture of hard and soft lumber, Type-writing, Printing and Tailoring.

"Students will devote two hours each day to the Industries. A record of their work in this Department is kept along with that of daily recitations, and counted as other studies for graduation."

Talladega College, Talladega, Ala., (1900-01).

"Training in the Industries has always received attention at TALLADEGA COLLEGE. It is believed that such training strengthens the power of observation, cultivates accuracy and skill, secures the formation of habits of industry and usefulness, and exerts an influence in the development of mind and heart. It is therefore made a part of the regular instruction given by the College. Its advantages are not offered to persons who do not wish to pursue the regular literary course, but desire simply 'to learn a trade.' Young men are taught Wood-working, Drafting, Forging, Agriculture, and, to some extent, Printing; while the young women receive training in Sewing, Dress-making, Cooking, Nursing and general housework."

Scotia Seminary, Concord, N. C., (1900-01).

In the industrial department of this school for girls the primary object "is domestic training. While the instruction given is such as to qualify the students to use their skill as a means of making a living, the end we keep most distinctively in view is to prepare them to be home makers."

"In the sewing room, systematic, practical instruction is given in plain sewing, especial attention being paid to patching, darning, hemming, button holes, cutting and making various garments. Fancy work is excluded as being so fascinating as to interfere with plain work, and requiring more time and money than our girls can afford.

"Fine dressmaking has also been introduced. Those who desire may give extra time to this, and when proficient will receive a certificate from this department.

"A text book on domestic economy has been introduced, and instruction in all pertaining to the care of a house and right ways of living is given. Practice is secured in the care of the buildings and in the kitchen and laundry work of the seminary, all done by the girls under careful supervision. Special lessons are given in cooking; from this department also certificates will be given to those who have come up to our standard of proficiency. These courses in plain cooking and domestic economy and in plain sewing are required as parts of the Grammar School course, and failure on the part of any one to complete them will be marked on the certificate.

"They are carefully graded on the neatness and thoroughness with which the domestic work is done, that it may have equal honor with other studies, thus raising the care of the home above mere drudgery."

LeMoyne Normal Institute, Memphis, Tenn., (1901-2).

In this school "manual training takes its place in the course of study on the same footing and is treated in every respect as of the same importance as any other branch of study." Through the ten years of the course the girls receive training in sewing for seven years, cooking two years, and nursing and hygiene, six months. The boys are trained in wood-working for three years. Both boys and girls are trained in printing in the Junior Normal year (the 11th year of the course).

Lincoln Institute, Jefferson City, Mo., (1902-1903).

"The object is to afford young men an opportunity to receive instruction in the mechanic arts, and to become proficient in the useful trades.

"To accomplish this industrial training is given as required work to young men of the Normal Course, while special courses are provided for those who desire to learn trades.

"The course is arranged parallel with the Normal and College Preparatory Courses and will be pursued as follows:

"Through the D Normal and Junior classes, woodwork; through the C Normal and Middle, blacksmithing; through the B Normal and Senior Preparatory Classes, machine work."

COURSE IN CARPENTRY. FIRST YEAR. FIRST TERM.

Joinery—Shopwork.
Mathematics—Algebra.
English—Grammar and Rhetoric.

SECOND TERM.

Turning—Shopwork.
Mathematics—Algebra.
Mechanical Drawing—Drawing.
English—Rhetoric.
Science—Physiology.

THIRD TERM.

Turning and Joinery.
Mathematics—Algebra.
Mechanical Drawing.
English—Rhetoric.

SECOND YEAR. FIRST TERM.

Joinery.
Mathematics—Algebra.
English—Grammar and Rhetoric.

SECOND TERM.

Turning.
Mathematics—Algebra.
Mechanical Drawing.
English—Rhetoric.
Science—Physiology.

THIRD TERM.

Turning and Joinery.
Mathematics—Algebra.
Mechanical Drawing.
English—Rhetoric.

THIRD YEAR. FIRST TERM.

Mathematics—Geometry.
Strength of Materials and Drawing.
English—English Literature.
Science—Chemistry.
Turning and Joining.

SECOND TERM.

Turning and Joining.
Mathematics—Trigonometay.
Mechanical Drawing—Architecture.
Science—Chemistry.
History—General History.

THIRD TERM.

Turning and Joining.
Mechanical Drawing—Architecture.
History—General History.
Science—Chemistry.

"Each student has one hour and thirty minutes shop practice each school day, which period may come early or late in the day, according to the class with which the student may be connected in other departments. The shops are open and in operation from 9 a. m. until 12 m. and from 1 p. m. until 4 p. m., thus giving accommodation to four classes each day in each shop.

"By special arrangements more time may be given to shop practice, provided this will not interfere with the program of the other departments.

"The young women are taught dressmaking, plain sewing and fancy needle work, and receive special instruction in matters pertaining to health, dress and deportment. Instructions will also be given in scientific cooking and in laundry work, for the ensuing year under a trained teacher."

Atlanta University, Atlanta, Ga., (1900-1901).

Atlanta University is a High School and College—the High School having two courses, the College Preparatory and Normal.

"All the boys in the Preparatory course receive instruction at the Knowles Industrial Building . . . . two triple periods each week. One year is devoted to wood-working; one term to forging; one term to free hand drawing; and one year and one term to mechanical drawing, including machine design and strength of materials.

First Year. In the Bench Room are thirty benches and vices: each bench being fitted with a case of wood-working tools—squares, planes, chisels, gauges, saws, hammer, mallet, bit and brace, draw-knife, dividers, screw-driver, oilstone, etc. All boys in the Preparatory course begin their industrial work here, and are instructed in the general principles of wood-working: marking, sawing, planing, boring, chamfering, mortising, tenoning, grooving, mitering, beveling, dovetailing. All students are advanced through a series of carefully graded exercises, which are fully shown by working drawings and models of the same. The exercises for the earlier part of the year are nearly all performed at the benches; later, the students do cabinet work and pattern making, and construct useful and fancy articles as may be best adapted for their individual advancement.

"Wood-turning is also introduced in the latter part of the year. The Lathe Room is fitted with twelve wood-turning lathes: each has a set of chisels, gauges, face-plates, chucks and centers, suitable for a large variety of work. The course follows a series of graded working drawings, and at its completion useful and ornamental articles can be made.

Second Year. The Forge Room is fitted with twelve forges and anvils and is thoroughly supplied with small tools suitable for doing ordinary blacksmith work and small machine forging. Instruction is given in heating, drawing, bending, upsetting, welding, annealing, tempering, etc. In iron-working, students are taught the correct ways of boring, turning, drilling, tapping, and finishing iron and steel; the use and care of the machines, and machine tools: the care and management of engine and boiler.

"The second term of this year is spent in free-hand drawing. The fundamental principles are taught by drawing from models, also the principles of shading, thus teaching the student to represent truly what he sees.

"The last term of this year is devoted to mechanical drawing. The students gain a familiarity with the use of drawing instruments through a series of geometrical constructions, orthgraphic projections, sections, line shading, development of helical curves, lettering, and blue printing.

Third Year. Mechanical drawing for the last year includes the working of problems in kinematics—cams, gear teeth outlines, screws, shafts, cranks, pulleys, etc. General and detailed drawings and tracings of the same are made. In all possible cases the kind and strength of material and cost of manufacture are considered. The course closes by each student making an assemblage drawing, upon some approved subject, called a thesis drawing.

FOR GIRLS.

"Instruction is given to all girls in the Normal and Preparatory courses in sewing, dressmaking, cooking, and household management.

First Year. Instruction is given in sewing, the stitches being learned on a sampler made of unbleached cotton cloth, with red and blue thread: including basting, stitching, backstitching, running, overcasting, hemming, oversewing, French seam, outline stitch, felling, gusset, napery stitch, combination stitch, tucking, binding, button hole, button, hemmed and whipped ruffle; then holders, sheets, pillow cases and aprons are made.

Second Year. Different kinds of darning and patching are taught, and various articles made, which the girls can buy at cost. Drafting, also, is taught during the year: also the cutting and making of undergarments.

Third Year. The work in cooking extends throughout the year. The care and management of a fire, the structure of a stove, the washing of dishes and cleaning of boards and closets are given careful consideration.

"The chemistry of cooking is illustrated by simple experiments and then given practical application in the cooking of eggs, meat, vegetables, cereals, batters, doughs, soups, etc.

"Sewing is continued through the year and includes hemstitch and fancy stitch, and the cutting and making of a shirt waist and simple skirt.

Fourth Year. An advanced course in practice cooking is given. The subjects considered theoretically are, the classification of food both chemically and physiologically, buying and care of food supplies, food economics, preparation of menus with reference to nutritive value and cost. Simple tests are given to prove whether food materials have been adulterated. Weekly papers bearing on the lessons are required.

"Instruction in the care and management of the house is given in lectures on sanitation, plumbing and ventilation, and practice in the different lines of household work.

"Dressmaking is taught during the year. Students are expected to buy a chart for cutting, also to buy inexpensive woolen dress goods, linings and trimmings for practical work.

PRINTING OFFICE.

"There is a large and well appointed Printing Office in the principal University building, in which instruction is given to optional classes, both of boys and girls, without extra charge. Type-setting, newspaper, book and job work are taught by an experienced superintendent. Two monthly papers are published: one by the Institution, THE BULLETIN OF ATLANTA UNIVERSITY; one by the students, THE SCROLL. Job printing is done for the Institution and others by student labor." This report was set up in this office.

Georgia State Industrial College, College, Ga., (1899-1900).

"Attention is given to stock raising and creamery. This department has been able in the past year to give employment to a number of young men for which they received extra pay. In this way several industrious young men made during the year more than all their expenses by extra work on the farm.

"The work in this department does not in any way interfere with the prosecution of the regular literary studies.

"Manual training is taught to the boys in the three Normal grade classes.

"It is believed that the minds of the students are thus aroused and quickened for their literary studies and that each student is also given a reasonable degree of skill in the use of different kinds of tools.

"Until the present year there has been no effort to give the student a trade. But in obedience to a growing demand for opportunities and facilities for trades, the Commission has organized trades in carpentry, blacksmithing, wheelwrighting, printing, shoemaking, tailoring, painting and dressmaking. They have placed competent instructors in charge of each shop.

"The entire department is under the management of an efficient director, and it is believed that the Georgia State Industrial College is prepared to give valuable aid to one who wishes to follow any of the trades named herein. The public is respectfully invited to examine our classes and work.

"Each student will be required to give eight hours a day to his trade. No one will receive any pay from any department, until he has reached the stage where he is of real assistance in the work of his trade. Students completing a course in any one of these trades will be given a certificate of proficiency.

"The courses of study in each department have been planned to cover three years."

9. *The Differentiation of Industrial Schools.* If now we refer back to page 31 and notice again the list and diagram we may attempt a rough classification of these industrial schools. We must remember that this is but a tentative classification based, for the most part, on the meagre data of catalogues and liable to some mistakes. It would seem that the schools represent the various phases of development about as follows:

1, 2.—Janitor and Repair Work with incidental industrial training.

Calhoun.
Benedict.
Paul Quinn.

3, 4.—House work.

Spelman.
Scotia.

(And courses for girls in nearly all the other schools).

5.—A. Industries given as courses of study more or less compulsory; trades not usually finished—the Unorganized Industrial School:

Howard,
Wilberforce,
Biddle,
Clark,
Scofield,
Rust,
Florida State,
Walden.

B. Co-operative Industry for gain and trade instruction—the School of Work.

Tuskegee,
Tougaloo,
Alcorn.
A. & M. College, Normal, Ala.

6.—Trade Schools.

A. & M. College, Greensboro, N. C.
Lincoln Institute, Mo.

9.—Manual Training Schools.

Shaw,
Tillotson,
Orange Park,
Prairie View,
Va. Union,
Knox,
Ballard.
Southern,
Talladega,
LeMoyne,
Atlanta University.

6, 9.—Manual Training and Trade Schools.

Hampton,
Claflin.

The first group are manifestly in the transition stage, either on account of primitive surroundings, as is the case of Calhoun, or because they are just beginning to introduce industrial training. The work for girls in Housework is important and permanent work which will improve in method as time passes. There is, of course, lurking beneath this work much drudgery and servant work of little or no educational value and at the same time a severe drain on the strength and good temper of the girls. Courses in housework ought to be really educational and not simply expedients for hiring less kitchen help.

The industrial schools under "5" are the ones which will, in the near future, show the greatest development. The history of those under "5 A" has been simple: they were ordinary schools of the older type. Under the impetus of the Slater Fund crusade they hired a carpenter or a shoemaker to instruct certain of their students and from this the work grew. The trouble with this sort of industrial school is the inevitable lack of harmony between the academic and industrial work. The studies of the two are not integrated—they have no common centre or unified object and the school must either seek a higher development of its work, as is the case at Wilberforce and Biddle, or the academic work will entirely overshadow the industrial, as at most of the schools, or the industrial work will overshadow the academic, as is the case with most of the schools under "5 B."

Dr. Haygood was soon able to point out that the "School of Work" idea must be pursued with caution: "I am entirely convinced," said he in his final report, "that we cannot make industrial training self-sustaining, without sinking, to a hurtful degree, the educative part of the work in the effort to secure 'profits.' With this view I believe all experienced teachers will agree." To bring a vast number of raw country lads together, give them a chance to work at a trade and learn it, study a little at the same time and partially support themselves while in school has in it much that is worthy and valuable. It is peculiarly the "Tuskegee Idea" and the one for which Mr. Booker T. Washington has labored faithfully and well. And yet the idea is a transitional one. The development of Tuskegee itself shows that it is moving toward a more definite and thorough organization. Two distinct ideas must more and more become clearly differentiated in such a school: (*a*) the education of youth and (*b*) the teaching of trades. To some small extent, or for short periods of time, these objects may be combined, but in the long run, and in any permanent educational system, they must be clearly seen as differing, and to an extent, incapable of complete combination. The so-called industrial schools will, therefore, in the next decade in all probability divide into two distinct parts: a department of common and grammar school training with perhaps higher courses, in which manual training, as an educative process, will play a pronounced part; and a department of Trade instruction to which only youth of a certain age and advancement will be admitted and which will turn out thorough, practical artisans. Paying industries and the student wage-system will play a very subordinate part in such schools.

10. *Manual Training.* Manual training, as it has come to be called, or the fashioning, handling, and studying of actual objects as a help to think-

ing and learning to think is perhaps the longest forward step in human education which this generation has taken. We have not, to be sure, learned to our entire satisfaction just how to combine for the best results the spoken word, the written letter and the carved wood or forged iron. And yet, gradually we are working toward this ideal, as the introduction of the kindergarten and of sloyd, nature study and laboratory methods into the common school rooms, abundantly testify. In the case of the Negro little has as yet been done in the public schools of the South. Public officials in the various states testify as follows:

Alabama. Superintendent of Education J. W. Abercrombie says: "Industrial training has not been introduced in the public schools of Alabama."

Arkansas. State Superintendent Dayne says: "Industrial training has been introduced into two or three of the city schools."

Delaware. The Secretary of the School Board writes that no industrial training at all has been introduced into the public schools.

Florida. Superintendent W. N. Sheats says: "Industrial training has not been introduced into the public schools."

Indian Territory. Superintendent John D. Benedict says: "Not much industrial training has been introduced, but we are gradually taking hold of that work now."

Louisiana. Superintendent J. V. Calhoun writes: "No industrial training has been introduced in the public schools."

Maryland. Superintendent M. Bates Stephens writes that private manual training schools are increasing but mentions no such work in the public schools. There is probably some such work in the Colored High School in Baltimore.

Mississippi. Superintendent H. L. Whitfield mentions no manual training work in the public schools.

Missouri. Superintendent Carrington says that outside St. Louis and Kansas City where such work is done, there is no manual training in the public schools.

North Carolina. Superintendent J. Y. Joyner writes: "As yet industrial training has not been introduced in the colored public schools to any extent. . . . . I think one great need of the public schools for the colored race is industrial and agricultural training. I shall be glad to have from you any suggestions as to how such training may be made practical for the lower public schools."

Oklahoma. Superintendent Baxter reports no industrial training save in the Normal University.

South Carolina. Superintendent J. J. McMahan writes: "Only a few town schools have introduced industrial features."

Tennessee. Mr. Rutledge Smith informs us that "no industrial training has been introduced in the public schools for the colored."

Texas. Superintendent A. Lefevre writes: "Industrial training in the colored public schools has had some beginning in a few localities, and the indications are that developments along this line may be expected in the near future."

Virginia. Superintendent Southall writes: "No systematic industrial training has been introduced into the colored public schools of the state. The introduction of industrial training is now receiving much attention at the hands of our school authorities, and we hope soon to make a start in all our public schools."

West Virginia. Superintendent Miller reports no manual training save in the higher state institutions.

No reports have been received from *Kentucky* and *Georgia* after repeated inquiries. It is known, however, in Georgia that manual training to some extent has been introduced in the colored public schools of Columbus and Athens. In the latter case the work is supported entirely by the colored teachers themselves.

In the private schools and state institutions manual training is made a prominent feature at

Hampton,	Knox,
Claflin,	Ballard,
Shaw,	Southern,
Tillotson,	Talladega,
Orange Park,	LeMoyne,
Prairie View,	Va. N. & C. I.,
Va. Union,	Atlanta University,

and at some other schools. As had been said, Atlanta University was the pioneer in this work and from the beginning the work has had one distinct idea: the using of a course of training in wood-working and iron-forging solely for its educative effect on the pupil. There have been many difficulties in carrying out this idea, chief among which is securing proper teachers and co-ordinating the work in the shop with that in the class-room. Probably Hampton has had larger success in this integration than any other of these schools. The Hampton manual training idea, however, has in mind not simply the educative value of the work but its value in furnishing skilled recruits for the trade school. It consequently gives a preponderance to the manual training courses such as schools for higher training could not afford to allow in justice to other work.

A much needed outcome from manual training is the preparation of teachers to instruct in such courses. Such a course is given at Hampton for simple work in the public schools. At Atlanta University, and probably at other schools, elective work outside the regular course accomplishes somewhat the same end less systematically.

So far as the public schools are concerned there is danger in the South that there will be introduced into the public schools some attempt at teaching paying "Industries" instead of manual training for its purely educative value. It would be a calamity if this were attempted. The public schools are designed primarily to awaken the child's mind and to teach him to read and write and the simpler uses of numbers. To this might cautiously be added a simple and carefully adapted course in sloyd, some lessons in plain sewing, and "busy" work in weaving, plaiting and modeling. This would cost little, is easily taught and above all easily co-ordinated and combined with the work in the three R's. Simple "nature studies" might also in these lower grades add diversion and instruction in the first elements of planting and plant life. Cooking as a study, in the Negro schools, would be more difficult to introduce and more costly. Probably a travelling cooking teacher in the homes of the parents themselves or at a mothers' meeting at the school house would accomplish the most good in the country. In the city schools experiments at teaching cooking might be tried. At any rate any attempt to introduce "Industries" in the public schools in the sense of imparting marketable skill or teaching handicraft would simply mean that reading, writing and arithmetic would get even less attention than they do now, that mental development would be lost sight of and the real mission of the public school system hopelessly blocked. It is sincerely to be desired that great care will be exercised by the friends of the Negro in warding off experiments in the wrong direction and promoting in the public schools real manual training for the sake of its intellectual value.

11. *The Post-Graduate Trade School*, (by Major R. R. Moton, Commandant of Cadets, Hampton Institute).

There is more or less confusion in the average mind as to the difference between industrial, manual and trade school training, although there is no question as to the importance of each. There is, however, a clear distinction to be made in their objects, if not in their underlying principles. Manual training is, as I understand it, a sort of laboratory in which abstract ideas are worked out by hand in a concrete, practical way. The shop work is given, not for its economic value, but purely for educational purposes. What is commonly called industrial training, on the other hand, is usually given for its economic value. It generally consists in teaching a man to work by rule and rote rather than by principle and method, its object being to make the work as profitable as possible and incidentally to teach the trade. This is not very different from the training the Negro got in slavery, under the old apprentice system. This is apt to mean a brainless training, producing, as a natural result, a generally brainless and unprofitable industry. The laborer is a machine and works as a machine.

The value of the work done in any branch of industry must and will depend largely upon the quality of brain that is put into it. It is not so much the number of men engaged in manual pursuits as the quality of men, that will dignify and make profitable the labor of the hands. It is not so much the number of men engaged in farming that will place agriculture among the most productive industries, as the quality of men engaged in it. It is very difficult to make a first rate artisan or farmer without a cultivated mind as a basis. In all the pursuits of life,—call them common, if you wish,—there are underlying principles which must be mastered, if one is to get the best results from his labor. The inventive mind, the originative and planning mind, is the trained mind. The proper industrial scheme for the Negro, or any other people, is one that emphasizes the right sort of education of the head, as a necessary preliminary, and uses his higher training as a subservient and tributary basis for his subsequent practical usefulness. To leave a thorough mental training out of any system of industrial training for the Negro of to-day is to produce a dwarfed and unprofitable workman. Under such a system, steam and electricity become useless, the shoemaker sinks into a cobbler and every workman becomes a jack-of-all-trades. This may have answered the demands once, but it will not to-day. Train the workman and you elevate his labor.

There are, scattered throughout the Southland, a number of industrial schools, many of which have done, and are still doing a magnificent work, and have sent out men who are accomplishing a great deal along industrial lines as teachers and artisans. We do not depreciate what has been accomplished, but there are three distinct differences between the trade school and the industrial school:—first, the difference in requirements for entrance, the trade school demanding a broader mental training, as a basis upon which its education shall be built; second, the difference in method of instruction, the stress being placed on what the shop produces in the boy, rather than upon what the boy produces in the shop; third, the difference in object, the aim being not merely to make mechanics and artisans who can build a house under supervision, but to turn out teachers of trades and captains of industry who can make the plans and execute them even in the most minute detail.

As the theological, medical and law schools fit men, who are usually post-graduates, for their respective professions, so the trade school should fit men (post-graduates) for their professions. A man's training may be that of a carpenter, blacksmith, wheelwright, machinist, or even of a polytechnic character, but if he comprehends the scientific principles underlying the trade, it should be dignified as a profession. In other words, the trade school should fit men for a higher grade of work than is done by the ordinary industrial school. Its standard and work should be so high as to attract the best and brightest youth of our land. Our best high schools and even colleges should be, in a sense, preparatory schools for professional trade school work. We can never reach the highest industrial ideal and elevate manual labor in the eyes of the Negro—and the white man as well—until a high intellectual and moral standard is demanded as an essential base upon which to erect a thorough, dignified and profitable industrialism. This will require no small amount of careful, thoughtful and often tedious work on the part of educators, but the end will without question justify the means.

It is not merely the comprehension of the three Rs which is necessary in the Negro's development. The complexity of our modern industrial system makes it essential that he shall comprehend more than the rudiments of reading, writing and arithmetic. All branches of study which will develop the intellect in the highest and most practical way should be included in his curriculum. The value of industrial education to the Negro and to the country in which he lives, will be largely in proportion to the training of the head which precedes it, or is acquired along with it. The skilfulness of his hand will depend largely upon the thoughtfulness of his brain.

While I do not believe that industrial education, or any other kind of education, is a panacea for all the ills of the Negro, I do believe that he especially needs to be thoroughly rooted and grounded in the underlying principles of concrete things. A man's education should be conditioned upon his capacity, social environment and the life which he is most likely to lead in the immediate future. The highest aim of education is the building of character, and any education which does not include the four cardinal factors in the building of character is false and misleading. Knowledge, skill, culture and virtue are essential elements in educational development. Knowledge suggests ideas and makes one original and inventive. Skill executes these ideas. Culture enjoys the inventions and executions of a superior skill. Virtue preserves knowledge, skill and culture, and brings man to a closer understanding of his fellow-men and his Maker.

The problem which presented itself to the industrial school two decades ago was simple in comparison with the problem of to-day. A farm and a laundry, and perhaps a sewing room, were enough to give a school its industrial character. Hampton, and Tuskegee as well, started very much in this way. But as those institutions grew, more varied industries became necessary and one industry followed another in rapid succession. At Hampton many of the young men used the shops, not only as a means of earning sufficient money to put them through the academic course, but devoted themselves for three or four years to learning a trade, at the forge or bench, much after the apprentice system. While this was good as far as it went, and enabled many to go out and accomplish a great deal of good by example and precept, often building with their own hands their own houses and their schoolhouses, and teaching their people the right ideas of life and duty, it was found inadequate to meet the increasing demands for men to fill positions in a higher realm of industrial activity and for teachers in the industrial schools that were and are still springing up all over the South and West. It was this demand that brought Dr. Frissell, the principal of the Hampton Institute, in the spirit of its great founder, Gen. Armstrong, to the idea of a trade school and a school of scientific agriculture, where the trades and agriculture should be taught upon a thoroughly scientific and intellectual basis.

We have in our trade school to-day men who have graduated from our own academic department or from other schools of equal or higher grade than Hampton who are learning trades with a view to becoming teachers of trades, or contractors and leaders of industry in a larger and broader sense than the average Negro artisan comprehends. Only since the Armstrong and Slater Memorial Trade School was opened six years ago, can Hampton lay claim to having been teaching trades. Before this, there were a number of men, Hampton students, who did work at trades, and some of them no doubt, as their subsequent work has clearly shown, did learn them, but Hampton can hardly claim to have *taught* them.

The importance of this higher trade training cannot be gainsaid, nor is it likely, at present at least, to be over-estimated. Since Hampton began, six years ago, to teach trades in a thorough, systematic way, ninety Negro boys have completed the course and left Hampton. Of these sixty, or eighty-one per cent., are either teaching or working at their trades. Four have died, five are studying in other institutions, nine are engaged in other occupations and twelve have not been heard from. Then, too, the demand for persons with this sort of training is still increasing. Hampton, alone, has had requests, within the last three months, for forty-eight of its trade school graduates to fill positions as instructors in mechanic arts.

What Hampton, Tuskegee and other schools of the same character, are trying to do for trade education is a simple but conclusive illustration of what can and should be done along the line of what might be called higher trade education. Hampton does not by any means approximate its ideal in trade school work, for it is necessary now—and probably will be for a long time to come—to teach trades to a large number of undergraduates, pupils who learn their trades while they are taking the academic course. But post-graduate work is without question the ideal toward which trade school work should be tending.

It is only through a clear understanding of the situation and a hearty co-operation on the part of the educators of the colored youth of our land, that we can get the best results from our various systems of education.

12. *Cost of Industrial Training.* It is not easy to estimate the cost of industrial training in all schools since the expenditures for industrial and academic teaching are not usually separated. The following table gives the total income (1899-1900) of all schools which give Negroes industrial training:*

*Re-arranged from the Report of the U. S. Commissioner of Education, 1899-1900.

INCOME OF INDUSTRIAL SCHOOLS, 1899-1900.

SCHOOLS.	Total Enrollment.	Students in Industries.	Value of Grounds, Buildings, &c	Income, 1899-1900. Gifts.	State Aid	Tuition.	Interest.	Other Sources.	Total.
Alabama.			$	$	$	$	$	$	$
Kowaliga A. and I. School	205	205							
Emerson N. Institute	201	100	18,000			1,087		2,452	3,534
State Normal School.	928	466	40,000		8,500	2,000		4,500	15,000
A. and M. College	499	499	30,119		4,000	0	0	10,776	14,776
Talladega College	618	195	134,000	1,682	0	1,500	7,500	5,000	15,682
Stillman Institute	45	35	8,000		0	100	784	3,116	4,000
Tuskegee N. and I. School	1,180	1,180	252,319	97,231	4,500	0	1,921	98,390	202,042
Arkansas.									
Shorter University	86	16	5,000					1,472	1,472
Arkadelphia Acad	92	20	15,000	223	0	175		519	694
Philander Smith Col.	388	95	32,000			1,873		2,450	4,323
Branch Nor. College.	214	109	63,000		3,500	460		6,860	10,820
Southland College	127	120	25,000	250	0	1,600	800	250	2,650
Arkansas Bap. Col	213	56	25,000			500		4,500	5,000
Delaware.									
State College for Colored Students	51	46	27,000		6,000				6,000
Dist. of Columbia.									
Howard University	768	223	700,000		35,100	0	8,000	6,000	49,100
Florida.									
Fessenden Academy.	206	130	5,000	1,000	500	200		800	2,500
Emerson Memorial Home and School	76	76	5,000	1,994	0	107		573	2,674
Orange Park Normal and M. T. School	79	79				640	3,000		3,640
State N. and I. Col	209	100	30,044		6,500	378	100	12,500	19,478
Georgia.									
Jeruel Academy	221	80	2,500	1,043	0	475		2,136	3,654
Knox Institute	270	114	8,000		0				
Atlanta University	263	233	255,000	28,000	0	2,000	1,575	100	31,675
Morris Brown College	499	83	75,000		0	1,315	0	8,685	10,000
Spelman Seminary	599	450	180,000	22,414		3,239	300	6,608	32,561
Haines N. and I. Inst.	460	208	20,000	4,500	0	900	150	4,450	10,000
The Paine Institute			43,733					10,111	10,111
Ga. State I. College	231	140	30,000		15,000		200		15,200
Ft. Valley H. and I. School	350	75	10,000		1,500	900	975	13,000	16,375
Dorchester Academy	408	209	12,900	403	0	709	0	2,947	4,059
Beach Institute	320	41	5,000		0	1,200		4,200	5,400
Clark University	476	310	250,000	1,700		2,600		9,400	13,700
Allen N. and I. Sch	210	78	9,079	193		677		1,000	1,870

INCOME OF INDUSTRIAL SCHOOLS, 1899-1900. (Continued).

SCHOOLS.	Total Enrollment.	Students in Industries.	Value of Grounds, Buildings, &c	Income, 1899-1900.					
				Gifts.	State Aid	Tuition.	Interest.	Other Sources.	Total.
Kentucky.			$	$	$	$	$	$	$
State N. School for Colored Persons.....	170	170	40,465		3,000	0	1,255	3,625	7,880
Chandler N. School...	220	111	17,904	155	0	1,222	240	2,155	3,772
Louisiana.									
Gilbert Acad. & I. Col	248	141	60,000			500	2,400	500	3,400
Leland University..	115	16	150,000	25,600	0	0	6,000	600	32,200
Straight University...	539	229	100,000	300	0	1,600	300	2,000	4,200?
Maryland.									
St. Frances Academy	59	27							
I. Home for Col. Girls	105	105							
Princess Anne Acad..	82	60	17,000	0	4,500	900			5,400
Mississippi.									
Mt. Hermon F. Sem...	60	60	25,000	1,000	0	400		1,000	2,400
Sou. Christian Inst...	87	43	35,000	4,000	0	150	0	3,850	8,000
State Normal School.	257	80	12,000	0	2,250	467	0		2,717
Rust University........	230	124	125,000	5,759		1,474		4,751	11,984
Jackson College........	102	60	35,000	177		498		141	816?
Tougaloo University.	436	221	80,000					15,000	15,000
Alcorn A. and M. Col.	339	339	130,000		12,850		6,815	19,161	38,826
Missouri.									
Lincoln Institute......	278	125	70,800		15,295			1,339	16,634
Geo. R. Smith Col.....	200	52	50,000	200		1,800	125	2,000	5,925
New Jersey.									
M. T. and I. School...	109	109				327	308	5,000	5,635
North Carolina.									
Washburn Seminary.	158	118	6,000						
Biddle University.....	236	107	150,000						
Scotia Seminary..... ..	290	290	65,000	11,000	0	618	100	5,000	16,718
Franklinton C. Col...	158	10	7,000						
A. and M. Col. for Col	174	174	66,600		7,500	350		8,954	16,804
High Point N.& I.Sch	276	66	130,000		1,200			2,000	3,200
Lincoln Academy......	235	155	55,000		220	252	0		472
Barrette C. & I. Sch..	111	75	5,000			1,500		250	1,750
Plymouth Sta.N.Sch.	87	37	0		1,875			100	1,975
St. Augustine's Sch...	323	100	50,000	6,000					6,000
Shaw University......	511	190	90,000	12,873	0	8,158		154	21,185
Livingston College...	266	9	125,000	4,000	50	500	200	5,500	10,250
Gregory Normal Sch.	228	100	15,000	300	0	1,100		2,900	4,300
Rankin-Richards Ins	80	16	11,000	525		250		525	1,300
Slater I. & S. N. Sch.	263	118	25,000		3,257	219		5,553	8,229

INCOME OF INDUSTRIAL SCHOOLS, 1899-1900. (Continued).

SCHOOLS.	Total Enrollment.	Students in Industries.	Value of Grounds, Buildings, &c	Income, 1899-1900.					
				Gifts.	State Aid	Tuition.	Interest.	Other Sources.	Total.
			$	$	$	$	$	$	$
Pennsylvania.									
Inst. for Col. Youth...	318	272							
South Carolina.									
Schofield N. & I. Sch	303	231	50,000	1,000	150	100	1,200	6,550	9,000
Browning Home Sch.	180	136							
Avery Normal Inst...	345	75	15,000		0	2,500	0	3,000	5,500
Brainerd Institute.....	205	205	10,000	0	0				
Allen University.	343	84	35,000	0	0	969		6,000	9,969
Benedict College......	488	213	76,000		0		6,000	4,359	10,359
Penn N. and I. Sch...	265	179	3,000	200	0	270		1,200	1,670
Brewer Normal Sch...	245	147	12,000		0	1,000			1,000
Claflin University.....	708	487	150,000	25,000		4,000		8,000	37,000
Tennessee.									
Warner Institute......	101	78	5,000		345	8		280	5,633
Knoxville College.....	304	68	100,000		2,900	300		14,000	17,200
LeMoyne Nor. Inst...	718	462	45,000	4,500	0	4,780		4,500	13,780
Morristown Nor. Col.	277	93	75,000	31,000		761			31,761
Central Tenn. Col......	540	70	19,000	7,500	625	6,169	500	8,500	23,294
Roger Williams Univ	268	100	200,000	1,235			1,823	8,190	11,248
Texas.									
Bishop College.........	337	327	100,000						
Wiley University......	411	200	30,000	1,200		5,600		1,680	8,480
Paul Quinn College...	276	149	77,000	2,008		4,410		3,821	10,239
Virginia.									
Ingleside Academy...	109	109	25,000	600				3,000	3,600
Gloucester A. & I.Col	97	97	20,000	3,700					3,700
Hampton N. & A.Inst	939	949	757,000	254,333	0	0	35,336	136,668	426,337
St. Paul N. & I. Sch..	318	230	60,000			3,500		8,500	12,000
Manassas Indus. Sch.	65	65	16,000	5,240				5,500	10,740
Norfolk Mission Col.	690	406	60,000		0	1,700		7,410	9,110
Va. Nor. and Col. Inst	343	183	157,000		15,000	1,103	672	300	17,747
Va. Union University	157	12	300,000	52,278		1,200	4,000		57,478
West Virginia.									
Storer College...........	142	105	50,000		1,000	387	3,123	0	4,510

13. *Results of Industrial Training.* It is always difficult to judge a system of human training, since in the nature of the case its results are spiritual rather than material and show themselves fully only after the lapse of time. Industrial training has changed the ideals of the freedmen, it has educated the hands and heads of his children and it has trained artisans. Of these we can only measure the last and that but imperfectly

by asking, How many of the graduates of industrial schools are actually following their trades?

Every school in the country which is especially designed to give industrial training to Negroes was sent the schedule of questions printed on page 11. Of the 98 thus questioned 44 answered, and partial data were obtained from the catalogues of 16 others, making returns from sixty schools in all. Of these sixty a number answered that they were unable to furnish exact data or had no graduates working as artisans:

G. L. Smith College, Mo: "We have not as yet made provision for Industrial work."

Mt. Hermon Female Seminary, Miss: "I am sorry I cannot answer your questions, but I really have not kept track of my former pupils."

Storr's School, Ga: "This is a grammar day school and has no industries except sewing."

Shorter College, Ark: "We have the Sewing and Printing Departments in connection with our school, but they have been recently connected and consequently we have no graduates, as yet."

St. Augustine's School, Raleigh, N. C: "We have classes in printing, in carpentry and in bricklaying. The classes have not been going long enough for us to have sent out more than a few boys, so that I am not able to give you any answer."

Normal School No. 2, Washington, D. C: "We have no trades [taught] in our school."

Roger Williams University, Nashville, Tenn: "This school has never been in any true sense an industrial school. . . . . . I have no list of our graduates who are artisans, though there are doubtless a good number who may be working in that way."

Emerson Normal Institute, Mobile, Ala: "Almost none [of our graduates are working as artisans] so far as I know."

Warner Institute, Jonesboro, Tenn: "We are teaching sewing only as industrial work at present."

Gloucester Institute, Cappahoosic, Va: "While we give elementary lessons in sewing, cooking and agriculture, with application upon a school farm of 148 acres, we cannot be correctly classed as an industrial school."

Straight University, New Orleans, La: "We have manual training in our school but do not teach trades."

Benedict College, Columbia, S. C: "At present it is impossible to make a report that will be accurate at all. Next year we hope to be able to give information in that line.',

Leland University, New Orleans, La: "This is not a trade school. I never want to manage shops, machines, foundries, kilns, plants, industries; I mean to use some of these on their educational side for various reasons, but book learning is our main aim. All of our graduates who are living as artisans learned that elsewhere."

Mississippi State Normal School, Holly Springs, Miss: "None [of our former students or graduates are artisans.] Ours is a normal school for the education of teachers. The only art we teach is dress-cutting and fitting."

Beach Institute, Savannah, Ga: "I have not found as yet records of addresses or occupations of former graduates. * * * * We have no industrial course."

Virginia Union University, Richmond, Va: "Our Industrial Department has been in existence only one year."

Florida State Normal and Industrial School, Tallahassee, Fla: Industrial lines of instruction "are just being organized."

Jackson College: This institution is being rebuilt and is "not at present an industrial school," but will be later.

Spelman Seminary: "On looking up our statistics of graduates and what they are doing, we find that we have so little knowledge of those engaged in industrial pursuits that we do not fill out the report asked for by you."

Scotia Seminary: "Our work being for girls only our industrial work is confined mainly to the domestic arts. Some who do not complete a literary course devote themselves to dress-making, but the literary graduates generally accept positions as teachers. The demand for industrial teachers far exceeds our ability to supply. Scotia girls, as a rule, do not get a chance for independent positions. They are in such demand for the high office of home-maker that nearly all of them are at that not very long after they graduate."

In addition to these 20 schools, probably all but a few of the 38 schools not heard from belong to the same category, i. e., they either teach sewing, cooking, farming, or simple manual training, or if they teach a few trades partially they have no record of their graduates. In the case of girls' schools like Spelman and Scotia it is not expected that they will send out artisans except possibly dress-makers, and teachers of manual training.

Turning now to trade schools and those that lay considerable stress on Manual Training, we have the following reports:

Hampton Institute, Va.

112 graduates or former students are working at their trades and 27 are teaching trades, making 139 in all. 227 have finished or practically finished their trades in the years 1885-1902. Of these 10 are dead, and 42 not heard from. Of the remaining 161 heard from, 139 are working at their trades or teaching them:*

HAMPTON TRADE STUDENTS.

	Left; trade finished.	Left; trade almost finished.	Total; left with trade practically finished.	Still here in school. Trade finished.	Total; trade finished or practically finished.	Left school; heard from.	Left school; not heard from	Left school; dead.
Blacksmiths	22	3	25	1	26	19	6	0
Bricklayers	2	0	2	2	4	1	0	1
Carpenters	69	1	70	4	74	50	12	8
Engineers	12	2	14	0	14	12	2	0
Harnessmakers	9	0	9	0	9	9	0	0
Machinists	6	1	7	1	8	6	1	0
Painters	7	0	7	1	8	4	3	0
Printers	15	4	19	1	20	18	1	0
Shoemakers	13	1	14	0	14	8	5	1
Tailors	13	3	16	1	17	15	1	0
Tinsmiths	2	0	2	0	2	2	0	0
Wheelwrights	23	2	25	3	28	14	11	0
Wood-working machinists	2	0	2	0	2	2	0	0
Manual training teacher	1	0	1	0	1	1	0	0
Total	196	17	213	14	227	161	42	10

*We are indebted to the authorities of Hampton Institute, and especially to Miss M. J. Sherman, for these tabular statements and other detailed information.

LOCATION OF FORMER STUDENTS KNOWN TO BE FOLLOWING THEIR TRADES.

		Blacksmiths.	Bricklayers.	Carpenters.	Engineers.	Harnessmakers.	Machinists.	Painters.	Printers.	Shoemakers.	Tailors.	Tinsmiths.	Wheelwrights.	Wood-working machinists.	Manual training teacher.	Total.
Virginia	Working	11	2	20	4	1	2	4	6	5	13	1	2	3		74
	Teaching	1	1	5		2			1	1			1			12–86
Alabama	W								2							2
	T			3		1				1			1			6– 8
Washington, D. C.	W	1			2				1	1	1					6
	T															0– 6
Georgia	W			1		1										2
	T															0– 2
Kentucky	W	1		1												2
	T			1												1– 3
Louisiana	W		1													1
	T				1											0– 1
Maryland	W						1		1							3
	T			1			1									2– 5
North Carolina	W	1		1							1		1			4
	T			1					1				1			3– 7
South Carolina and Tennessee	W															0·
	T			2												2– 2
Texas	W	1					1						1			3
	T															0– 3
In the North	W	1		3	2	1	1			2	3					13
	T															0–13
In the West	W								1							1
	T														1	1– 2
In the U. S. Navy	W						1									1
	T															0– 1
Total working at trades	W	16	3	26	9	3	6	4	11	8	18	1	4	3	0	112
Total teaching trades	T	1	1	13	0	3	1	0	2	2	0	0	3	0	1	27
Total heard from		17	4	39	9	6	7	4	13	10	18	1	7	3	1	139

"This list includes those Negro students with trades wholly or partially completed about whom we have had definite information within a year and a half. The present addresses and occupations of a still larger number, especially of those who did not finish their trades, cannot be found."

No report is available as to dress-makers, nor as to graduates and students who are earning a living partially as artisans. In tailoring and blacksmithing the graduates have experienced no difficulty in obtaining work, and in other trades "no serious difficulty." They do not as a general thing join trades unions.

Tuskegee Institute, Ala.

"We have been keeping a record only of our academic graduates and those who have certificates from the industrial department. I send you under separate cover to-day our catalog which contains our alumni record. The institution cannot be fairly judged only by those who are referred to in the catalog as there are many others who have been working regularly at their trades of whom no record is made."

In the catalogue the occupations of graduates of the school are given as follows:

Total graduates.......................................423

Painters	1	Harnessmakers	1
Tinners	5	Plasterers	1
Dairymen	2	Shoemakers	2
Butchers	1	Wheelwrights	1
Tailors	11	Machinists	1
Brickmasons	8	Blacksmiths	3
Carpenters	4	Milliners	4
Dressmakers	2	Firemen	1

Artisans.......................................48

Teachers of Trades in Industrial Schools..........28

Students in Industrial Schools..................2

Persons who work at their trades when not employed at some other principal occupation:

Carpenters	8	Wheelwright	1
Dressmakers and Seamstresses	16	Plasterers	1
Blacksmiths	1	Painters	1
Shoemakers	2	Printers	1
Mattressmakers	1	Tailors	1

Total.......................................33

Other occupations of graduates*:

Cashier	1	Farmers	9
Book-keeper	1	Trained Nurses**	7
Teachers†	157	Railway laborers	1
Students	31	Steward	1
Pharmacists	4	Laundress	1
Physicians	8	Miners	3
Preachers	11	Drayman	1
School officials other than teachers	9	Merchants††	6
Other professions	6	Clerks	8
Newspaper work	2	U. S. Army	4
Civil Service	6	Housekeepers‡	29

*Including the 33 who work at their trades only a part of their time. They are here counted under their principal occupations.

**Including 3 who also keep house.

†Including 27 who practice trades in vacation, 16 who teach and keep house, 4 who teach and keep store, 9 who teach and farm, and 2 who teach and preach.

††Not counting 4 who teach and keep store.

‡I. e., Housewives?

Summarized we have:

Artisans	48	
Teachers of trades	28	
Students of trades	2—	78
Casual artisans, (33, recounted below).		
Teachers, students and school officials	197	
Professional men	44	
Merchants, Clerks, &c	16	
Farmers	9	
Miscellaneous	40	
Dead, unknown and at home	39—	345
Total graduates		423

Claflin University, S. C.

The following graduates and former students have been sent out with trades:

Carpenters	16	Iron and steel workers	6
Blacksmiths	6	Shoemakers	3
Masons	22	Painters	6
Engineers	2	Plasterers	20
Dressmakers	11	Tailors	2
Harnessmakers	1	Machinists	2
Teacher domestic science	1		

Total 98; 60 of these are following their trades. 12 or more graduates besides these earn a living partially as artisans, usually combining teaching and farming with the trade. Fourteen of the graduates* are instructors in industries.

These artisans are working principally in South Carolina. They are usually preferred by contractors and have had no difficulty in obtaining work. They do not usually join trades unions, as there are not many unions in the state.

A. & M. College, Normal, Ala.

This institution has no record of its undergraduates. The following have graduated as artisans:

Carpenters	15	Shoemakers	6
Blacksmiths	10	Painters	2
Engineers	3	Tailors	3
Dressmakers	25	Printers	10
Iron and steel workers	10	Total	84

The number of these who are following their trades at present is not known; some of these combine teaching with their trades, but the exact number is not stated. The chief difficulty encountered by these artisans is the "Trades Unions, which, in some localities, control labor and will not admit them to membership." In any case they seldom join the unions. Ten teach industries in schools.

*Probably included in the above 60. The report is not explicit on this point.

Bishop College, Texas.

This institution sends a partial report. "The incompleteness of the report is not due to lack of students at work as artisans, but to the lack of method in keeping track of them."

Carpenters	3	Printers	10
Blacksmiths	1	Total	15
Brickmakers	1		

A. & M. College, Greensboro, N. C.

This institution which graduated its first class in 1899 reports as follows:

Carpenters	4	Earning a living partially as artisans	6
Machinists and architects	3		
Teaching trades in schools	2		

"One of our graduates—a machinist with less than two years' experience—is employed in a Northern factory at $5 a day."

Most of the other graduates are located in North Carolina. The six mentioned above usually combine teaching with their trade. They do not usually join trades unions and have no difficulty in getting work save "their own imperfections or lack of energy."

Tougaloo University, Miss.

"While we have done much industrial work we have not had special graduation from industrial courses, but have co-ordinated the hand work with the other as part of an all-round education. Until comparatively recently the call for artisans has not been so strong in this state as in some others. It is predominantly an agricultural state."

The artisans reported are:

Carpenters	18	Dressmakers	4
Blacksmiths	7	Iron and steel workers	2
Masons	1	Painters	3
Engineers	3	Total	38

Three in addition teach industries in schools. They do not join trades unions and find work with but little difficulty.

Schofield N. & I. School, S. C.

This school returns "a partial list, but there are many more who have entered and are following trades." The following are known to be pursuing these trades:

Blacksmiths	5	Painters	20
Brickmakers	10	Harnessmakers	20
Masons	15	Plumbers	5
Tailors	3	Printers	15
Carpenters	30		

Total 123

"Very many" others are following their trades, but there are no exact records; 6 are teaching industries in schools.

These persons are located in South Carolina, Georgia and Florida. Some are in the North.

Barrett C. & I. Institute, N. C.

This institution has trained 157 artisans, chiefly blacksmiths, masons, dressmakers, plasterers and carpenters. Of these "about 10 or more" are earning their living entirely as artisans. Others are combining their trades with teaching. They do not join trades unions and meet little difficulty in getting work.

Haines Institute, Ga.

"Ours is simply a manual training school and makes no pretense at teaching trades. The following are earning a living at their trades, not having studied them elsewhere than here."

Printers	2	Dressmakers and Seamstresses	6
Tailors	2		

They are in Georgia, New Jersey and District of Columbia.

Knoxville College, Tenn.

This institution reports among its graduates:

Blacksmiths	1	Dressmakers	2
Masons	1	Iron and steel workers	4
Civil Engineers	1	Total	9

Eight are teaching industries in schools. Others, formerly students, are working as artisans, and "a large number" are gaining a living by combining a trade with teaching or other pursuits.

Institute for Colored Youth, Penna.

This institution reports:

Carpenters	8	Tailors	6
Brickmasons	16	Printers	8
Shoemakers	8		
Plasterers	4	Total	50

Two teach industries in schools.

Most of these artisans are at work in Philadelphia and vicinity. They do not join the trades unions.

Fort Valley H. & I. School, Ga.

This institution reports:

Carpenters	5	Shoemakers	2
Masons	1	Painters	1
Dressmakers	4	Coopers	1
Tailors	1	Total	15

One is teaching industries.

17 are earning a living partially as artisans. They are located in Georgia, have no trouble in getting work, and do not join Trades Unions. "Our industrial departments have not been established long enough for us to make a very good showing in the industries yet."

State Normal School, Montgomery, Ala.

"This institution has graduated 320 in the past twenty-two years. Of this number twelve had died, sixty-four women are married and house keeping, 185 are teachers, four merchants, one millwright, eight medical doctors, twenty-one farmers, one house plasterer, two carpenters, one each, dentist, blacksmith, house painter, two in Government service, three bookkeepers, eight dressmakers, two teachers of music, seven students in higher schools."

This makes 14 artisans in all. Three others teach trades. About 25% of the graduates and former students practice their trades casually. They often combine teaching or farming with the trade. They have no difficulty in finding work and are located mostly in Birmingham and Montgomery, Ala. They usually join trades unions.

Ballard Normal School, Ala.

One graduate of this school is an architect and builder at Norfolk, Va.; another learned his trade after leaving and was instructor in tailoring at Tuskegee. Most of the graduates teach.

Alcorn A. & M. College, Miss.

The industrial departments here are of recent establishment and only two or three classes have been sent out. There are among these:

Carpenters	3	Shoemakers	8
Blacksmiths	9	Painters	2
Total	22		

Washburn Seminary, N. C.

This school reports:

Carpenters (combined with general labor)	4
Teacher of industries	1

Clark University, Ga.

This school gives among its graduates, as published in its catalogue:

Dressmakers	6	Teachers of industries	5

Avery Institute, S. C.

The catalogue of this school gives the following artisans:

Shoemakers	1	Blacksmiths	2
Carpenters	6	Plumbers	2
Bricklayers	2	Tailors	2
Barbers	6	Butcher	1
Pattern-makers	1	Machinist	1
Total	24		

Apparently none of these were trained at this school, but took up the trades after leaving. The principal was unable to give any accurate information.

Rust University, Miss.

This institution reports:

Carpenters	7	Dressmakers	10
Brickmakers	1	Shoemakers	5
Masons	3	Painters	5
Engineers	6	Plasterers	5
Firemen	7	Coopers	2
Tailors	2	Total	53

Two teach industries in schools. They do not join trades unions.

Arkansas Baptist College, Ark.

This institution has trained in all 79 artisans, but does not report the number of these following their trades. They meet color prejudice in getting work and their own "lack of superior preparation" is a disadvantage.

The following institutions sent no reports, but on consulting their catalogues a list of artisans has been made out as there given: Benedict College, S. C.; Lincoln Institute, Mo.; Wilberforce University, O.; Biddle University, N. C.; Walden University, (Central Tenn. College), Tenn.; Tillotson College, Tex.; Orange Park N. & I. School, Fla.; State Normal School, Miss.; Knox Institute, Ga.; LeMoyne Institute, Tenn.

Among the graduates of these schools are:

Printers	2	Students of industries	2
Carpenters	5	Mason	1
Civil Engineer	1	Barbers	2
Machinist	1	Blacksmith	1
Dressmakers, &c	3	Milliners	1
Photographer	1	Tailor	1
Teachers of industries	5	Total	19

Two urgent requests for reports were sent to all other industrial schools but no replies were received. It may be taken for granted that most of them have very little real trade teaching and no records of the few graduates who have acquired trades after leaving them. A few others have only manual training and the record of their graduates is interesting in this connection only as showing how far such training turns students' ideals toward trade-learning. The most conspicuous of the larger institutions with manual training and without trade departments are Shaw University,* N. C., and Atlanta University. The latter has among its graduates and former students:

1. Superintendent of Industries, Biddle University, N. C.
2. Superintendent of Mechanical Department, Prairie View State Normal School, Texas.
3. Instructor in Manual Training, Knox Institute, Ga.
4. Instructor in Carpentry, Brick N. & A. School, N. C.
5. Superintendent of Manual Training, Talladega College, Ala.
6. Instructor in Manual Training, V. N. & C. I., Va.
7. Instructor in Bench Work, LeMoyne Institute, Tenn.
8. Instructor in Printing, " " "
9. Instructor in Carpentry, Kowaliga I. Acad., Ala.
10. Instructor in Manual Training, Haines Inst., Ga.
11. Teacher of Sewing, Fort Valley H. & I. School, Ga.
12. Teacher of Cooking, " " " " "

Three others are heads of industrial schools but ought rather to be counted as teachers than as artisans. Several former students are artisans but the exact number is unknown.

*The report from Shaw University unfortunately arrived too late for insertion.

Combining these reports we have:

ACTUAL ARTISANS GRADUATED FROM INDUSTRIAL SCHOOLS.

Schools	Hampton.			Tuskegee			Claflin.	Normal, Ala.	Barrett, N. C.	Arkansas Baptist.	Bishop.	Tougaloo.	Schofield, S. C.	Inst. for Colored Youth, Pa.	Montgomery.	Alcorn.	Avery.	Rust.	Other Institutions.	Atlanta University.
	Living graduates.*	Working.	Teaching.	Living graduates.†	Working.**	Teaching.	Total liv'g graduates.				Total graduates working at trades.									Teaching trades.
Blacksmiths	26	16	1	7	3	1	6	10	20	6	1	7	5		1	9	2		2	
Masons	3	3	1	13	8		22		30			1	15	16			2	3	3	
Carpenters	68	29	13	15	4	1	16	15	15	12	3	18	30	8	2	3	6	7	15	3
Engineers	14	9					2	3				3						6		
Harness-makers	9	3	3	3	1		1						20							
Machinists	8	6	1	3	1		2										1		2	
Painters	8	4		3	1	1	6	2	15	6		3	20		1	2		5	1	
Printers	20	11	2	19		3		10		25	10		15	8					4	1
Shoemakers	13	8	2	6	2	1	3	6	10					8		8	1	5	2	
Tailors	17	18		9	11	3	2	3	2				3	6			2	2	5	
Tinsmiths	2	1		4	5															
Wheelwrights	28	4	3	5	1															
Iron & steel workers							6	10				2							4	
Brickmakers				6		1			15		1		10					1		
Dressmakers and Milliners				30	6	1	11	25	25	12		4			8			10	22	1
Other artisans	1		1	11	4	2	20		25	18			5	4	2		10	14	8	7
Total graduates	217			134			98	84	157	79										
Total work'g at trades		112			48		46		10		15	38	123	50	14	22	24	53	68	
Total teaching trades			27			28	14	10				3	6	2	3			2	13	12
Total work'g & teach'g		139			84		60		10		15	41	129	52	17	22	24	55	81	12

There are reported 623 artisans at work, and 120 teaching them trades or teaching manual training. The proportion which those at work and teaching bear to the total trade graduates is not easily ascertained. Some are working at trades who did not graduate: Hampton, for instance, reports

*Of the Trade school only, not of other departments.

†Not including those graduates before 1890.

**Including all graduated.

4 bricklayers and wood-working machinists graduated and 7 working at these two trades. No report at all is made of other than trade school graduates. Tuskegee gives no record of her trade graduates before 1890, and Claflin's report of 60 at work is an estimate and not a detailed report. However, we may make the following table:

Tuskegee:

Total graduates, 423, or 100%.
Of these 11% work at trades,
and 6.5% teach trades.
Total trade graduates, about 150*, or 100%.
Of these 32% work at trades,
and 19% teach trades.

Hampton:

Total trade graduates, 217, or 100%.
Of these 51.5% work at trades,
and 12% teach trades.

Claflin:

Total trade graduates, 98, or 100%.
Of these about 47% work at trades,
and about 14% teach trades.

Possibly it would be fair to say that in the best industrial schools something less than a quarter of all the graduates, and about three-fifths of all the trade graduates, actually practice their trades or teach them.

If to the 743 artisans working and teaching we add for the school at Normal, Ala., and the Arkansas Baptist College an estimated number of 60 additional artisans, we have 803 artisans. The unreported artisans would bring this number up to at least 1,000, so that it would be a conservative statement to say that the hundred schools giving industrial training have in the last twenty years sent one thousand actual artisans into the world, beside a large number who combine their mechanical skill with other callings.

14. *Five Faults of Industrial Schools.* We may now summarize this study of the Industrial School by pointing out briefly certain faults and accomplishments. Twenty years or more ago it was evident that the great problem before the Negro was that of earning an income commensurate with his expanding wants. The Industrial School attempted to answer this problem by training farmers and artisans. How far has it accomplished this work?

The various adverse criticisms against the work of Industrial Schools may be catalogued as follows:

(1.) *Their work has cost too much.*

The total incomes of the industrial schools so far as reported on pages 66-68 was $1,514,793. This includes all schools giving industrial training on any scale. Of this sum $628,379, or 41%, went to Hampton and Tuskegee. Perhaps in all about one million dollars went actually to industrial train-

* i. e., 134 since 1890 and an estimated number of 16 before that time who finished their trades.

ing and the rest to academic and normal work. One might estimate that in the last twenty years the industrial training of Negroes has cost something between five and ten millions of dollars.

The total income including gifts and benefactions of the schools* aided by the Slater fund was in 1899-1900:

Hampton	$426,337	939 students.
Spelman	32,561	599 "
Tuskegee	202,042	1,180 "
Claflin	37,000	708 "
Shaw	21,185	511 "
Montgomery	15,000	928 "
Tougaloo	15,000	436 "

It is clear that while manual training is not very costly, and instruction in sewing and cooking need not be expensive, that on the other hand the teaching of trades and the conduct of "schools of work" are very expensive. It costs as much to run Tuskegee a year as it does to conduct the whole Southern work of the Freedmen's Aid and Southern Education Society†, with their 43 schools, 413 instructors and 10,146 pupils.

So, too, Hampton received in 1900 more than was spent on the whole Negro public school system of the state of Virginia. Such facts are no argument against industrial training, but they do raise the question if its cost today is not unnecessarily excessive. The largest items of expenditure are for tools and machinery, materials, and furnishing work for students. In the first item it is doubtful if there could be any saving: modern industrial appliances are growing more and more elaborate and costly, and if the student is to be properly trained according to the best methods, he must handle and learn the use of such machinery. There must be too in all trade teaching a large consumption of material from which no return can be expected. The old idea was that the industrial school could sell its products and partially, if not wholly, support itself, but this has proven fallacious. In the third item alone, the furnishing of work for students, there is the largest field for retrenchment. The theory in several schools is to charge no tuition and allow the student to work out his education by crediting him with wages for work in the shops. As a matter of fact every $100 thus earned by the student was proven in one school to have cost over $300. Consequently, as has been noted before, there is less emphasis put on this phase of industrial school life to-day than formerly. It is to be hoped that in the future the system will wholly disappear. It was undoubtedly some moral value to the student, but this is more than offset by the waste of time and energy in requiring a student to learn a difficult trade and earn a living at the same time. If he learns the trade well the living "earned" will be simply disguised charity; and if he really earns a living he will scarcely master his trade in any reasonable time. An industrial school should be like other schools: the student or his parents should be required to pay his tuition, board and clothes, and scholarships

*Except Straight and Bishop; no available data for these.

†Christian Educator, May 1902.

should be granted the brightest and most deserving pupils who cannot do this. Others should work and earn the necessary sum before they come to school. In the school all time and energy should be given to learning the trade and mastering the accompanying studies. Any attempt to go further than this is a dangerous experiment which must be costly either in time, energy or money.

(2.) *The lines of study have not been differentiated.*

Most graduates of industrial schools teach; this means that teacher-training should be an important part of the curriculum. In many schools, however, the attempt is made to train a teacher and an artisan at the same time. This would seem to be a mistake: teachers should be trained as teachers and given normal courses in manual training, while separate trade courses should train artisans.

"If carpenters are needed it is well and good to train men as carpenters; if teachers are needed it is well and good to train men as teachers. But to train men as carpenters and then set them to teaching is wasteful and criminal; and to train men as teachers and then refuse them living wages unless they become carpenters is rank nonsense."*

(3.) *There is undue insistence on the "practical."*

Industrial schools must beware placing undue emphasis on the "practical" character of their work. All true learning of the head or hands is practical in the sense of being applicable to life. But the best learning is more than merely practical since it seeks to apply itself, not simply to present modes of living, but to a larger, broader life which lives to-day, perhaps, in theory only, but may come to realization to-morrow by the help of educated and good men. There still lurks in much that passes for industrial training to-day something that reminds us forcibly of Dotheboys Hall and Mr. Squeers:

"We go upon the practical mode of teaching, Nickleby; the regular education system. C-L-E-A-N, clean, verb active, to make bright, to scour. W-I-N, win, D-E-R, winder, a casement. When the boy knows this out of book, he goes and does it."

The ideals of education, whether men are taught to teach or to plow, to weave or to write must not be allowed to sink to sordid utilitarianism. Education must keep broad ideals before it, and never forget that it is dealing with Souls and not with Dollars.

Along with this goes a certain indifference to the artistic side of industry. Industrial art is a most important line of study and one peculiarly suited to the aesthetic Negro temperament. Yet Beauty as "its own excuse for being" has had little emphasis in most industrial schools.

Of the same character is the unfortunate opposition of advocates of industrial education toward colleges. The colleges at first looked askance at the industrial schools until they began to prove their usefulness; and this was a natural attitude. On the other hand no one in the light of history can doubt the necessity of colleges in any system of education.

*Atlanta University Publications No. 6: "The Negro Common School," p. 117.

No adequate system of industrial schools and common schools can be maintained without a proper number of Negro colleges of high grade and efficiency, and this fact all men ought frankly and openly to acknowledge.

(4.) *The changing industrial conditions are often ignored.*

The journeyman artisan, the small shop and the house industry are being replaced by the large contractor, the factory system and power machines; the central fact in the world of labor is the rise and development of the Trade Union. The courses of study in many schools do not sufficiently recognize these changes but prepare workmen for conditions of work that are passing. Especially are these artisans ignorant of the extent and meaning of the great labor movement.

(5.) *Few actual artisans are sent out.*

This criticism is less valid to-day than when it was first made,* and in another decade may disappear as industrial schools improve. Still it has some weight to-day.

Roughly speaking it has cost above five million dollars to establish the industrial schools and send out a thousand workmen. What has hindered the one or two thousand other recipients of some considerable degree of industrial training from following their trades? It may be answered, three considerations:

1. Poor trade instruction. 2. The demand for teachers. 3. The factory system and trade unions. Many schools undoubtedly give a training in "trades" which is not really worthy of the name. When, as is true in one case, only 6 in every 100 artisans trained are following their trades the inevitable conclusion is that the training is very poor. Even the better grade of industrial schools have come to teaching the main trades thoroughly only in the last few years and many other trades are still inadequately taught.

When the graduate of an industrial institute leaves school he is tempted to go to school teaching. As long as the school does not distinctly separate teacher-training and trade-training, and as long as the average teacher is of low efficiency, this temptation will remain and take many artisans from their callings.

There are many callings, however, which Trade Schools, be they ever so efficient and careful, cannot fill with their graduates. This is due to two causes: first, the factory system with its minutely developed division of labor which renders it absolutely essential that the apprentice should learn his trade in the factory; secondly, the strong opposition of trade unions to Negro labor in all lines save those where the Negro already has a foot-hold.

Of these five faults careful consideration would seem to indicate that while all have some weight the first three are most serious; and that careful organization and experiment will likely remove most of these faults in time.

*Cf. Report of the U. S. Commissioner of Education, 1894-5, p. 1360.

15. *Five Accomplishments of Industrial Schools.* Turning now to favorable criticism we may note that Industrial training has:

(1.) *Rationalized Negro Ideals.*

The first result of these schools, as of all schooling, has been spiritual rather than economic. It has made Negroes think; turned their attention from mere aspiration to the concrete problem of earning a living and emphasized the truth that labor is honorable; and while this thinking has not yet shown itself to any great extent in increased avenues of employment and greater skill there is no doubt that future decades will show vast improvement.

(2.) *Begun the co-ordination of hand and head work in education.*

We have not yet reached altogether satisfactory results in this new education but the Negro industrial school has given great and needed emphasis to the movement and has to some extent taught the whole nation.

(3.) *Reached out into the Country Districts.*

The mission schools and the schools of the Freedmen's bureau were primarily city and town schools and reached the select classes largely. The industrial schools have appealed especially to the neglected county districts and to the "field-hand" class.

(4.) *Improved Domestic Work in the Home.*

The first industrial work was with girls in sewing and cooking, and already the results of this training are seen in the first-class town homes.

(5.) *United Races and Sections on one Point.*

Progress is largely compromise. The attitude of the South toward the Negro is not what the best thought of the North or of the Negroes could wish. The attitude of the Negro toward the South and of the North toward the Negro is not what the dominant thought of the South wishes. It is, however, an omen of unusual importance that amid this difference of opinion and bitterness of spirit there is some common ground on which North and South, black and white, can meet, viz: common school, manual and trade training for black children. This does not mean that the race problem can be settled on this basis, but it does mean that its settlement can be auspiciously begun. Negroes can and will demand some college and professional training in addition; fair minded men can and will demand equal rights for all Americans despite color, and the Southern people can and will demand safeguards against ignorance and crime; but all happily will agree on the importance of industrial training. And this is no little step from January 1, 1863.

16. *The Higher Education and the Industries,* (by Dr. J. G. Merrill, President of Fisk University). The higher education is essential to the very existence of any education and it is only in lands where education is found that the industries thrive. The higher education may be likened to the head as part of the body; the life of the body terminates when it is removed from it; it may be likened to the key stone of the arch, a very small matter as far as material goes, but it makes efficient the aggregate mass in the structure that can bear untold weight.

The mental quickening which the college graduate gives a rural village, the breadth of view which he helps a municipality to take, the larger conceptions of business life due to the men of letters are every day verifications of the value to all of the training received by the few. It is such an atmosphere as this that quickens the mind of the inventor so that he may produce new instruments for human progress, the intellect of the architect on whose success depends the daily bread of the carpenter, and mason, and even the teamster and the hod-carrier; the ambition of the farmer who learns how to make two blades of grass where one has grown before, and is kept from being merely "the man with the hoe."

Or look at the matter in another way. The large proportion of the children of the artisan and the laborer are to obtain their training in the common school; this training will be of value to them in proportion to the worth of the teaching force in the school. A stream cannot rise higher than its fountain; a teacher with only a common school education is not equipped for such work; a high school graduate or normal teacher is sought for. But who is to teach the industrial, the high, or the normal school? There must be a source higher than they to put in requisition, and so on until we reach the superlative—the highest educators, those whom God has endowed with the loftiest of gifts, who have had the privileges of post graduate training such as have made Germany and England and, of late, the United States, famous in the realms of knowledge.

It remains to note the counter movement, the help received by the higher education from the industries. This has been well-nigh phenomenal. As the years have gone by wealth has increased; the number of millionaires has multiplied; very many of them having amassed their fortunes by means of the industries. But better than this has been the earning power of the average man which has risen in the United States from ten cents per day in 1800 for each man, woman, and child, to 30 cents in 1850, over 50 cents in 1890, and much higher than that in 1900, we are sure compilations when made from the last census will show. Now, because of this state of affairs higher education prospers, the normal schools and universities supported by the state and the princely benefactions given to endow colleges, universities and post graduate schools are a sign of the times, pointing to a future that is very bright when, in all our land, the opportunity to obtain a common school education will be afforded to all, an industrial training to the many, who by native gifts or inclination can earn a livelihood and bless the state by use of their physical powers, the higher education to those whose mental equipment is matched by tenacity of purpose and the high moral aims which alone can make of value any education.

17. *The Industrial Settlement at Kowaliga, Ala.* The thesis of Dr. Merrill as developed in the preceding section is illustrated clearly in the case of Negro education. Industrial training in the South is peculiarly the child of the College and the University. Samuel Armstrong and Dr. Frissell were College-bred men, and the majority of their teachers also; Tuskegee "is filled with College graduates, from the energetic wife of the principal down to the teacher of agriculture, including nearly half of the executive

council and a majority of the heads of departments"* and so, too, in every one of the hundred industrial schools the College graduates are the leading spirits. Further than this one College graduate, William Benson, of Fisk and Howard, has, at Kowaliga, developed an industrial settlement of Negroes on a business basis which is the longest step toward the economic emancipation of the Negro yet taken. The "Dixie Industrial Company" is the name of the enterprise and this is a description of its work:

"We are sitting in the spacious chapel of a new school building. The walls and columns are decorated in bunting and flags, in three colors. In every direction which the eye may gaze is to be seen an air of cheerfulness, except the long line of dark, care-worn faces before us. It is the occasion of the county fair which is held annually on the premises of the new community school. On the grounds outside we have seen exhibits of live-stock and poultry; the recitation rooms are filled with specimens of corn, cotton, potatoes, fruit and other products grown in the region. On the floor above the women have arranged their handiwork of sewing, cooking, preserving, canning and quilting; and now we are to witness the awarding of prizes to successful competitors.

"The farm group seems divided into four classes; those who rent land, live stock and implements, furnishing only their labor and dividing their products half and half; a smaller class who have been frugal enough to pay for live stock and implements and give a stipulated amount for the rent of a given number of acres; a still smaller class who own land of their own, and lastly, those who are buying land under a form of lease and option contract. An enterprising man, a College-bred Negro, secured a tract of one thousand acres of land, which he sub-divided into twenty-five farm lots of forty acres each. Neat and inexpensive cottages were built, being grouped as closely as possible, with the view of overcoming the disadvantages of sparsely settled rural life. These farms, including improvements, are sold at four hundred dollars each. The payments are arranged in annual installments covering a period of eight years—not much exceeding what they have heretofore paid as rent. This group we notice from the reports just read, is more prosperous because they work under intelligent supervision. It is a part of their contract. They cannot take more land than they can handle thoroughly, and they make more with the same labor than under the old system with a big crop, half fertilized, and half-cultivated. They must raise an abundance of food supplies, take care of their live-stock and improve their farms. They work better and live better, because they have a personal interest in all they do. One man works at the saw mill, another at the oil mill and another at the brick yard. Every buyer, be he farmer or mill-hand, will be given a clear title to his home when he has completed his payments as specified.

"Our community began with a single group, and now we develop another. The establishment of minor industries supplements the farm life and add to the material prosperity of the community. Much of the viciousness of an isolated rural population is due to idleness. A few pay-

*Atlantic Monthly, Sept., 1902, p. 295.

ing industries utilize waste material and keep in the community thousands of dollars which must go out. But you say that we are too far from a railroad, and the expense of finding a market for our products would be too great. Whatever opportunities might ultimately open to us in this direction, it is certain that our present welfare depends upon making the community self-sustaining and self-relying. We shall make our own market and supply our own demand. We cannot export; we will not import.

"We are spending annually an aggregate of five thousand dollars for wagons, furniture and implements. A saw mill and general wood-working plant would utilize our timber, first in building homes and making as near as possible all the cheap furniture required in furnishing these homes. A small oil mill plant can be equipped at an outlay of ten thousand dollars. This does not represent the cost of last year's fertilizer, to say nothing of the thousands of bushels of cotton seed carted away to a foreign market. The oil mill man takes the lintings, the hulls and the oil, and sells back again the meal alone to the farmer at an advance of $6.50 to $12.00 per ton more than he has given for the whole product. Our mill will save the community the cost of its fertilizer, and the hulls as a valuable feed. These industries can be operated entirely independent of trusts, because we saw our own trees, and use the houses, make our own seed and use the fertilizer.

"Now follows the development of other groups in fast succession. One finds it profitable to make a specialty of gardening, another dairying and another poultry raising. The aesthetic taste of the female population demands better made dresses, and they like to have ribbons tied to their hats by a milliner. Our community life becomes a centre of industry, and then a centre of commerce to its own immediate region, selling its products and buying its necessities. This brings us to the point where we touch the life of our white neighbor. The moment we rise to the plane where our business interests are mutual, we strike a common meeting-ground. The Negro teacher, minister and professional business man finds his patronage almost exclusively among the people of his own race. The Negro business man is the only one who crosses the line, and it is here that his contact with the white man is closest and most congenial.

"The first direct effort toward this new agricultural, industrial and domestic activity was through the enlargement of the community school, and the perfection ot a plan by which the community that enjoys its benefits, might more largely participate in its burdens. The people had little money, so one gives land, another material, and others labor. Thus the cabin school-house was torn down and in its place erected a fine structure, with the appointments of a modern institution. We are introduced to several new teachers—a nice set of young men and women, well trained for the work of leading those who live around them to a more intelligent life of Christian manhood and womanhood.

"We have presented this sketch of settlement life, with the simple hope that it may suggest to your minds a practical scheme for preventing the Negro from drifting from the country to foreign fields, and a fair way to start him on the road to independence where he is. If you are skeptical as to its feasibility, let us remember that the father of the young Collegian who directs this community, has demonstrated every feature of life and industry which we have advanced. He began a pioneer in the woods, and now we find him the owner of three thousand acres, with two hundred and fifty people cultivating his land. He operates a saw mill, a grist mill and cotton gins. He has a plantation store, horses and cattle. He has given his children a good education at the best schools afforded them in the South, and they in turn are helping others. We are surprised to find that he not only has the patronage, but indeed the friendship, of the best white men of the region. His problem is solved, and he has given us the hope of the ideal community, and his son is widening and developing it."

18. *General Statistics of Negro Artisans.* The occupations of American Negroes in 1890 have been discussed in a general way on pages 23 to 26.* Let us now consider more specifically the distribution of Negro artisans in 1890, taking certain typical employments and giving the figures first for the United States and then for the Southern States in detail.**

NEGRO ARTISANS IN THE UNITED STATES.—Census of 1890.

Occupation	Number	Occupation	Number
Carpenters	22,318	Shoemakers	5,065
Barbers	17,480	Mill and Factory operatives	5,050
Saw-mill operatives	17,230	Painters	4,396
Miners	15,809	Plasterers	4,006
Tobacco factory employees	15,004	Quarrymen	3,198
Blacksmiths	10,762	Coopers	2,648
Brick-makers	10,521	Butchers	2,510
Masons	9,647	Wood-workers	1,375
Engineers and Firemen	7,662	Tailors	1,280
Dressmakers	7,479	Stone cutters	1,279
Iron and Steel workers	5,790	Leather-curriers	1,099

There were in the United States in 1890 about 175,000 Negro skilled artisans in the main classes enumerated above. If we take the chief skilled workmen in the Southern States we have:

*Cf. Gannett: Occupations of Negroes—Publications of the Slater Fund Trustees.

**The figures for 1900 are not yet available. The figures in the tables contain a negligible number of "Chinese, Japanese, and civilized Indians."

SKILLED NEGRO LABORERS (BY STATES)—1890.

	Alabama.	Arkansas.	Delaware.	District of Columbia.	Florida.	Georgia.	Kentucky.	Louisiana.	Maryland.	Mississippi.	Missouri.	North Carolina.	South Carolina.	Tennessee.	Texas.	Virginia.	West Virginia.	Totals.
MALE.																		
Engineers (Civ. & Mech.)	16	2		10	9			37					26		6	16	3	125
Barbers	520	392	51	450	263	899	657	369	480	326	909	482	380	871	816	835	220	8,920
Eng. & Firemen (Stationary)	452	165	27	122	169	520	359	309	220	703	321	432	344	558	212	521	36	5,470
Steam Railway Employees	4591	1013	88	89	1536	7440	2492	1593	467	2736	703	3534	3052	4039	2658	7648	1401	45,080
Apprentices	73		3	54	67	247	36	190	57		25		255			186	5	1,198
Blacksmiths & Wheelwrights	891	364	23	121	150	1328	592	699	206	665	206	831	832	1032	537	1554	97	10,022
Boot & Shoe Makers	272	68	23	234	95	632	143	138	155	130	52	384	353	348	85	849	39	4,300
Brick Makers	514	269	146	442		977	491		1143	355		443	286	849	466	1213	22	7,616
Butchers	136	64	7	62	91	299	80	141	130	128	65	144	274	132	174	231	7	2,165
Carpenters	1703	581	20	316	988	3761	886	1611	374	1476	263	1789	2730	1361	917	2017	51	20,844
Cotton & Other Textile Mill Op.	281	83	15		183	771	225	263	57	76		564	369	201	330	462		3,880
Iron and Steel Workers	1749		186	16		270	240	30	68		177	88		982		793	13	4,612
Machinists	54	91	3	15	31	71	27	24	13	41	19	46	42	66	41	61	2	677
Marble & Stone Cut'rs & Mas'ns	618	198	37	188	211	1344	586	766	231	296	281	827	889	1429	298	913	76	9.198
Mechanics	64	59				154				85		74	58	48				542
Millers	166	26	6		62	160	77		76	63	35	158	108	130	34	212	4	1,317
Painters	280	85	6	141	165	676	181	280	59	153	66	297	482	287	133	206	20	3,517
Printers	40	17	1	64	26	78	23	39	27	22	32	56	57	43	22	44	5	606
FEMALE.																		
Dress Makers & Seamstresses	859	266	32	1411	593	1632	576	2490	990	759	311	705	2193	915	425	1412	37	15,606
Printers	3	0	0	17	2	1	1			5	3		0	2	0	6	0	40
Tailoresses	16		0		12	22	2	137	7		2	8	21	3		30	2	262

The steam railway employees include many section hands and semi-skilled workmen, and also the colored firemen. The carpenters are the largest body of skilled workingmen and it will be seen that 20,800 of the 22,300 are in the South. Next come the blacksmiths and wheelwrights with 10,000, the masons and stone cutters with 9,000, the barbers with 9,000 and the brickmakers, stationery engineers and firemen. The states differ considerably in the proportion of different kinds of workingmen: Steam railway employees and carpenters lead in Virginia, the Carolinas and the Gulf States; iron and steel workers outnumber all but the railway men in the mining state, Alabama, and the masons and stone cutters are numerous in Tennessee. The city population of the District of Columbia has barbers and brickmakers as its chief Negro artisans. Among the women the skilled work is almost wholly confined to sewing and working in tobacco factories.

We may further study the black artisan by noting his distribution in the large cities where most of the white artisans are located. For this purpose let us take 16 large cities with an aggregate Negro population of nearly half a million. There are many curious differences to be noted here. The great Northern cities, like New York, Chicago and Cincinnati, are conspicuous for scarcity of black artisans, having only barbers.

The border State cities show the Negroes in some of the important skilled occupations, as in brickmaking in Baltimore, Wilmington and Philadelphia; and iron and steel-working in Louisville, Wilmington, Pittsburg and Richmond. Stationary engineers are prominent in St. Louis. In the more typical Southern cities, like Atlanta, Charleston, Memphis and Nashville, the carpenters, railway men and masons are most conspicuous, while New Orleans shows its peculiarities in a considerable number of carpenters, masons, railway men, shoemakers and painters:

SKILLED NEGRO LABORERS (BY CITIES)—1890.

MALE.	Atlanta, Ga.	Baltimore, Md.	Charleston, S. C.	Chicago, Ill.	Cincinnati, O.	Kansas City, Mo.	Louisville, Ky.	Memphis, Tenn.	Nashville, Tenn.	New Orleans, La.	Philadelphia, Pa.	Pittsburg, Pa.	Richmond, Va.	St. Louis, Mo.	Wilmington, Del.	New York, N. Y.
Engineers (C. & M.)	5		10	3	2	2	7	6	5		3	2	3	4	0	3
Barbers	162	317	148	229	150	185	120	123	193	200	423	105	195	293	38	111
Eng. & Firemen (S.)	49	145	76	41	87	28	82	106	122	117	59	33	43	180	19	61
Steam R'y Employ's	387	48	251	45	43	38	104	389	239	367	79	10	252	173	27	28
Apprentices	27	36	107	1	0	2	8		0	123	31	3	24	6	0	4
Blacksmiths and Wheelwrights	140	35	129	21	23	14	48	120	113	116	18	16	139	13	10	9
Boot & Shoemakers	120	88	90	11	8	4	19	47	82	366	63	2	128	19	15	6
Brick Makers	59	981		8	2	88	184	109	121		406	35	96	103	128	
Butchers	18	90	144	8	4	4	5	18	26	48	27	1	32	10	3	15
Carpenters	503	85	681	37	33	37	122	369	198	603	61	17	150	56	2	33
Cotton & Other Textile Mill Operators	28	22	62	13	13		30	41	22	88	22	22	93	0	6	3
Iron & Steel Workers	43	46	12	16	4	8	158	25	19	17	22	207	293	137	171	9
Machinists	11	9	8	24	21	2	11	11	16	10	9	3	13	7	2	7
Marble & Stone Cutters & Masons	245	128	224	50	13	83	66	126	404	495	53	24	93	37	31	23
Painters	74				5	24	41	80	99	200			28	20	4	99
Printers	25	37	171	19	0	7	9	8		29	28	8	9	6	1	21
Cabinet Makers and Upholsterers	16	24	9		2	2	17	21	19	92	59	5	28	6	4	18
Harness, Saddle and Trunkmakers	10	59	24			2	6	84	7	239	73	17	1	2	3	10
Plasterers	116		48	21		45	47		83	59		2	165	0	1	20
Tailors	32	87	105	13	5	4	6	6	18	36	32	0	3	5		3
Tinners & Tinware Makers	2	60	44	1	0	0	5	4	13		2		4	4		
FEMALE.																
Dressmakers, Milliners, Seamstresses	197	814	1,822	232	136	62	183	341	271	1,689	746	55	270	147	25	522
Printers	0	0	0	5	2	0	0	0	1		2	0	2	0	0	2
Tailoresses	3	6	21	1	2	0	1	0	1	132	130	1	24	0	0	3
Negro Pop'lat'n 1890	28,098	67,104	30,970	14,271	11,655	13,700	28,651	28,706	29,382	64,491	39,371	7,850	32,330	26,865	7,644	23,601

We may turn now to the few available figures which show the general condition of these artisans, as illiteracy, steadiness of employment, age and conjugal condition.

In the Manufacturing and Mechanical industries throughout the United States there are 146,153 colored persons of whom 43.8% were illiterate in 1890. Of the 143,371 in Trade and Transportation 43.4% were illiterate. The illiteracy of the artisans by selected trades for 1890 was as follows:*

MALE.	TOTAL.	ILLITERATE.	% ILLITERACY.
Blacksmiths and Wheelwrights	11,156	5,916	53.
Boot and Shoe Makers	4,982	1,868	37.5
Butchers	2,508	1,023	40.7
Carpenters	22,310	9,789	43.8
Cotton Mill Operatives	820	369	45.
Machinists	838	213	25.4
Masons	9,645	3,732	38.6
Miners and Quarrymen	18,986	9,466	49.8
Printers	829	89	10.7
Steam Railway Employees	47,316	26,321	55.6
Tailors	913	139	15.2
Textile Mill Operatives	3,260	1,673	51.3
Tobacco and Cigar Factory Opera's	10,480	4,190	40.
FEMALE.			
Dressmakers, M'ners, Seamstresses	19,753	4,228	21.4
Tobacco and Cigar Factory Opera's	4,524	2,596	57.3
Tailoresses	367	83	22.6

These figures throw interesting sidelights on the character of the workingmen. Blacksmith miners, steam railway section hands, those employed in rougher kinds of textile work and those in the tobacco factories are largely ignorant. On the other the machinists, printers, tailors and dressmakers are a younger and more intelligent set.

Not all of these artisans are employed steadily. In two great divisions of industry we find the Negroes employed as follows:

	UNEMPLOYED DURING THE YEAR.		
	1-3 MONTHS.	4-6 MOS.	7-12 MOS.
Manufacturing and Mechanical Industries	18,955 12.9%	16,184 11.7%	2,831 1.8%
Trade and Transportation	11,321 7.8%	6,414 4.4%	1,437 1. %

Taking the number and percentages by separate callings we have:

*Only those of Negro descent are here given, making some slight discrepancies between these and other tables.

ARTISANS—EMPLOYMENT—1890.

	UNEMPLOYED.		
	1 to 3 mos.	4-6 mos	7-12 mos.
MALE.			
Blacksmiths & Wheelwrights	644	443	145
Boot and Shoe Makers	245	219	98
Butchers	118	92	25
Carpenters and Joiners	2,820	2,302	487
Cotton Mill Operatives	80	87	12
Machinists	63	30	6
Masons	1,381	1,487	283
Miners and Quarrymen	4,149	2,559	467
Printers	60	30	11
Steam Railroad Employees	5,247	2,378	452
Tailors	70	52	17
Textile Mill Operatives	420	239	35
Tobacco & Cigar Fac. Operat's	1,718	2,541	250
FEMALE.			
Dressmakers, Milliners and S	1,101	877	218
Tobacco & Cigar Fac. Operat's	759	1,433	126
Tailoresses	28	25	9

PER CENT. UNEMPLOYED DURING THE YEAR.

	1 to 3 mos. Per Cent.	4 to 6 mos. Per Cent.	7 to 12 mos. Per Cent.
Blacksmiths and Wheelwrights	5.7	3.9	1.3
Boot and Shoe Makers	4.9	4.4	1.9
Butchers	4.7	3.6	1.
Carpenters and Joiners	12.6	10.4	2.4
Cotton Mill Operatives	9.7	11.1	1.4
Machinists	7.5	3.5	.71
Masons	14.3	15.4	2.9
Miners and Quarrymen	21.8	13.4	2.4
Printers	7.2	3.6	1.3
Steam Railroad Employees	11.	5.	.9
Tailors	7.6	5.5	1.8
Textile Mill Operatives	12.8	7.3	1.
Tobacco and Cigar Factory Operatives	16.3	24.2	2.4
FEMALE.			
Dressmakers, Milliners, Seamstresses	5.	4.4	1.1
Tobacco and Cigar Factory Operatives	16.7	31.6	2.7
Tailoresses	7.6	6.8	2.4

Carpenters, masons, miners and tobacco hands show the largest irregularities in employment.

We may next consider the question of the ages of Negro employees:

Ages.	Manufacturing and Mechanical Industries.	Trade and Transportation.
10-14	3,438	3,858
15-24	36,762	46,490
25-34	35,165	41,908
35-44	28,449	26,787
45-54	22,319	14,817
55-64	11,852	5,375
65 and over.	6,499	2,436
Age unknown.	1,669	1,700

Considering the chief sorts of artisans we have:

ARTISANS BY AGE—PERIODS.—1890.

AGE—PERIODS. MALE.	10-14 years	15-24 years	25-34 years	35-44 years	45-54 years	55-64 years	65 yrs & o'er	Total*
Blacksmiths, W'wrights.	54	1,360	1,799	2,156	2,569	1,940	1,173	11,051
Boot and Shoe makers...	22	606	730	1,141	1,299	715	421	4,934
Butchers....................	39	783	596	474	329	174	87	2,482
Carpenters and Joiners...	31	2,354	4,147	5,103	5,364	3,281	1,816	22,096
Cotton Mill Operatives...	47	243	220	163	94	35	9	811
Machinists....................	3	163	258	212	118	53	20	827
Masons.......................	43	1,847	2,299	2,076	1,811	999	468	9,543
Miners and Quarrymen...	360	6,757	6,121	3,114	1,595	540	187	18,674
Printers.	15	367	233	107	63	27	15	827
Steam R'road Employees	337	18,693	16,164	7,399	3,184	778	182	46,737
Tailors	9	243	225	157	148	77	49	908
Textile Mill Operatives...	144	1,305	941	486	242	69	45	3,232
Tobacco and Cigar Factory Operatives...........	1,231	4,140	2,314	1,448	813	331	138	10,415
FEMALE.								
Dressmakers, Milliners and Seamstresses.........	189	7,275	5,794	3,486	1,808	751	364	19,667
Tobacco and Cigar Factory Operatives...........	478	2,007	990	581	304	96	43	4,499
Tailoresses....................	4	149	86	68	34	17	7	365
Total	3,006	48,292	42,917	28,171	19,775	9,883	5,024	157,068
Percentage..................	1.9	30.7	27.3	17.9	12.5	6.2	3.1	100.

The average age of Negro artisans is not as high as one would expect; this is probably owing to the large number of young people in semi-skilled occupations, such as section hands, miners and tobacco operatives. The carpenters and blacksmiths, on the other hand, are mostly between 35 and 55. Younger men are becoming masons, printers and tailors.

Of the general conditions of family life among Negro artisans we can only judge by the statistics of conjugal condition; the conjugal condition of all Negroes engaged in manufacturing and mechanical industries was as follows in 1890:

	Single and unknown.	Married.	Widowed and Divorced.
15-24 years...........	80.4 per cent.	19.1 per. ct.	.4 per cent.
25-34 years...........	27.1 " "	69.8 " "	2.9 " "
35-44 years......	12.2 " "	81.7 " "	6. " "
45-54 years.......	7. " "	83.5 " "	9.2 " "

We add to these the figures for the selected classes of artisans before studied:

MALE.

	Single and unknown.	Married.	Widowed and divorced.
15-24 years...........	80.4 per cent.	19.1 per ct.	.4 per cent.
25-34 years...........	28.9 " "	68.3 " "	2.6 " "
35-44 years...........	15.9 " "	77.8 " "	6.1 " "
45-54 years...........	7.1 " "	83.9 " "	8.8 " "

*Omitting those of unknown age.

FEMALE.

	Single and unknown.	Married.	Widowed and divorced.
15-24 years..........	78.5 per cent.	17.2 per ct.	4.1 per cent.
25-34 years..........	36.5 " "	44.1 " "	19.2 " "
35-44 years..........	19.6 " "	45.9 " "	34.3 " "
45-54 years..........	12.7 " "	33.5 " "	53.6 " "

The artisans naturally marry earlier than the College-bred Negroes and exhibit no marked peculiarities save in the large number of widows forced to earn a living for themselves.'

19. *Social Conditions: A study in Memphis, Tenn.*, (by Henry N. Lee, of Le-Moyne Institute.) In Memphis the chief Negro artisans are carpenters, blacksmiths, brickmasons, plasterers, painters, dressmakers, plumbers, tailors and shoemakers. There are also a few glaziers, paper hangers, electricians, stone cutters, engineers, milliners, sculptors and printers.

This is a study of 123 Negro artisans made by a personal canvass in the spring of 1902. The carpenters are the most numerous group of artisans. Of the twenty studied ten are over forty years of age; of the fifteen painters, nine are over forty. This fact is true of the sixteen trades studied except among the printers. Six of the sixteen trades have no workmen under thirty years of age. As there are few apprentices it is to be feared that the number of black artisans in Memphis is decreasing.

Twelve of the 20 carpenters studied, own their homes; 6 of the 15 brickmasons, 4 of the 9 plumbers, 6 of the 15 painters, 4 of the 11 plasterers, 1 of the 8 glaziers and 4 of the 7 dressmakers. These owners are all middle-aged people whose chance for future accumulation is small. There are three prosperous contractors among the carpenters, and 6 men who work for themselves. There are five men who contract for painting and do some of the best work in the city; 7 of 10 blacksmiths have their own shops and employ at least one man.

There are 4 brickmasons who work for themselves, but Mr. Hodges, who is one of the officers of the union, says that there is a great need for a reliable Negro contractor, who would be a leader for the Negro brickmasons; while now the colored and white masons belong to the same union, yet there are many changes going on in the Memphis unions as we shall see later.

6 of 11 plasterers contract for plastering. There are only three colored apprentices in this trade. This number is fixed by the union, which passed a law that each contractor could employ one apprentice. White contractors do not take colored apprentices any more. I learned that one apprentice is employed by a white contractor, and he is retained because his apprenticeship is nearly completed.

There is a great difference in the wages for colored and whites in all the trades except that of the plasterers and brickmasons. These belong to the same unions with the whites and have the same privileges, both in wages and work.

The examination is so difficult that only two colored plumbers have passed. Therefore most of the Negro plumbers are not recognized as competent because they have not passed the examination; yet, I am told, that many of these men can do excellent work.

The colored carpenters, except those who work for colored contractors, are forced to do the rough and drudgery work, while the finishing is left to the whites. This robs them of every chance to be or become first-class workmen. Yet, if one is first-class he receives only a little more than half wages as compared with the whites.

The engineers and electricians are a little more than a name. They are not given the opportunity to show their ability nor to do that class of work which would be of very much use to them as skilled workmen. The wages are such that a young man would not be induced to brave the disadvantages to fit himself for the trades.

There seems to be a difference of opinion as to whether the Negro is gaining or losing in skilled work. But we think that from the fact that there is such a great discrimination in wages which would possibly force the best mechanics to seek other employment more remunerative, and because of the low class of work which the Negro is forced to do in many of the trades, which robs him of any chance to do fine work and to become an all-round workman in his trade, and from the many limitations and unjust laws passed by the labor unions, the Negro in our section is losing. This may not be seen very much now but will be one of our sad awakenings.

Those who think the Negro of Memphis is losing, credit it not so much to inefficiency, as to organized labor unions which direct, in many instances, all their energy against the Negro. It is safe to say, said a leading Negro artisan, that 20 years ago the Negro followed largely all the trades and about five-eighths of all the laborers were Negroes. If the Negro had been inefficient in his labor then other labor would have been imported; but this was not done.

Yet it seems very clear that with the introduction of electricity and modern machinery and with these restrictions of labor unions, the Negro has had no chance to advance with the times along many industrial lines and increase his skill as was demanded by this new order of things. And sad to say it is growing worse instead of better. Until one who is the least pessimistic is almost ready to say the Negro will indeed before very long be "hewers of wood and drawers of water," or in other words be reduced to the lowest place among skilled workmen. The unions do not as a rule protect the Negro, not only in Memphis but elsewhere. At present there are only two trades in which both white and colored belong to the same union, the brick masons and plasterers. And the privileges of these are curtailed by what is known in Memphis as the Builders' Exchange, to which Negroes do not belong. Recently this exchange passed a law that no contractor could sublet his work to a contractor who did not belong to the exchange. This law completely shuts out the Negro. A colored plasterer was refused a contract, although his bid was least, and the parties cited this law of the exchange as their reason for not letting the work to him.

Not very long ago the union for horse shoers dissolved itself into two branches—one for whites and one for colored. Shortly after this had been done the white union passed a law that no colored shoers should be employed in white shops.

I bring a very strong plea from Memphis for one or more competent Negro architects. The contractors desire a leader. They are not permitted to go to a white architect's office, look over his plans and make their bids. So they think they are at a very great disadvantage.

I also bring a very urgent plea for the combination and profitable investment of Negro capital that the Negro artisans may have permanent means of support.

When we note that of 123 artisans reported from Memphis only six received their training in Industrial schools. When we see from the catalogues the comparatively small number of those graduating from Industrial Schools actually following their trades, we wonder what the cause is.

The thinkers of Memphis believe that the causes for this state of affairs are these. (1). Young men do not receive sufficient encouragement and are not made to feel the importance of their sticking to their trades while at school. (2.) In most of the trade schools the training is antiquated and impracticable, thus the young men are handicapped and forced to the back ground in many of the trades when they meet the competition of those laborers who have received a more adequate and modern training. (3.) Many of the young men can not find employment at all, either because their training will not permit them to compete with other skilled laborers, or because they are prohibited from working in manufactories and machine shops which give employment to men of their trades. Or if they are employed it is at starvation wages and for drudgery work with no chance of advancement.

We want many skilled laborers in every line of work, for no race can be prosperous and progressive without a large number of men who are producing the necessities of life. But if we do not want this class either to leave their trades for other work, as many are doing, or lead lives of idleness and, in many cases, lives of absolute worthlessness, as a race we *must* do something for the employment of our boys and girls. This fact is more and more clear each year. And every business enterprise established by a Negro giving employment to the Negro youth is a sacrifice for the salvation of our boys and girls and a step in the solution of these important questions which confront us.

SELECTED NEGRO ARTISANS OF MEMPHIS, TENN.

Trade.	No.	Av. Wages Per Day.	Own Real Estate.	Own Tools.	Other capital invested.	Ages—20-30.	Ages—30-40.	Ages—40 and over.	Have Attended Industrial School. No	Have Attended Industrial School. Where.	Wages of Whites.	Works for himself.	Works for others.	Education—Read.	Education—Write.	Higher training.	Remarks.
Carpenters	20	$2.50	12	20		4	6	10			$3.50 to $4	9	11	18	18		4 Contractors.
Painters	15	$2.50 to $3	6	6	1		6	9				5	10	14	14		5 Contractors.
Tailors	5	$2.50	2	4		1	3	1				4	1	5	5		4 have shops and own fixtures.
Plumbers	9	$3.50	4	9		2	2	5			$3.50 to $4	6	3	7	7		Only two passed examination.
Blacksmiths	10	$2 to $3	3	6		3	2	5			$2.50 to $3	7	3	7	7		Can't work in white shops.
Brick Masons	15	$4.50	6	10		5	4	6	1	Tuskegee, Ala.	$4.50	4	11	12	12		No reliable contractors.
Plasterers	11	$4 to $6	4	10		2	4	5			$4 to $6	6	5	10	10		Belong to white union.
Glaziers	8		1	8		1	3	5			$1.75 $2.25		8	7	7		Six are intemperate.
Paper Hangers	3	$2.00					1				$2.50 to $3	1	1	2	2		Cannot join union.
Electricians	1		1	1			1				$2.50 to $3		1	1	1		
Stone Cutters	3	$3.50	1	1			1	2			$4 to $6	1	2	3	3		Began as helpers.
Engineers	3	$2 to $2.50	2	3			2	1			$3 to $4.50		3	3	3	1	Passed examination; have little chance.
Seamstresses	7	$1 to $2.50	4	7		1	3	3	1			4	3	7	7		Young girls do not take to sewing.
Milliners	1	$1 to $1.50		1		1			1	Tougaloo.	$1 to $3	1		1	1	1	Teaches part of time.
Sculptors	1	$3.00	1	1				1				1		1	1		Work chiefly on tomb stones.
Printers	5	$2.50 $3.50	3	4		3		2	3	Clark U. & Le M. I.	Union Price	4	1	5	5	4	
Shoe Makers	6	$1.50 $2.75	1	6		1	1	4	1	Clark University	$2 to $3	5	1	6	6	1	One went to Middle Prep. Class.
Total	123		51	97		12	43	59	7			58	64	109	109	7	

20. *Local Conditions: Texas* (by E. H. Holmes of the Prairie View Normal school).

We have always had among us some men who have been more or less skilful in the use of tools. During the days of slavery these men built the houses, made the plows, carriages, wagons, etc., and performed nearly all that class of labor. The constant doing brought to them experience and experience ripened into a degree of skill. Slavery was their trade school and experience their instructor. After the Civil war these workmen followed the trades—they had the field to themselves at first.

In the course of time labor saving machines were introduced and new methods of doing things were adopted—the old workman enters a new era—he finds himself face to face with new conditions—his school did not give instruction in the use of machines and he is unable to keep step with the onward march. Some of them who did keep up have finished their work and gone to their reward. No one has taken the vacant places and to-day the ranks of Negro Artisans need—sadly need—recruiting.

Texas offers great opportunities to skilled workmen in various trades. Her natural resources surpass those of any state in the Union. It is her proud boast that within her broad domain is to be found everything from a salt mine to an oil geyser. These resources are but partially developed—some not at all. The Negro Artisan has had a share in this development and will have a larger share in the future, provided he will fit himself for this larger share. I have had opportunity to observe conditions among artisans only in the cities, towns and country districts of southern Texas.

Ours being an agricultural state, blacksmiths are in greater demand than perhaps any other tradesman. You will find a Negro blacksmith in nearly every town and at every country cross-road. They are found managing shops on many of the large cotton and sugar plantations. One of the largest sugar farms in the Southwest, located at Sugarland, Texas, employs a Negro foreman of their blacksmith shop at a salary of $1,080 per year. In the towns the majority of them are doing business for themselves, a few own their own shops, are making a living and accumulating property. There are still others who work by the day in shops owned by whites. These receive wages according to their skill. White men having the same degree of skill would receive no more. There is such a shop at Brenham, Texas. Some weeks ago the owner of this shop stated that he worked a few colored men, that he would employ more if they could do superior work—that there was no discrimination practiced in his shop and he also expressed the hope that our school would send out more students who could make drawings and work from drawings. It is difficult to tell the per cent of Negro artisans in the towns for this reason: they do not register their occupations. Whatever is known must be learned by inquiry or from personal contact. Let us consider conditions at Houston, Texas. This is a city having a population of 60 thousand. One-third are Negroes. It is in every respect a liberal and representative city. There are seven blacksmiths there who own and run their shops. Two of these shops employ from three to five regular workmen. The proprietors make a good living and nearly all of them own their homes. The largest carriage and iron repair shop owned by a white man employs 5 Negro blacksmiths on his working force. Two of these manage their own fires. They are paid according to skill—sometimes discrimination is made on account of color. Two boiler and foundry shops employ Negro workmen. They receive the regular moulders' wages, $4.00 per day, and a few of them have been in the service of the firms for years. The Southern Pacific Railway System employs them in two of their shops. In these shops are some who manage their fires, one who operates a steam hammer, some who build and repair cars and a large number of helpers who rank several grades above common laborers. A few of these men have been steadily employed for twenty-five years, some longer. The wages range from 15 to 25 cents per hour, according to skill. It might be of interest to remark just here that one of the helpers long years ago was foreman of the shop. Time and improved machinery forced him down. So far as employment goes there is practically no discrimination against blacksmiths and I do not know of any blacksmith's union in the whole state.

Carpenters are fewer in number than blacksmiths. In the small towns they are journeyman workers. As a class they do inferior work. Their wages range from $1.25 to $2.00 per day. White journeymen do the same poor quality of work but receive higher wages. Their pay ranges from $1.50 to $2.50 per day. The best carpenters drift to the cities because the people there appreciate and demand good work and live in better houses. Competition is sharp and the labor unions are strong. In the city of Houston we have four men who contract for themselves. They do good work and find ready employment. They get contracts not exceeding $2,500. In the same city are several old contractors who have been forced to retire on account of close competition. Two white contractors work a force of Negro and a force of white carpenters—separate of course. They pay according to skill, white and black alike. More discrimination is shown against carpenters than is shown against any other class of tradesmen. Negro carpenters have been urged to form unions which would affiliate with white unions, but have not thought best to do so. They know that they would be called upon to strike in concert with the other unions and they feel that in the end they would get the worst of it. As long as they find employment they prefer to work independent of the unions.

Brickmasons are fewer than carpenters. This class of workers are in demand, wages are high and discrimination is reduced to a minimum. There are no brick contractors in Houston, and only one or two in the state. Bricklayers in the towns are journeymen and most of them do a good grade of work—wages are from $3.00 to $4.00 per day. In the cities wages are a little better. I know of no plasterers. Sometimes they are called from New Orleans to do that sort of work. The finest plastering in our state Capitol was done by Negroes brought from Chicago. Nearly all the employees in the cotton seed oil mills and cotton compresses are Negroes. They are not all common laborers. It requires skill to operate some of the machines and to get these mill products ready for market. Wages are $1.50 to $3.00 per day. In some of the trades we do not find the

Negro at all, or if found they are so few that they do not count in trade competition. Houston has no shoemakers, no plumbers and harness-makers, and I know of but one tinner in the state. These are the conditions as they now exist among Texas artisans. I have observed that any man who knows how to do something and knows how to do that something well and is willing to do something, will find ready employment. Opportunities are not wanting, but many times when these opportunities present themselves we are not able to grasp them because of lack of training. The world wants trained workmen, men whose trained minds will direct skilled hands—masters of their craft. Not more than 3 per cent of our young men in Texas are entering the trades, and at the present death rate among the old workmen, it will not be long before we shall be conspicuous for our absence from all the trades. On the other hand a very large per cent of young white men enter the trades. We have a great influx of emigrants from Europe. They come and work the farms. They are better farmers than any one else—they make a crop rain or no rain. The American needs rain to make his crop, and in a few years he finds that he cannot compete with the foreigner, his land is too poor. He abandons the farm and seeks refuge in the trades, or he moves to another county to begin farming anew. There are some reasons why our young men avoid the trades. Let me mention a few of them. There is a class of young men who, after finishing some school course, do not believe in manual labor, skilled or unskilled. When the slaves were emancipated their first thought was to send their children to school like the white folk, to dress them like white children and to keep them from work like the white children. To do any sort of manual labor was to their minds a badge of humility and a relic of slavery. The old master was a gentleman and he did not work, their sons must be like him and like his sons. This idea was taught the children, it has grown up in them and still remains in them. If a record could be made of all that these dear old parents suffered and endured, of how they toiled and what sacrifices they made, that their children should be ladies and gentlemen, who did not have to work, it would make a tale far more pitiable than "Uncle Tom's Cabin." They passed from the slavery of the white man to the slavery of their own children.

Another hindrance is that society looks down upon a man who works with his hands, no matter how much skill he may possess or how much that skill commands. This class distinction does not exist among us alone. It is hard to see how a man can be intelligent and at the same time be a mechanic. We cannot associate the two ideas. Fear of non-employment keeps another class from entering the trades. Those who oppose industrial education never fail to present this argument and they have made an impression on some, which nothing but time and changed conditions will ever efface. Another class would enter the world of working men but for this fact: They are ambitious to excel in whatever line of work they may choose, but to become an intelligent artisan requires years—long years of hard work and patient study on short pay. They cannot wait, results are too long coming. They forget that men begin at the bottom and that the man who succeeds must toil early and late with all his powers of body and mind, he must realize that if he masters his chosen work he must perform the necessary amount of drudgery required in all cases to prepare a suitable foundation upon which to build a successful career. Many of our young men who do follow the trades are not living up to the full measure of their opportunities. In the first place the employer can not always depend upon them. They are just as likely not to come to work at the appointed time as they are to come. It matters not how busy the employer may be or how anxious he is to finish the job, our young workman feels that he is under no obligation to see him through. He feels free to take a day off and go a-fishing or to enjoy himself in some other way. That's his idea of liberty. When the next Negro workman comes along and asks for a job, the contractor says, No, we don't want any more Negroes. Then we say that that man is prejudiced. I used to think so, too, but I do not think so any more. I have hired some of them myself and I know that unreliability has kept more Negroes out of good jobs than incompetency ever did. Unsteadiness is another barrier to success. In the lumber district of Eastern Texas, there are numerous saw mills which run the year round. The owners employ Negro workmen for places requiring skill, whenever they can be found. I have in mind one man who has been with a certain firm for 18 years. In fact, he has been with the company so long and has given such faithful service, the managers have forgotten that he is a Negro. He is now a competent sawyer and receives $6.00 per day. The sawyer's place at these mills is perhaps the best paying place of all, outside the management. The wages run from $4.50 to $6.00, according to skill. The places are open to Negroes and occasionally they take them, but after working for 10 or 12 months they conclude that they have made enough and retire. The job is too steady. I do not mean these general statements to apply to all our workmen, but I do say that they will apply to the majority. Our artisan must be more competent faithful and reliable. It's the only way to hold on to that which we have. We must be progressive. We have clung to the old ways too long—methods of half a century ago. If we do not make the best use of these trade advantages which are now ours, we not only shut ourselves out but we close the door of opportunity in the faces of our boys who expect to enter. I grant that there are obstacles. One finds them in every trade and every profession. They seem to be necessary evils. None are too great for our strength. Capacity will be allotted an appropriate place and that speedily. If all the paths are closed to us, we will find a way or make one. Faithfulness to duty, however small that duty may be, is simply irresistable. It is so in every walk of life. Greatness in every direction is an accumulation of little faithfulnesses towering into sight of the world. All we need are those qualities which have made and are still making men of other races successful along these lines. We need men who have been trained—men who are able to do things and know why they are done. In every line of work it is the man who knows most about the thing he is doing, other things being considered, who comes out ahead.

President Roosevelt, speaking to the graduates of the New York trade school, said: "Success will come to the man who is just a little bit better than the others. There are plenty of workmen who can do pretty well, but the man who can do his work right up to the handle is the man who is in demand." Mental and manual training combined will in the long run open wide to us the avenues leading to usefulness and power in the material world.

21. *Local Conditions: A Negro Contractor of Atlanta, Ga.*, (by Alexander Hamilton, Jr., of the firm of Hamilton & Son, building contractors). It is a matter of great pride to me, and I think sometimes I am a little over boastful of the fact, that I learned the use of tools at Atlanta University; and to this intelligent beginning I attribute my success as a carpenter and contractor.

I was enabled when I left school to begin my trade as an advanced workman, and when I was a journeyman, and now when I have the occasion to use my tools, I ask no artisan in my line any odds. As I say I credit this to my early training here. I am now associated with my father in business as contractor and builder. We enjoy a good business; our patrons are among the best people in this city. I am proud to say that we have been able to maintain a reputation which gives us a preference often in the awarding of contracts.

The opportunity for wage earning for the Negro artisan is good; he is always in demand. I can bear witness to this fact for I have been frequently hampered in carrying out my work on account of being unable to secure extra hands, as all were busy. This demand does not exist for the reason that their services are obtained for a smaller wage for, as a rule, they get the prevailing scale of wages. They are in demand for the reason that in their class they are generally swifter workmen than those of the other race. Some contractors, white contractors I refer to, won't employ other than Negro workmen as they realize that they will earn them more money. Some of them employ Negroes from the foreman down, and but very few, to my knowledge, have their force entirely white. One firm employs both white and colored.

Though wages here are small as compared with some other cities, the Negro artisans as a rule are making good use of their money. They have comfortable homes and are educating their children. I know of several who own their own homes, and of some who not only own their homes but have other property, and still others who are buying homes. Some I know who have saved enough to lay down their tools and enter mercantile life. I know several who have tried mercantile life but found there was more money for them as artisans, so they are back at their trades. One who has been with us 15 or 16 years, who is a preacher, occasionally lays down his tools and takes a charge somewhere, but he doesn't stay long before he is back looking for his old place.

With all this, there is nevertheless, in many cases, a lack of an intelligent conception of the work which the Negro artisan is to perform; he is ready, willing and able to execute that laid out for him as long as he has constant supervision, but sometimes when left to himself he is lacking in pride as to the execution of his work. Ofttimes this may be due to an overzealousness to get so much accomplished. I have heard artisans, whose intelligence and honesty ought not to allow such a view of things, say, "On, that will do," when nothing should answer short of as near perfection as is possible, for I believe that a man can do a thing properly as easily and quickly as he can do it poorly, and I am sure the results are far more satisfactory. I have always found that if one has that view of it and performs a piece of work and satisfies himself as to the execution, he will find that his employer, however critical, will be satisfied.

As to the capability of the Negro as an artisan one only needs to visit the many buildings in course of erection in our city and see Negroes employed at all trades.

Of course I do not have much chance for personal observation, but I am informed of these few instances of which I cite. There is a "sky scraper" in course of erection in this city on which the Negro workmen have been in the majority since its beginning, from the putting up of the iron frame until now. There are at present on that particular building more than a score of plasterers at work, all of whom are Negroes. Now, this only applies to one building, the same conditions exist on many others. On another job of considerable proportions, the contractor (who is white) discharged all his white employees and substituted Negro artisans, and I am informed that the plastering, which will amount to some 30,000 yards, has been awarded to a Negro contractor. I am not in any sense crowing over the displacement of anybody, but simply cite these cases to show that there is a demand for the Negro artisan. Some argue that this demand prevails because the Negro is cheaper, but in the last case I cited, the men who were put in the place of those deposed were paid the same wages.

I must confess that I haven't had a great deal of experience as an artisan, pure and simple, though I worked at my trade as a carpenter several years when I was practically my own boss, and my greatest experience has been as a contractor. I have had some degree of success in that vocation. I had the advantage, on entering that business, of a standing established by my father through 20 years or more of endeavor. We enjoy the confidence and respect of all the people with whom we deal. We always try to merit this confidence and respect. We are invariably told when a prospective customer thinks our figures are a little high: "Hamilton, your figures are high, but I am told you do good work and will do what you say." On that reputation, as I said before, we have preference shown us very often in the awarding of work. A great many say that we are awarded a greater number of contracts than most contractors get. Of course we do not take any very large contracts, as we haven't the capital to handle them. We rarely take other than residence contracts, though we can show quite a number of stores, warehouses, mills, etc., built by us. The largest contract we hád last year was a house which cost about $10,000. Our contract amounted to about $7,500, as the steam fitting, plumbing and electrical work were under separate contracts. We are general contractors and usually contract for the house entire, but some architects let contracts under different heads, separately.

Last year, which was a good year for work, we were awarded a little over 100 contracts. Of course we did not have competition on half of that number. Much of it was what we call job work. Of that number about 55% of them were for amounts less than $100, 20% ranged from $100 to $500, 15% from $500 to $1,000, 10% from $1,000 to $7,500. In all we did nearly $35,000 worth of work.

A large majority of the houses we build are from our own plans and specifications, as very often, unless a person wants an original or an elaborate design in a house, he doesn't care to employ an architect. And there is where my ambition lies, that is if a customer should want an original design I could be able to meet his requirements. I only attempt pencil floor plans and once in a while a crude elevation plan; but my desire is to take a course in architectural drawing, which desire there seems small hope of gratifying.

I am a staunch friend of higher education and at the same time I am glad that so much stress is being laid upon manual training. There is a broad field for intelligent artisans. I only wish that more young men would apply themselves to a trade on leaving school. If so much can be accomplished by artisans who have not had the advantages of school training, how much more success could be achieved by those intelligently prepared for their vocations.

22. *Local Conditions: Indianapolis, Ind.*, (by W. T. B. Williams*.) All the figures I give below were obtained in June, 1900, from foremen and mechanics and from the offices of large manufacturing plants. Though they are meagre, yet I think they are thoroughly reliable. They come, too, from representative establishments and laborers.

Indianapolis had, in 1900, a Negro population of 15,931 in a total population of 169,164.

The mass of Negro population has come to Indianapolis from the South during the last thirty years. The greater part are fairly recent comers. Many of the whites are also from the South. In fact, Indianopolis is in some respects very much of a Southern city. Being in the North, however, the relations existing between the whites and blacks relating to labor savor of both sections.

By far the great majority of Negro laborers are unskilled. But representatives of the ordinary trades are found in appreciable numbers.

The following are the results of my investigations. They refer to the city only:

BLACKSMITHS.

Four shops run by Negroes.

Boss Mechanics	6
Journeymen	2
General work	1
Carriage work	1
Special Horseshoer	1
Total	11

*Submitted through the courtesy of Mr. A. F. Hilyer, of Washington, D. C., at whose suggestion the study was made.

The Blacksmiths' Union is open to Negroes. J. K. Donnell, a Negro, is corresponding secretary of the union. He is also a member of Master Horseshoers' Protective Association.

FOUNDRIES.

Moulders	3
Moulders' helpers	2
Cupola tenders	5
Furnace men melting iron	12
Total	22

I found also

Firemen	2
Common laborers	125

My conclusion after visiting a number of foundries is that there is no uniformity in their attitude toward Negro laborers. Most foundries employ no Negroes. Some employ a few. Most claim that no Negroes apply as skilled laborers. One admitted having received one application which was rejected only because there was no vacancy. Wherever Negroes were employed they were spoken of as efficient and satisfactory.

Negro foundrymen do not belong to the unions. Employers, however, say no trouble comes from that. Whites and blacks in all cases are given work together.

CARPENTERS.

Boss Carpenters and Contractors	5
Journeymen	20
Total	25
Besides the above there are men who make a living at carpentry, but who are not thorough mechanics	30

Carpenters' Union admits Negroes, but the Negroes do not join. They say that while they may join the unions yet the boss carpenters will not look out for work for them and that white carpenters will not work with them, though they are union men. Negroes gain in times of strikes by not belonging.

BRICKLAYERS.

Boss Mechanics and Journeymen	14

Bricklayers' Union admits colored men but none join for the same reason given by the carpenters.

PLASTERERS.

Boss Plasterers	10
Journeymen	20
Total	30
Galvanized iron and cornice workers	1

WOOD WORKERS.

Running planing machine	1
Turners	2
Total	3

Very good feeling seemed to exist at the factory where the two turners worked. The foreman declared that the factory could not tolerate interference from unions and that men were advanced according to merit.

CEMENT WORKERS.

Making walks, cellars, sewers, etc	34

No organization in city.

HOD CARRIERS.

Number in city	350
" " union	200

Union mainly composed of Negroes, but a few whites belong. This union is not affiliated with the National Association.

PAPER HANGERS.

Can not give exact figures, but not more than	6

Indianapolis has a fine industrial training school with good courses in wood-work, i. e., making of joints, etc., and turning, and in iron forging and machine fitting, etc. An appreciable number of colored boys attend this school, but I was unable to learn of any one's having applied to any of the factories or foundries for work. Some mechanics felt that the school has not been in existence long enough to have exerted any marked influence upon the quantity or quality of skilled laborers in the market.

From all I could learn Negro carpenters are decreasing in number. But in every other trade there is an increase. This is very marked though the gain in actual numbers is small in the factories and foundries.

A probable cause of the increase of skilled laborers in this locality is the steady emigration northward of the Negro from the South. It is not due to any considerable number of younger men of the city entering the trades. This will probably be changed in a few years for the industrial training offered by the city in one of its high schools seems to appeal strongly to the colored youth who enter the high school. And though there is much prejudice against the Negro as a skilled laborer yet I think he has a fighting chance in Indianapolis.

23. *Alabama.* The state of Alabama had 678,489 Negroes in 1890 and 827,307 in 1900. In 1890 there were reported the following skilled and semi-skilled laborers: *

*These figures include a negligible number of "Chinese, Japanese and civilized Indians."

The figures given here and in succeeding sections are from the census of 1890, volume on population, part 2. Just how far these are accurate there is no means of knowing. In some cases I have had grave suspicions of their validity, in others they seem reasonable. At any rate they are only available figures and are given for what they are worth. The plan followed in these state reports was to select those occupations most largely represented in the state; in this way it often happens that those occupations given are not necessarily those in which Negroes are most largely engaged. This should be borne in mind.

MALES.

Occupation	Number
Lumbermen	415
Miners	3,687
Quarrymen	369
Engineers (civil, mechanical, etc.)	16
Barbers	520
Engineers and Firemen (stationary)	452
Boatmen, pilots, etc	223
Steam railroad employees	4,591
Telegraph and Telephone operators	3
Apprentices	73
Blacksmiths and Wheelwrights	891
Shoemakers	272
Brick-makers	514
Butchers	136
Carpenters	1,703
Charcoal and lime burners	499
Textile mill operatives	281
Iron and steel workers	1,749
Machinists	54
Marble and stone-cutters and masons	618
Mechanics	64
Millers	166
Painters, etc	280
Printers	40
Saw and planing mill employees	1,163

FEMALES.

Occupation	Number
Telegraph and telephone operatives	1
Textile mill operatives	22
Dressmakers, milliners, etc	859
Printers, etc	3
Tailoresses	16

A special report from Tuskegee says that a "consensus of best opinions" agree that in that region the Negro artisan "is gaining for the past six or eight years." Up to that time and since the War he had been losing. His losses were due to neglect and reaction. To-day inefficiency and increased competition still hamper him. "Competent colored laborers are too few for the demand." The sentiment among the colored people in regard to entering the trades has "greatly changed in this and surrounding states" during recent years. Prejudice still is an obstacle before the young mechanic and yet the difference in wages is due largely to the fact that competent colored laborers are too few to supply the demand, hence cannot command highest wages; and also to the further fact that colored laborers' standard of living is lower and they are consequently willing to work for less. These Negro mechanics can and do join the labor unions, some 5,000 being members throughout the state, chiefly in the United Mine Workers. They have separate local organizations however. There are at Tuskegee, including the teachers at the Institute, the following artisans:

Shoemakers 4
Harnessmakers 2
Brickmasons 11
Tinsmiths 2
Tailors 3
Blacksmiths 3
Wheelwrights 2
Pattern-maker 1
Seamstresses & Dressmakers 5
Architects 3

Printers 4	Electrical Engineers 1
Carpenters 14	Mechanical Engineers 3
Woodturners 1	Bakers 1
Painters 3	Milliners 1

Unfortunately no detailed report is available from the great industrial centers like Birmingham, Anniston, etc.

24. *California.* There were in California 11,322 Negroes in 1890, and 11,045 in 1900. The colored artisans reported in 1890 include both Negroes and Chinese:

MALE.	
Lumbermen and Raftsmen	94
Miners	4,871
Engineers (civil, mechanical, etc.)	1
Barbers and Hairdressers	817
Engineers and Firemen (stationary)	32
Boatmen, Canalmen, Pilots and Sailors	73
Steam Railroad Employees	2,044
Apprentices	14
Bakers	72
Blacksmiths and Wheelwrights	65
Boot and Shoemakers	1,269
Butchers	220
Carpenters and Joiners	141
Iron and Steel Workers	24
Machinists	39
Marble and Stone Cutters and Masons	43
Painters	60
Plumbers	4
Printers	43
Saw and Planing Mill Employees	191
Tailors	2,139
Tobacco and Cigar Factory Operatives	2,380
FEMALE.	
Cotton and Other Textile Mill Operatives	2
Dressmakers, Milliners, Seamstresses, etc	239

There are four colored carpenters in San Francisco in a Union of 2,500, and about 100 colored members among the teamsters', stablemens', longshoremens', seamens' and laborers' unions. In Pueblo there are a few lathers, building laborers, plasterers and stationary engineers, and also barbers. In Stockton there are a few longshoremen and hod carriers; in Los Angeles there are a few cement workers, plasterers, lathers and painters. Fresno has a butcher and several mortar mixers. On the whole a Negro mechanic is a rare thing in California.

25. *Colorado.* There were 6,215 Negroes in Colorado in 1890 and 8,570 in 1900. There were reported in 1890 the following artisans, including a few Chinese, etc.:

MALE.

Lumbermen and Raftsmen	11
Miners	142
Engineers (civil, mechanical, etc.)	2
Barbers and Hairdressers	193
Engineers and Firemen (stationary)	12
Steam Railroad Employees	106
Telegraph and Telephone Operators	2
Bakers	1
Blacksmiths and Wheelwrights	19
Boot and Shoemakers	7
Brickmakers, etc	37
Butchers	2
Carpenters and Joiners	27
Iron and Steel Workers	4
Machinists	4
Marble and Stone Cutters and Masons	33
Painters	17
Plasterers	49
Plumbers	1
Printers	2
Saw and Planing Mill Employees	2
Tailors	5
Tinners and Tinware Makers	3

FEMALE.

Confectioners	1
Dressmakers, Milliners, Seamstresses, etc	51
Printers	1

Nearly half the Negro population of the state is in Denver. Here a special report says that the artisans are chiefly in the building trades, although there are not many. The leading artisans include 3 bricklayers, one of whom is a contractor, 7 plasterers, 4 carpenters, 1 ink-maker, 1 machinist and 4 printers. "Master mechanics can enter the trades but there is no opening for apprentices."*

26. *District of Columbia.* There were in 1890, 75,572 Negroes in the District of Columbia, and 86.702 in 1900. This is in many ways a remarkable population, nearly three-fourths being in domestic and personal service and the other fourth containing a considerable number of clerks and professional people. The census of 1890 reported:

MALE.

Engineers, (civil, mechanical, etc)	10
Barbers and Hairdressers	450
Engineers and Firemen (stationary)	122
Boatmen, Canalmen, Pilots, and Sailors	82
Steam Railroad Employees	89
Street Railway Employees	23
Apprentices	54
Bakers	17
Blacksmiths and Wheelwrights	121

*Report of Dr. P. E. Spratlin.

MALE (continued).

Boot and Shoemakers	234
Brickmakers, etc	442
Butchers	62
Cabinet makers and Upholsterers	55
Carpenters and Joiners	316
Iron and Steel Workers	16
Machinists	15
Marble and Stone Cutters and Masons	188
Painters	141
Plasterers	152
Plumbers and steam-fitters	76
Printers	64
Tailors	16
Tinners and Tinware makers	36

FEMALE.

Barbers and Hairdressers	15
Stenographers and Typewriters	4
Telegraph and Telephone Operators	6
Apprentices	13
Confectioners	18
Dressmakers, Milliners, Seamstresses, etc	1,411
Printers	17

The Union League Directory, compiled by Mr. Andrew F. Hilyer, reported the leading Negro artisans as follows. This is not an exhaustive list, but gives the more prominent men in 1902:

Bakers	4	Electricians	1
Barber shops	142	Locksmiths	1
Barbers	411	Painters, contractors	5
Bicycle shops	9	Painters	56
Blacksmith shops	13	Paper hangers	1
Blacksmiths	27	Photographers	3
Shoemakers	74	Plumbers	1
Bricklayers, contractors	4	Printers, shops	9
Bricklayers	91	Printers	34
Cabinet maker	1	Stove repairers	3
Carpenters, contractors	4	Tailor shops	9
Carpenters	29	Tailors	57
Cement workers	1	Roofers	1
Cigar manufacturers	1	Tinners	4
Building contractors	17	Trussmakers	1
Dressmaking shops	89	Typewriters, etc	5
Dressmakers	140	Upholsterers	9
Dyers and cleaners	11	Kalsominers, etc	46

It is probable that a list like this is more reliable as a guide to actual effective artisans than the census of 1890, where helpers and casual artisans and those claiming to be artisans are set down under the various trades. The directory referred to has a further study of these artisans by Mr. George W. Ellis, as follows:

YEARS AT WORK.

Trades.	Under 1 year.	1-3 yrs.	3-5	5-10	10-20	Over 20.	Total.
Barbers	3	31	25	27	28	17	131
Blacksmiths and Wheelwrights	1	1	3		3	3	11
Shoemakers		6	3	11	15	19	54
Bricklayers			3	5	24	11	43
Carpenters			1	2	7	9	19
Dressmakers	10	4	11	23	14	7	69
Dyers and Cleaners	1	2	1	2	3	1	10
Painters			1	1	10	15	27
Plasterers, Kalsominers, &c.			4	3	9	7	23
Printers	1	2	2	2	2		9
Tailors	1	2	3		2	1	9

NUMBER OF EMPLOYEES, CAPITAL AND RECEIPTS.

Trades.	Employees.	Capital.	Annual Receipts.
Barbers	407	$56,490	$200,800
Blacksmiths and Wheelwrights	27	4,575	11,800
Shoemakers	74	9,950	28,570
Bricklayers	91		
Carpenters	29	2,850	15,750
Dressmakers	140	8,445	23,170
Painters	56	2,015	22,800
Printers	34	10,700	18,050
Tailors	57	9,325	25,900
White-washers, etc.	46	752	15,730

In his report to the Hampton Conference in 1899 Mr. A. F. Hilyer said: "In Washington there are over 500 skilled colored workmen not including barbers. There are about 100 bricklayers, 75 carpenters, 80 painters, 75 plasterers, 100 stationary engineers, 100 of various other skilled occupations. There are also many skilled brickmakers. Only the engineers and barbers are organized. * * * * During the last ten years over 500 houses have been built in Washington almost entirely by colored labor, some of them costing as high as fifteen thousand dollars. Many of them are fine specimens of the mechanic's art."*

27. *Florida.* There were 166,180 Negroes in Florida in 1890, and 230,730 in 1900. The census of 1890 reported the following Negro artisans:

MALE.

Miners,	323
Engineers, (civil, mechanical)	9
Barbers and hairdressers,	263
Engineers and Firemen, (Sta.)	169
Boatmen, canalmen, pilots, and sailors,	570
Steam railroad employees,	1,536
Telegraph and telephone operatives,	2
Apprentices,	67
Bakers,	51
Blacksmiths & wheelwrights,	150
Boot and shoemakers,	95
Butchers,	91
Carpenters and joiners,	988
Cotton and other textile mill operatives,	183
Machinists,	31
Marble and stone cutters and masons,	211
Millers,	62
Painters,	165
Printers,	26
Saw and planing mill employees,	858
Tobacco and cigar factory operatives,	937

*Report of the 3rd Hampton Negro Conference, 1899, p. 20.

FEMALE.

Dressmakers, milliners, seamstresses, etc.,	593	Starch makers,	22
Printers,	2	Tailoresses,	12
Saw and planing mill employees,	7	Tobacco and cigar factory employees,	97

There were in the Florida labor unions in 1902 about 2,000 Negro cigar makers, 1,000 carpenters, 1,200 building laborers, 200 painters, 800 longshoremen, 200 bricklayers and 300 plasterers. In Jacksonville a prominent Negro contractor and builder* reports that there are a "great many" Negro skilled laborers, and that the Negroes are represented in more trades than formerly. The 33 leading Negro artisans include 7 carpenters, 9 masons,2 blacksmiths,2 engineers,4 tailors and 8 tinners. The Negro is gaining in skilled trades, and in the trades mentioned meets little opposition. Usually, too, there is no discrimination in wages, but this is not always true. These are the following Negro union men in Jacksonville:

Bricklayers .... 75 Painters 50
Carpenters ....250?

In some of the unions there are a number of colored women.

In Pensacola the skilled work is about evenly divided between black and white. Of the 169 leading Negro mechanics there are 95 carpenters, 19 painters, 7 blacksmiths, 23 plasterers and bricklayers, 5 tailors, 8 cigar makers, 7 shoemakers, 2 tinners and 3 cabinet makers. There is "no perceptible loss or gain here," the Negro mechanic "is measurably holding his own." Almost all the artisans "have come up as apprentices" and there are few from the industrial schools. As to general conditions Mr. M. M. Lewy reports: "Carpenters and bricklayers work side by side and receive the same union wages; some times, and quite usually, Negroes are the contractors on private and business buildings. Blacksmiths, stonecutters, tailors and shoemakers do a good business here without the semblance of friction between the races. There are several noted cases of Negroes doing contract for large firms." In St. Augustine there is a colored painters' union of 30 members and Negro members of the masons', plasterers' and carpenters' unions. In Tampa there are 20 colored carpenters in the union, and a number of cigar makers.

28. *Georgia.* There were 858,815 Negroes in Georgia in 1890 and 1,034,813 in 1900. The census of 1890 reported the following Negro artisans:

MALE.

Lumbermen and raftsmen,	412	Cotton and other textile mill operatives,	771
Miners,	402	Iron and steel workers,	270
Barbers and hairdressers,	899	Machinists,	71
Engineers and firemen, (Sta.)	520	Marble and stone cutters	101
Steam railroad employees,	7,440	Masons,	1,243
Telegraph and telephone operators,	5	Mechanics,	154
Apprentices,	247	Millers,	160
Blacksmiths & wheelwrights,	1,328	Painters,	676
Boot and shoemakers,	632	Plasterers,	398
Brickmakers,	977	Printers,	78
Butchers,	299	Saw and planing mill employees,	2,471
Carpenters and joiners,	3,761	Wood workers,	198
Coopers,	363		

*Mr. S. H. Hart.

FEMALE.

Stenographers and typewriters,	2	Dressmakers, milliners, seamstresses, etc.,	1,632
Telegraph and telephone operators,	7	Printers,	1
Cotton and other textile mill operatives,	139	Tailoresses,	22

There are about 1,500 Negroes in the unions of Georgia, chiefly carpenters, masons, stone-quarrymen, lathers and plasterers. At Greensboro the leading 13 colored artisans include 4 blacksmiths, 6 carpenters, 1 mason and 2 shoemakers. There is neither gain nor loss in number, and the artisan "might do better if his opportunities in early life had been more favorable." Industrial schools "are cultivating a higher respect for manual labor." The chief obstacle of the Negro is his own inefficiency. At Milledgeville the 10 leading artisans include 1 contractor, 2 masons, 2 stationary engineers, 2 tinsmiths, 1 blacksmith and 2 painters. The Negro artisan in this town "is gaining. All the painters and blacksmiths are colored and they are in the majority in all the trades." So far as industrial schools are concerned the report says*: "I cannot yet see the result of industrial training which I would like to see. Many of our artisans are young men and some of them have attended industrial schools but preferred to complete their trades at home." As to obstacles the report continues: "In my opinion he has no obstacles in the South and especially in small towns and villages. The whole field is his. What he needs to do is to equip himself and occupy it." At Washington, there are about 35 Negro artisans, the 8 leading ones being 3 masons, 1 carpenter, 3 painters and 1 kalsominer. As to numbers "there may be some falling off due to lack of work." There is little interest manifested in industrial training. "The Negroes at Washington do excellent work but there is not sufficient work to keep them all employed. Some are in Augusta, quite a number in Crawfordville, and some in South Carolina at work." At Marshallville there are a few artisans, chiefly carpenters, masons and blacksmiths, and they are gaining. "There were only two Negro artisans here before the civil war, now there are fourteen." At Albany, Ga., there are many skilled laborers; the 17 leading artisans include 6 carpenters, 3 blacksmiths, 1 carriage maker, 6 masons and 1 painter. "In this community the Negro seems to be losing in skilled work," chiefly because of "the great growth of the South in industrial lines; the poor white man is taking to the trades in large numbers." Moreover, "there are very few young men here who have had the advantage of industrial school training. Some are now in these schools. Most of the younger men in the trades, however, entered under the apprenticeship system." Competition and color-discrimination are considerable obstacles for the Negro. "The discrimination is very marked in wages: white artisans receive from one-fourth to one-third more for the same kind of work."

All of the above towns are small semi-rural communities. In the larger cities of Georgia—Atlanta, Savannah, Macon and Augusta—the Negro artisan is conspicuous. In Savannah there are 7 trades unions composed

*From Mr. A. B. Cooper.

entirely of Negroes:—the bricklayers, carpenters, coopers, building laborers, lathers, painters and tinners. There are also colored members in some of the other unions. Both Macon and Augusta have large numbers of artisans. The condition of all of these may be judged from the special study of the Negro artisan in Atlanta given below.

Some general information as to the three chief sections of Georgia has come to us by correspondence. Miss E. E. White says:

"From a gentleman who has spent much time in South-western Georgia I learn that this section of the state being devoted to fruit, turpentine, and cotton does not require many artisans, and those who follow the carpenter and brick mason trades are unemployed for perhaps six months. In several places there is very little discrimination shown toward good workmen, although sometimes the wages of colored are less than those of the whites; in other places there is much prejudice toward colored workmen and most of their dealings must of necessity be with their own race."

In Northeastern Georgia the following wage scale for 42 artisans was reported by the artisans themselves; they could all read and write and were from 30 to 40 years of age:

OCCUPATION.	NUMBER.	WAGES.
Engineers	2	$ 8.00 a week
Tinners	1	1.50 a day
Contractors	1	1.25 a day
Brick and Stone Masons	4	2.00 a day
Blacksmiths	2	
Florists	1	450.00 a year
Machinists	2	300.00 a year
Harness-maker	1	
Bridge builders	1	2.00 a day
Barbers	4	
Tailors	1	2.50 and 2.75 a day
Paper-hangers	1	
Painters	2	1.00 a day
Firemen	4	30.00 a month.
Shoemakers	7	
Carpenters	8	2.50 a day.
Total	42	

From eastern Georgia, Miss L. D. Davis reports:

"The relations with the whites in most communities are friendly. Few communities have trades unions. In Athens Negroes can join some of the unions with whites: none are organized among themselves. Augusta has several Negro trades unions. The painters, brickmasons and carpenters are well organized. Negroes cannot join white unions in Augusta.

"At first I had a little trouble to get the question of wages received answered. Negroes do not receive the same wages as whites, there were some exceptions, but generally whites receive from 25c to 50c more than Negroes. (1.) Carpenters get from $1 to $2.50 a day. (2). Brick masons and stone cutters get the same wages of whites in the same trade, from $2.00 to $4.00 per day. (3). Plasterers get 33½c per hour. Barbers, tailors and blacksmiths conduct their own business, and did not as a general rule tell their profits.

"Those reporting who own real estate, by trades, were: Barbers, 0; Blacksmiths, 6; Printers, 1; Shoemakers, 0; Tailors, 1; Plumbers, 1; Plasterers, 3; Tinners, 4; Painters, 4; Mechanics, 4; Telegraph linemen, 0; Brick masons, 15; Carpenters, 16."

29. *Atlanta, Ga.* In the spring of 1902 a number of seniors from Atlanta University were given sections of the city to investigate as to the number and condition of Negro artisans. Extracts from these reports are appended and form the best general picture obtainable of industrial conditions as seen by young observers.

Mr. H. H. Pace says:

"The first person from whom I obtained any real information was a brickmason who received me cordially and who was inclined to talk. He was at home then (the middle of the afternoon) and said that it was the season when he never did much. He was a Union man and said that colored brickmasons were well received by the white unions 'if they knew their business,' although the initiation fee was larger for colored men and the sick and death benefits much smaller for them than for whites. I next saw a machinist who lived in a tumble down house in a rather poor locality. But he said he owned the house. I found a carpenter who was almost totally despondent. He couldn't get work, he said, and was sorry he ever came to Atlanta. 'I own a farm in Jackson county,' he said, 'but quit farming and came here thinking to do better at my trade. But if things don't change soon I think I'll go back to it.'

"The next thing of particular interest to me was a gang of men, white and black, at work upon ten or twelve three-room houses. The person in charge of the work was a colored man who gave his name and address as Tom Carlton, Edgewood, Ga. He talked to me himself but refused to let me talk to his employees. He was willing to give me plenty of information about himself, still I was unable to persuade him to let me interview those at work. He said he could join the white union now, they were after him every day to do so. But he wouldn't, because once awhile back when he was working for wages he was refused admission. As soon, however, as he became his own boss they wanted him.

"A tailor, who conducted a small shop at * * * * told me that he cleared one hundred and twenty dollars a month from his business. But from his confession that he owned no real estate, the appearance of his shop and its location I concluded that he did well to collect one hundred and twenty dollars *altogether* in six months. In comparison with this shop was another small tailoring establishment farther up the street which was neat and progressive. The proprietor told me he had been there only six months and averaged now, from his business, an income of about fifty dollars a month. He had another man at work and seemed to have enough work on hand to keep him employed for some time.

"Of the whole number questioned except, of course, shoemakers and tailors who ran their own shops, all had worked at some time or did work sometimes with whites in the same work. The painters said that the white painters were not very friendly disposed toward them, and did not allow them to join their union under any circumstances. The plumbers were under somewhat the same ban.

"Not one of the artisans in my territory had been to a trade school. Nearly every one had simply 'worked awhile under a first-class brickmason' or 'carpenter,' etc. Several had learned their trades during slavery and followed them ever since. One had learned his trade of blacksmith in the U. S. Army. None answered 'Yes' to the question of any 'higher training.'

"The most interesting bit of information in regard to color discrimination was obtained from a colored fireman on the Southern Railway. He said the Company refused to sign a contract and wage scale with his union but did sign one with the white union. Moreover, he said, 'If I take a train from here to Greenville, S. C., I get for that trip $2.60, the white engineer gets $6.00. But if that same train had the same engineer and a *white* fireman, the engineer would get his $6.00 just the same but the fireman would get $3.25. He gets 65 cts. more for doing the same work I do. At the end of the run we have to make out our time on a card, which, with the other necessary wording has two spaces marked 'white' and 'colored' respectively. I cross out the 'colored' and get $2.60; he crosses out the 'white' and gets $3.25. That's all the difference there is between our work."

Mr. Pace interviewed 67 artisans in all. Mr. J. F. Lemon studied 89 artisans. Twelve per cent of them owned property, 5% owned several pieces of property; 27% were married, 4% were illiterate, 25% had respectable homes and 10% were first-class workmen. He says:

"During my tour of research, I did not find many high-class artisans; most of the shoemakers, carpenters, and barbers, being hardly more than 'botchers.' There were, however, among the brickmasons, carriage-workers, painters, etc. some good workmen. Most of them are married and have families to support.

"About one-fifth of the artisans lived in nice homes of their own, well furnished, and comfortable; another third lived in fair homes of three or four rooms fairly well furnished, but the remaining half of the total number of artisans lived in homes too poor and ill-kept to warrant their being called artisans who might earn enough to decently support a small family.

"Most have children in the public schools. Many of the wives of male artisans are laundresses, helping to earn the needed running expenses, while a few wives are in good paying work, as school teachers, etc.

"Many of the men belong to secret orders, but I found only two who belonged to any labor union, although they knew of the International to which Negroes are admitted.

"Only three of my artisans attended trade schools, most of them having learned as helpers, apprentices or 'picked it up.'

"Almost all could read and write, but only about half a dozen had any higher training. I found several who had attended Atlanta University, Spelman, and other schools, none, however, being graduates. I found two enterprising and successful contractors, who do the best work, have plenty to do and own property themselves as a result of their success.

"Many of the poorer artisans are old ex-slaves and some cannot read or write and they are no credit to their trades. The better class of artisans are the young who were born since slavery.

"The different trades pay, per day, from an average of 75c for the seamstress to about $3.00 for brickmasons and carriage-workers, the others varying between these figures. The wages of whites in like trades are slightly better in most cases."

Mr. A. C. Tolliver was "very much surprised at the poor condition of some of the artisans' homes, particularly of men whom I know to be good workmen and engaged nearly the year round."

"Very few, if any, of the artisans, as you will see from the statistics, learned their trade at a Trade School. I found one, a glazier, at Woodward Lumber Co., West End, who had attended Tuskegee Everything seemed to be learned by apprenticeship.

"The plasterers all seemed to have served under the same man, who was a noted workman in his day. The molders whom I found worked at the Southern Terra Cotta Works. Of the 53 artisans I studied, 35 were illiterate.

"The following table shows a comparison of the average wages of the white and colored artisans engaged in the same trade, per day.

Trade.	Per day Average wages of colored.	Per day Average wages of white.
Painter,	$1.80	$2.30
Molder,	1.95	2.05
Rock-mason,	2.40	2.70
Carpenter,	1.82	2.07
Blacksmith,	1.83⅓	2.25
Tile-layer,	1.25	2.50
Electrician,	3.50	5.00

"The wages of the whites are computed as given by the colored men themselves; in a few instances I think the amount given is a little too large. It seems to be the opinion of every colored artisan that he gets from 25 to 75 per cent less than his white brother for his work.

"Very few artisans seem to own any real estate, and if they do, they will not always tell you of it for fear of the tax collector; of the 53 artisans of my district only 8 owned any property. Those houses from outside and inside appearance were in very good condition.

"The fellow who gave his trade as an electrician learned what he knew by correspondence. I questioned him very closely. He can only put in electric bells, which he worked at all of last summer, but for a living and regular work, he cleaned cars in the Southern Railroad shops. Yet he makes extra money by putting in electric bells when the days are long."

The number of Negro artisans by age, conjugal condition and trades was reported by the canvassers as follows:

ATLANTA ARTISANS.

CONJUGAL CONDITION AND AGE.—MALES.

Conjugal Condition	Under 20	20–30	30–40	40 & over	Unknown	Total
Single	17	83	32	19		151
Married		118	223	263	9	613
Widowed		8	10	24		42
Separated		3		5		8
Unknown	3	4	5	7	10	29
Total	20	216	270	318	19	843

FEMALES.

Conjugal Condition	Under 20	20–30	30–40	40 & over	Unknown	Total
Single	4	7	3			14
Married	1	3	6	6	1	27
Widowed		2	1	6		9
Separated		1		1		2
Unknown		1	1		1	3
Total	5	24	11	13	2	55

Those designated as "separated" are not divorced and not in all cases permanently separated, although usually so. About thirty per cent. of these artisans are under thirty, and about sixty per cent. are under forty years of age.

We may now separate these 900 artisans according to the trades they follow.

OCCUPATIONS OF ATLANTA ARTISANS.—MALES.

	U. 20	20–30	30-40	40 & O.	Unknown	Total
Painters	1	10	7	13	4	35
Plumbers		3	6	8	1	18
Barbers	1	30	33	17	1	82
Blacksmiths	1	7	16	31	2	57
Shoemakers		14	17	52	1	86
Carpenters	3	25	55	92	3	178
Masons	1	17	27	24	4	73
Tailors	3	20	12	3	1	39
Plasterers	2	9	16	24	1	52
Bakers	1	9	2	1		13
Moulders	1	1	3			5
Lathers	1	4	2	2		9
Machinists	1	4	5	6		16
Candy-makers	1	6	4			11
Broom-makers	1	1				2
Mattress-maker	1	1	1			3
Dyers	1		2			3
Firemen		11	15	12		38
Printers		2	1			3
Telegraph linemen		1	1			2
Paint-makers		1				1
Tinners		1	1	1		3
Electricians		1				1
Glaziers		2	1	1		4
Contractors & builders			5	2		7
Iron workers			1			1
Gun-makers			1			1
Wheelwrights			1	2		3
Harness-makers			1	1		2
Miscellaneous		36	32	26	1	95
Total	20	216	270	318	19	843

FEMALES.

	U. 20	20–30	30-40	40 & O.	Unknown	Total
Dressmaking	3	11	7	7	1	29
Tailoring	1			1	1	3
Seamstresses	1	12	3	2		18
Pastry-cooks			1			1
Milliners				1		1
Miscellaneous		1		2		3
Total	5	24	11	13	2	55

The chief artisans are carpenters, shoemakers and barbers; after these come masons, blacksmiths and plasterers, tailors and painters. The firemen are both stationary and locomotive; the plumbers are usually helpers and not many are masters of the trade.

The wages of artisans in the city are reported as follows:

ATLANTA ARTISANS: WAGES PER MONTH.

	U. $15	$15–24	$25-29	$30–39	$40-49	$50 & O.
Painters		6	9		8	7
Plumbers		2	1	7	3	2
Barbers	1	17	4	7	27	12
Blacksmiths		7	1	16	13	11
Shoemakers	1	18	7	16	19	5
Masons		2		5	7	50
Carpenters		4		46	76	42
Tailors		3		3	7	12
Plasterers		1	1	5	7	32
Bakers	1	5		1	3	
Molders				1	2	
Lathers		1			6	2
Machinists		2	2	3	6	1
Candy-makers		2	2	2	2	
Broom-makers		1				1
Mattress-makers		1	1		1	
Firemen		1	1	15	8	8
Dressmakers and Seamstresses		7	1	5	5	1
Miscellaneous		10	6	21	21	11
Total	3	90	36	153	221	197
Percentage	5%	13%	5%	22%	31.5%	28%

Probably in the wages of $50 and more there was exaggeration due to the desire to appear prosperous. On the whole, however, the returns seem reliable and the earnings of the Negro artisan are seen to be small.

There is no very satisfactory way of ascertaining the growth or decline in number of the Negro artisans in Atlanta. One method tried by the class in economics in Atlanta University was to count the number given in the directories for a series of years. The directories, however, are inaccurate and especially careless in regard to Negroes. The following table, however, is of some interest:

REPORTED NUMBER OF NEGRO ARTISANS IN ATLANTA.

	1885	1890	1895	1902
Carpenters	208	245	199	181
Barbers	84	93	139	158
Shoemakers	80	103	127	113
Masons	77	98	96	91
Blacksmiths	65	95	59	50
Painters	30	9	26	43
Tailors	9	29	20	30
Plasterers	17	54	38	28
Firemen	15	21	50	58
Bakers	4	25	9	10
Printers	4	10	4	3
Machinists	1	7	9	6
Plumbers	1	4	10	7
Contractors and builders	4	7	10	3
Other trades	39	60	93	67
Total	638	860	889	848

The apparent slight decrease in number of Negro artisans is offset by two considerations: 1st. The increased competition of later years has had the effect of sifting out the poorer Negro artisans so that the survivors in 1902 are probably better artisans on the average than those of 15 or 20 years earlier. 2nd. There is in South Atlanta a settlement of Negro artisans and home-owners centering about Clark University who are really a part of the city life. The number and wages of some of these artisans is reported as follows in 1902:

ARTISANS AND MONTHLY WAGES—SOUTH ATLANTA.

	$20-29	$30-39	$40-49	$50 & O
Bakers	1			
Barbers		5	1	1
Blacksmiths			2	
Candy makers			1	
Carpenters		3	1	9
Engineers		1		
Firemen		1	1	
Harness makers				1
Masons		1		5
Plasterers				7
Plumbers			1	1
Shoemakers		2	2	
Dressmakers	1	3		
Total ..51	2	16	9	24

The artisans of Atlanta proper reported that 301 of them are accustomed at times to work with whites at these trades; 594 were not. 238 artisans work usually for white patrons; 101 for Negroes, and 266 for both; 210 of the artisans were illiterate, 631 could read and write; 53 had some higher training; 290 own real estate, 494 own none, and 111 gave no answer; 26 had attended trade schools at Spelman Seminary, Tuskegee Institute, Clark University and Atlanta University. Only 85 artisans reported themselves as belonging to trade unions; however, there are some others who also belong. They reported as follows as to their work:

Trades	Works for himself	Hires others	Works for wages	Works f'r himself & f'r wages
Painters	3	3	18	1
Barbers	6	11	47	1
Blacksmiths	7	9	23	1
Shoemakers	36	9	20	
Carpenters	33	17	88	2
Masons	8	6	40	4
Tailors	6	8	6	
Plasterers	6	8	25	2
All others	18	15	155	
Total	123	86	422	11

30. *Other Towns in Georgia.* Detailed reports covering over four hundred artisans were received from other towns in Georgia. The ages of these artisans were as follows:

Years of Age	Male	Female	Total
Under 20	5	1	6
20–30	89	1	90
30–40	111	3	114
40 and over	159	2	161
Unknown	37	13	50
Total	401	20	421

Their trades were as follows:

MALE

Trade	Number	Trade	Number
Brickmasons	71	Firemen	5
Carpenters	86	Telegraph linemen	3
Painters	18	Electric linemen	2
Printers	5	Horse shoers	2
Tailors	11	Mortar mixers	1
Barbers	31	Florists	1
Blacksmiths	32	Tie cutter	1
Shoemakers	31	Glazier	1
Engineers	3	Dyer	1
Plumbers	7	Stationary firemen	2
Mechanics	14	Cabinet maker	1
Wheelwrights	3	Baker	1
Machinists	7	Wood worker	1
Plasterers	13	Paper hanger	1
Bill posters	1	Jeweler	1
Tinners	9	Musician	1
Contractors	5	Trained nurse	1
Basket makers	1	Crockery worker	1
Bridge builders	1	Undesignated	25
Harness makers	2	Total	401

FEMALE

Trade	Number	Trade	Number
Tailoress	3	Printer	1
Seamstress	11	Undesignated	3
Dressmaker	2	Total	20

Of these 426 artisans, 6 had attended trade school. The wages received by 122 men were as follows, per month, not counting unoccupied time:

	Under $20	$20–30	$30–40	$40–50	$50–60	$60 & O
Masons and plasterers			1	6		10
Shoemakers	2	3	2		1	4
Blacksmiths & wheelwrights		5	5	5	1	1
Engineers and firemen	1	3	2			1
Barbers	1	3	3	1		2
Painters		2	2	7	1	4
Tinners		2	2	1		1
Tailors						
Mechanics		2	7	2	1	
Miscellaneous	1	6	7	7	4	
Total (males)	5	26	31	29	8	23

251 of the men were accustomed once in a while to work along side of whites in pursuing their trade; 59 never worked thus. 148 work primarily for whites, 35 for Negroes, 157 for both; 69 belong to trade unions, 240 do not; 98 said they could join the same trade unions as the whites, 128 said they could not, 180 did not know; 274 could read and write; 44 had had some higher training; 240 owned real estate, 125 did not, 49 gave no answer.

The following extracts from letters and reports give an idea of the condition of these artisans:

LaGrange—Bridge Builder. "For 20 years I have worked for the LaGrange Bridge Co. Have done very well. Save but little. Live very well. Have 6 girls, all in school."

Darien—Tailor. "There is but one other tailor in this locality. Our town is not very large, hence we two workmen do the work of our town. Neither of us hire others."

Augusta—Tinsmith. "I started at the trade in 1853 as an apprentice, and served same five years. From that time I worked by the day until 1867 at $2 per day. Since that time I have been engaged in business of my own up until the present. I also have a son who learned the trade under my instruction, and is now in business with me. He is 33 years old. I have been successful in my business up to the present time. Since I have been in business I have turned out 72 good workmen that served under me at the trade."

Bricklayer. "We, as Negroes, have to work mostly for what we can get, and the whites always gets the best of all."

Augusta—Brickmason. "I have saved with my labor in cash $800 and that with what I have in real estate all makes a total of $1,200."

Gainesville—Brickmason. "I have helped to build 'Vesta' and 'Pacelot' mills here, and also was a foreman over both colored and white in Spartanburg, S. C., on Enaree mill."

St. Mary's—Brickmason and Plasterer. "Mr. —— was among the mechanics that laid the foundations of Atlanta University, and worked there until the building was ready for use, working for $3.00 per day, and also for $3.50 on the Kimball House."

Athens—Carpenter. "No contracts from whites are given to colored carpenters in Athens, but colored and white carpenters work together."

Augusta—Carpenter. "I am not contracting this year. I am foreman for one of the leading contractors in this city. Prejudice is very strong between the white and colored mechanics here. Even the architects are against us. I get there just the same."

Athens—Carpenter. "Work almost entirely for non-union white contractor, who employs and pays white and colored alike. There has arisen within the last three years a feeling on the part of white union carpenters against my present employer for using on equal terms and wages, white and colored mechanics."

Carpenter. "I have been working at the trade for 40 years and can do any kind of finishing, and can get a reputation from any contractors who know me. I have worked both North and South."

Augusta—Painter. "The Negro painters are doing well."

LaGrange—Carpenter and Contractor. "I learned my trade under my father. I have been a contractor and bridge builder for 30 years. My contracts for 1901 amounted to $10,000."

Augusta—Plasterer. "Negro workmen have very little competition in this line of work, as this kind of work is too hard for whites."

Eatonton—"I am a painter at $1.50 per day. The white men get $2.00 per day. I work 10 hours per day, and keep pretty busy all the year. I began work in 1889."

Buena Vista—Turner and Glazier. "This boy is a fireman, glazier and turner. I have been knowing him some 12 or more years as a fireman. He has the certificates of his trade."

Quitman—Carpenter. "I am employed almost the entire year, mostly for whites. I work with white and colored. There is very little discrimination shown toward good workmen."

Thomasville—Tinner. "We have several skilled workmen here, such as carpenters, blacksmiths, and shoemakers."

Marietta—Blacksmith. "In they ear 1890 I went to work at the American Marble Co., as a yard hand, and in three weeks I was sent to the shop as a helper to make and dress marble tools and in three months I was given a forge. In the year 1894 I was made foreman and machinist. My first wages were 90c per day. Then my wages were $1.25 during the part of the year 1894. Afterward I went to Canton, Ga., to work for the Georgia Marble Finishing Works for $1.50 and my expenses of travel paid. In the year 1895 I went into business of my own. In 1897 I was offered $2.00 per day by the McNeal Marble Company of Marietta, Ga. Now I am working for the Butler Brothers, of Marietta Ga., and others."

Fort Valley—"The town is being benefited no little by the different trades that are taught the boys and girls at the Fort Valley High and Industrial School."

Athens—Carpenter. "I fail to work about one-third of the year. I get $1.50 up to $2.00 per day. There is a white union here but the colored do not belong to it."

Darien—Contractor and Builder, now Post Master. "This is my third term as post master, but I continue with my trade. I have men working now. I pay them $1.00, $1.50 and $2.00 per day."

College—Mason and Plasterer. "I am instructor in Ga. State College. Have erected $20,000 brick dormitory with student labor. Under my supervision students work for both white and colored around the College."

Wrightsville—Carpenter. "There is some discrimination as to color where the colored mechanic is not of high standard."

Savannah—Contractor. "When I first went out to learn the trade I received 50c per week; as my trade advanced, wages advanced, and now I am foreman of my work."

Augusta—Bricklayer. "I am a bricklayer by trade. I have been working for the leading contractor of Augusta for 20 years. I work regularly when it is so we can work."

Eatonton—Contractor of Brick, Tile and Plastering. "I own property and real estate. I am a competent and active contractor and have been engaged in it for 35 years. I have learned nearly 50 young men to be first-class workmen, together with my two sons."

LaGrange—Blacksmith and Machinist. "I worked in one shop two years, and where I am now I have been working 13 years, and I am the only colored man in the shop, and I stand equal to any man in the shop; if you need any references you can get them."

Roberta—Carpenter. "I have been engaged in this trade for about 14 years and follow it about half of my time now. I farm and carry on my trade whenever called on to do a job of work."

Valdosta—Painter. "As to unions, we can have separate branches and co-operate with whites in cases of a strike or regulation of hours per day or wages, by a committee."

St. Mary's—Carpenter. "I have contracted for work and worked quite large gangs, both colored and whites, but have been working for ——— for 10 years at Cumberland Island, Ga."

Augusta—Plumbers. "There is no union among the colored laborers here at all. I wish there were. At the shop where I am employed, Mr. ——— and myself are the only two that are reliable. We both work right along by the side of the white men. We do gas and steam fitting just the same as the white men. But still we don't get the same wages for the work. Of course there are a great many others that will work, but they work only as helpers with white men."

Marietta—Plumber. "I have been a steady workman under others for nine years. I can do tin work of any kind; I can set bath tubs, toilets, rough a job on new houses; can fit up any kind of steam work in the line of plumbing; make steam quirls, can wipe a pretty good joint, and most any other work in common plumbing. I am sorry I cannot give you a more interesting sketch. A man must have a good head to run that trade for himself to make anything out of it. I have a home, and I like the farm and the country the best. I have no idle time through the year, for when I am out of the shop I am in the field."

Marietta—Plumber. "I have worked at the trade for ten years, and have found many discouragements. It is a known fact that the whites do everything they possibly can to prevent a Negro from getting into the plumber's trade, and after he gets in he can get no employment in a white shop. I have been doing business for myself as a plumbing and tinning contractor for 2½ years and have had as much work as I can do."

31. *Illinois.* The state of Illinois had 57,028 Negroes in 1890 and 85,078 in 1900. Over a third of these persons (30,150) live in the city of Chicago. The census of 1890 reported the following artisans:

MALE.

Miners,	556	Carpenters and joiners,	128
Barbers and hairdressers,	762	Coopers,	19
Engineers and firemen, (stationary)	243	Harness, saddle and trunk makers,	9
Boatmen, canalmen, pilots and sailors,	73	Iron and steel workers,	67
Steam railroad employees,	243	Machinists,	27
Street railway employees,	3	Marble and stone cutters & masons,	110
Telegraph and telephone operators,	4	Painters,	79
Apprentices,	22	Plumbers,	16
Bakers,	17	Printers,	29
Blacksmiths and wheelwrights,	103	Saw and planing mill employees,	85
Boot and shoe makers,	35	Tailors,	20
Brick makers, potters, etc.,	69	Tinners and tinware makers,	8
Butchers,	32	Tobacco and cigar factory operatives,	54
Cabinet makers and upholsterers,	15	Wood workers,	26

FEMALE.

Telegraph and telephone operators,	1	Dressmakers, milliners, seamstresses,	329
Apprentices,	2	Printers,	5
Cotton and other textile mill operatives,	6	Tailoresses,	2
		Tobacco and cigar factory operatives,	2

The Negroes are found in the trades as follows in various towns:

In Chicago there are carpenters, bricklayers, blacksmiths, stationary engineers, plasterers, butchers, coopers, etc. They are slowly gaining in the trades. The lack of leading contractors and the restrictions on apprentices keep the Negroes out of the trades, as well as their own lack of appreciation of the advantages of mechanical trades. In Springfield there are over 400 Negro miners and a number of hod-carriers, plasterers and barbers. In Centralia, Streator, Pontiac, Rock Island and Danville many Negro miners are reported; at Alton there are hod-carriers and a few firemen and masons; at Peoria, barbers, building laborers and firemen; at Galesburg, building laborers.

32. *Indiana.* There were 45,215 Negroes in Indiana in 1890, and 57,505 in 1900. Over a fourth of these persons live in Indianapolis, which has already been spoken of in § 22. The census of 1890 reported the following Negro artisans:

MALE.

Miners and quarrymen,	185	Cotton & other textile mill operatives,	34
Barbers and hairdressers,	699	Glass workers,	56
Engineers and firemen (stationary)	154	Harness, saddle and trunk makers,	5
Steam railroad employees,	128	Iron and steel workers,	162
Telegraph and telephone operators,	2	Machinists,	15
Apprentices,	24	Marble & stone cutters and masons,	92
Blacksmiths and wheelwrights,	81	Millers,	12
Boot and shoe makers,	31	Painters,	40
Brickmakers, potters, etc.,	130	Plasterers,	90
Butchers,	12	Printers,	14
Cabinet makers and upholsterers,	18	Saw and planing mill men,	124
Carpenters and joiners,	133	Tailors,	7
Carriage and wagon makers,	9	Wood workers,	39
Coopers,	11		

FEMALE.

Stenographers and typewriters,	1	Tailoresses,	2
Cotton & other textile mill operatives,	6	Tobacco & cigar factory operatives,	1
Dressmakers, milliners, seamstresses,	161	Wood workers,	2

Indiana has but a small number of Negro artisans and the opposition of Trade Unions is strong. A report from Mount Vernon says there are several bricklayers, masons and engineers there and that the Negro is gaining in the trades. The chief obstacles are "prejudice among the masses and the hostility of organized white artisans." There is some discrimination in wages and Negroes are barred out of the unions. Before the war there were no artisans in the place. Since then artisans have come from the South, the most conspicuous one from Alabama. "He is a very fine mechanic and engineer."

33. *Indian Territory and Oklahoma.* These two territories had a Negro population of 21,609 in 1890, and 55,684 in 1900. Oklahoma* with 2,873 Negroes in 1890 had the following artisans:

MALE.

Engineers, (civil, mechanical, etc),	1	Carpenters and joiners,	10
Barbers and hairdressers,	18	Confectioners,	1
Steam railroad employees,	1	Marble and stone cutters,	1
Blacksmiths and wheelwrights,	11	Masons,	6
Boot and shoe makers,	2	Painters,	1
Brick makers,	2	Plasterers,	4
Butchers,	1		

FEMALE.

Dressmakers, milliners, seamstresses, etc., 1

A report from Ardmore, Indian Territory, says there are not many skilled Negro laborers there; the leading ones include 3 blacksmiths, 4 carpenters, 2 printers, 2 shoe makers and a type-writer. The Negro mechanics are gaining, however, and young men are entering the trades. Only lack of skill hinders the black artisan. There are no trade unions and "white men have been let out of jobs for colored mechanics of greater ability."†

*There was no report for Indian Territory.

†Report of Mr. S. T. Wiggins.

34. *Iowa and Kansas.* Kansas had 49,710 Negroes in 1890 and 52,003 in 1900; Iowa had respectively 10,685 and 12,693. There were the following artisans reported in the two states in 1890:

MALE.

Miners,	815	Lead and zinc workers,	108
Barbers and hairdressers,	637	Machinists,	7
Engineers & firemen, (stationary)	91	Marble & stone cutters & masons,	234
Steam railroad employees,	287	Millers,	25
Telegraph & telephone operators,	4	Painters,	43
Bakers,	2	Plasterers,	151
Blacksmiths and wheelwrights,	151	Printers,	27
Boot and shoe makers,	27	Tailors,	7
Butchers,	37	Tinners and tinware makers,	14
Carpenters, joiners and coopers,	157	Apprentices,	5
Carriage and wagon makers,	3	Brickmakers, etc.,	13
Harness, saddle & trunk makers,	10	Saw & planing mill employees,	19
Iron and steel workers,	45		

FEMALE.

Stenographers and typewriters,	1	Dressmakers, milliners, seamstresses,	141
Cotton & other textile mill operatives,	9	Printers,	2

In Atchison, Kansas, there are very few Negro artisans, and they are chiefly blacksmiths. Nevertheless, the Negro is gaining and numbers of young people are entering the industrial schools. In Kansas City there are a number of stationary firemen and beef-butchers. The trade unions are the chief obstacles. In Iowa there are a large number of Negro miners and many in the building trades. In Ottumwa there are hod-carriers, steel and metal workers, plasterers, carpenters, and miners in considerable numbers.

35. *Kentucky.* In 1890 there were 268,071 Negroes in Kentucky and 284,706 in 1900. The census of 1890 reported the following artisans:

MALE.

Lumbermen, raftsmen, etc.,	114	Cotton & other textile mill operatives,	225
Miners,	976	Harness, saddle & trunk makers,	19
Barbers and hairdressers,	657	Iron and steel workers,	240
Engineers and firemen,	359	Machinists,	27
Steam railroad employees,	2,492	Marble & stone cutters & masons,	586
Apprentices,	36	Millers,	77
Blacksmiths and wheelwrights,	592	Painters,	181
Boot and shoe makers,	143	Printers,	23
Brickmakers, potters, etc.,	491	Saw and planing mill employees,	312
Butchers,	89	Tailors,	19
Cabinet makers and upholsterers,	29	Tinners and tinware workers,	31
Carpenters and joiners,	886	Tobacco & cigar factory operatives,	857
Coopers,	169	Wood workers,	51

FEMALE.

Apprentices,	7	Dressmakers, milliners, seamstresses,	576
Boot and shoe makers,	2	Printers,	1
Cotton and other textile mill operatives,	29	Tailoresses,	2
		Tobacco & cigar factory operatives,	162

The chief artisans are miners, tobacco workers, hod-carriers, marine firemen, carpenters, railway men, etc. At Paducah there are many artisans; the 22 leading ones include 9 carpenters, 3 bricklayers, 4 plasterers, 3 painters and 3 blacksmiths. The black artisans are gaining here. In Lebanon there are carpenters, blacksmiths and masons, but they are losing ground on account of inefficiency. "Old artisans are dying out and no young men are taking their places." At Danville, Ky., the leading artisans include carpenters, masons, painters and plasterers. They are gaining as a result of industrial training and the entrance of young men into the trades. In Georgetown the leading artisans include 2 contracting carpenters, 4 contracting masons, 1 cabinet maker and 1 paper hanger. Young men are entering the trades and the Negro is gaining. In Louisville there are perhaps 500 artisans of various kinds. They are not gaining perceptibly.

36. *Louisiana.* There were 559,193 Negroes in Louisiana in 1890, and 650,804 in 1900. The census of 1890 reported the following artisans:

MALE.

Lumbermen and raftsmen,	484	Carpenters and joiners,	1,611
Engineers (civil and mechanical)	37	Coopers,	605
Barbers and hairdressers,	369	Cotton & other textile mill operatives,	203
Engineers and firemen (stationary)	309	Iron and steel workers,	30
Boatmen, canalmen, pilots, sailors,	660	Machinists,	24
Steam railroad employees,	1,593	Marble and stone cutters and masons,	766
Apprentices,	100	Painters,	280
Bakers,	145	Printers,	39
Blacksmiths and wheelwrights,	689	Saw and planing mill employees,	948
Boot and shoe makers,	438	Tailors,	70
Butchers,	141	Tinners and tinware makers,	44
Cabinet makers and upholsterers,	111	Tobacco & cigar factory employees,	539

FEMALE.

Apprentices,	6	Dressmakers, milliners, seamstresses,	656
Bakers,	18	Tailoresses,	45
Cotton & other textile mill operatives,	22	Tobacco & cigar factory operatives,	21

In New Orleans there are large numbers of artisans in the building trades and in shoe making, cigar making, blacksmithing, coopering, etc. The impression seems to be that the Negro artisan here is either gaining or at least not losing There are about 4,000 Negroes in the trade unions. The influx of white mechanics is increasing the competition, however, and "the brief life, so far, of the industrial school among the colored people will not permit one to see any large results as yet. It is promising, however, and ought to be encouraged." There is no apparent discrimination in wages in this city and the trade unions are open to Negroes in most cases. One report says: "There is no way of telling the number of Negro artisans in this city. The directories do not distinguish them from others. Before and since the war they have built some of the best structures of our city. They work in various shops and in cigar factories,but have been lately crowded out of machine shops. The new stone library of Tulane University is now being erected by Negroes entirely."*

Another report says: "The city of New Orleans comprises among its population Negro artisans who receive recognition in their respective trades, are widely employed and paid remunerative wages. Contractors of public buildings and private work appreciate the Negro workmen and a majority of the most imposing structures in the city were built by colored men. The number of artisans has increased since the war, and their

Report of Mr. F. B. Smith.

condition is better. A large proportion of them are property-holders."* Baton Rouge is said to be "an exceptionally good community for Negro artisans" and they are gaining there. "The old slave time plasterers, masons and carpenters trained up an array of youngsters to fill their shoes and they are doing it most admirably."** Among the buildings erected entirely by Negro mechanics are a $25,000 dormitory, a $25,000 public school building and a $10,000 bank building.

There are many strong Negro trade unions in Louisiana, especially the Longshoremen's Benevolent Association, the Screwmen, the Cotton Yard men, the Teamsters and Loaders, the Excelsior Freight Handlers, the Round Freight Teamsters, etc.

At Shreveport there are carpenters, hod-carriers and bricklayers organized in unions. On the whole the Negro artisans seem better organized and more aggressive in this state than in any other. The colored secretary of the Central Labor Union says: "By amalgamation of organizations and through International connections we expect to have the color line in work removed."

37. *Maine and Massachusetts.* These two states have a comparatively small proportion of Negroes: Maine had 1,190 in 1890, and 1,319 in 1900; Massachusetts had 22,144 and 31,974. The report of artisans in 1890 for both states was:

MALE.

Lumbermen, etc.,	83	Cotton & other textile mill operatives,	89
Engineers (civil, mechanical, etc.)	12	Gold and silver workers,	2
Barbers and hairdressers,	390	Iron and steel workers,	22
Engineers & firemen (stationary)	53	Leather curriers, dressers, tanners, etc.,	42
Boatmen, canalmen, pilots, sailors,	156	Machinists,	46
Steam railroad employees,	83	Marble and stone cutters,	12
Street railway employees,	9	Masons (brick and stone)	93
Apprentices,	15	Painters,	59
Bakers,	11	Paper mill operatives,	16
Blacksmiths and wheelwrights,	34	Piano and organ makers,	5
Boot and shoe makers,	159	Plumbers,	16
Brickmakers, potters, etc.,	18	Printers,	30
Butchers,	20	Rubber factory operatives,	11
Cabinet makers and upholsterers,	27	Tailors,	66
Carpenters and joiners,	103	Wood workers,	28

FEMALE.

Stenographers and typewriters,	3	Printers,	4
Boot and shoe makers,	38	Rubber factory operatives,	2
Cotton & other textile mill operatives,	64	Straw workers,	1
Dressmakers, milliners, seamstresses,	271	Tailoresses,	31

In Portland, Maine, there are five skilled workmen in the unions and they stand well.

In Massachusetts the meat handlers, longshoremen, and building trades are represented and a great many are in the unions. In Boston the Negroes are in the building trades, cigar makers', meat handlers', and a few in the machinists' unions. In Springfield there are masons and mason tenders and barbers; but not many. They are good workmen. Brockton has a few electric linemen, stationary firemen, boot and shoe makers and laundry workers. In the smaller towns there is here and there an artisan.

*Report of Mr. E. Bones. **Report of Mr. A. H. Colwell.

38. *Maryland.* There were 215,657 Negroes in Maryland in 1890, and 235,064 in 1900. There were reported in 1890 the following artisans:

MALE.

Miners......................................139
Barbers and hairdressers.. 480
Engineers and firemen (sta.) 220
Boatmen, canalmen, pilots and sailors..................................1,085
Steam railroad employees.........467
Street railway employees.......... 4
Apprentices..... 57
Bakers.......... 21
Blacksmiths & wheelwrights.....206
Boot and shoe makers...............155
Brickmakers, potters, etc........1,143
Butchers......................................130
Carpenters and joiners............... 96
Cotton and other textile mill operatives 57
Iron and steel workers.......... 68
Machinists....................... 13
Marble and stone cutters and masons........ 231
Millers....................................... 76
Painters.................... 59
Plumbers.. 13
Printers.. 27
Saw and planing mill employees.. 230
Ship and boat builders.............. 96
Tailors 22
Tinners and tinware makers...... 68
Tobacco and cigar factory operatives...... 18

FEMALE.

Apprentices.............. 9
Confectioners 3
Cotton and other textile mill operatives........ 10
Dressmakers, milliners, seamstresses, etc............................. 990
Hat and cap makers...... 1
Meat, fish, and fruit packers, canners, etc...... 19
Tailoresses....... 7

The Negro population of this state centres in Baltimore, where over a third of the colored people live. Here the Negroes have had an interesting industrial history.* Before the war the Negroes made brick, shucked oysters, loaded ships and did the caulking; there were also carpenters and blacksmiths. Then came foreign competition and the war until gradually by skill and prejudice the Negroes were more and more forced out. There are still painters and building laborers, brickmakers and other artisans, but the trades unions have largely confined these to job-work. The hod-carriers are still strong and there was a strong union of caulkers in 1890. The brickmakers, too, are well organized and have white and black members.

There have been in Baltimore some interesting experiments in industrial co-operation, the most noted of which was that of the Chesapeake Marine Railway. There was a brickmakers' strike after the war which led to colored men organizing a brick yard which flourished awhile and died. A strike against colored caulkers and stevedores followed which forced most of them out of work; as a result the Negroes raised $10,000, bought a ship yard and marine railway and several hundred caulkers went to work. The capital was soon raised to $30,000. The venture was successful until it was found that instead of having been purchased outright the yard had only been leased for 20 years and at the end of that time the yard passed into the hands of whites and left the Negroes with nothing but the two or three dividends that had been paid.

*Cf Brackett: Notes on the Progress of the Colored People of Md., etc., J. H. U. studies, 8th series, 1890.

As an example of the situation of Negro artisans in the country districts in Maryland we may take the village of Sandy Spring* with about a thousand Negroes. There were here in 1900:

2 barbers.	1 miller.
6 blacksmiths.	3 shoemakers.
2 carpenters—$1.25 a day.	1 shingle maker.
3 engineers—$12-$24 a month.	2 masons—$2-$2.50 per day.

Five of these own their homes.

39. *Michigan, Minnesota and Wisconsin.* Michigan had 15,223 Negroes in 1890 and 15,816 in 1900; Minnesota had 3,683 and 4,959 in those years, and Wisconsin 2,444 and 2,542. The following artisans were reported in these states in 1890:

MALE

Lumbermen and raftsmen	235	Coopers	39
Miners	4	C'ton & o'er textile mill operat's	6
Barbers and hairdressers	731	Harness, saddle & trunk makers	8
Engineers and firemen (sta.)	85	Iron and steel workers	28
Boatmen, canalmen, pilots and sailors	82	Machinists	15
Steam railroad employees	56	Marble & stone cut'rs & masons	111
Blacksmiths & wheelwrights	40	Millers	3
Boot and shoe makers	18	Painters	55
Butchers	19	Printers	16
Cabinet makers & upholsterers	7	Saw & planing mill employees	82
Carpenters and joiners	122	Tailors	9
Carriage and wagon makers	2	Tobacco & cigar fact'y operat's	7
		Wood workers	13

FEMALE.

Telegraph & telep'ne operatives	2	Dressmakers, milliners, seamstresses, etc	194
Cotton & other textile mill operatives	7	Printers	1
		Tailoresses	3
		Wood workers	3

In Michigan there are about 500 barbers, engineers, plumbers, bricklayers and coal-miners in the unions. In Grand Rapids there are building trades laborers; in Detroit there are longshoremen, engineers and carpenters. This is one of the few cities where there are several colored motormen and conductors on the street railways. They were forced in by political influence but have proven excellent workmen. In Sault Ste. Marie there are several good mechanics. "We have no toughs in the race here." There is an excellent Negro plumber at Flint, and several good mechanics in Ann Arbor. One in the latter city does considerable small contracting. In Kalamazoo there are bricklayers and masons.

In Minnesota there are few Negroes and fewer artisans; there are a number of barbers in the twin cities, a few cigar makers, printers and carpenters.

In Wisconsin there are few artisans except barbers here and there. In Milwaukee there are a few cigar makers.

---

*Cf. U. S. Bulletin of the Department of Labor, No. 32.

40. *Mississippi.* There were 742,559 Negroes in Mississippi in 1890 and 907,630 in 1900. The census of 1890 reported these artisans:

MALE

Occupation	Number
Lumbermen and raftsmen	192
Barbers and hairdressers	326
Engineers & firemen (sta.)	203
Boatmen, canalmen, pilots and sailors	275
Steam railroad employees	2,736
Telegraph and telephone operators	1
Blacksmiths & wheelwrights	665
Boot and shoe makers	130
Brickmakers	355
Butchers	128
Carpenters and joiners	1,476
Charcoal, coke & lime burners	94
Cotton and other textile mill operatives	76
Machinists	41
Marble and stone cutters and masons	296
Mechanics	85
Millers	63
Painters	153
Printers	22
Saw & planing mill employees	1,387
Tinners and tinware makers	16
Wood workers	53

FEMALE.

Occupation	Number
Basket makers	26
Cotton and other textile mill employees	8
Dressmakers, milliners, seamstresses, etc	759
Printers	5

A report from Westside says: "Our population is mostly rural, but the towns are growing constantly in number and importance; and, whereas heretofore few skilled artisans were needed in Mississippi the demand for them grows constantly.

"As there are no trades unions in the state to interfere colored mechanics find work without difficulty. There appears to be few labor organizations in the state; there is one at Vicksburg. I presume it was instigated by white mechanics, who induced colored men to organize with them in order that they, the whites, might then more easily obtain work where they were thrown into competition with colored mechanics. They thus procured work through the aid of colored men. There is no trouble whatever on the part of colored men to obtain work in this state as carpenters, blacksmiths, brickmasons, brickmakers, shoemakers, painters or plasterers.

"There is a brickmasons' union at Meridian, Miss. The colored masons are allowed to join it, there being only two such masons in the city. There is somewhat of a dearth of colored masons in the state. This fact being appreciated by the authorities of this institution arrangements are now being made to give instructions in brickmaking and brickmasonry."

A report from Ebenezer mentions blacksmithing as the chief trade and thinks the status of artisans is about the same as in the past although they "may be gaining." There is general lack of efficiency, but students from industrial schools are entering the trades. There is some color discrimination in wages. In Woodville the leading 14 artisans include two builders and contractors, two carpenters, four blacksmiths, one smith and carpenter, three machinists, and two painters. They are competing with white labor and are gaining. The effect of industrial training is apparent; but there is a lack of leading contractors with capital. In all lines but brickmasonry there is discrimination in wages. There are so few white masons that the differences do not extend to this trade. Gloster has a number of carpenters, blacksmiths, painters, engineers and bakers. The writer of the reports "cannot say the Negro is losing as an artisan, but his gains are not satisfactory." There is a demand for better artisans, but there are no industrial schools near and young men are not entering the trades. There is very little discrimination in wages. "We have no organized unions but the colored men generally confer and have certain mutual understandings with each other." The great drawback is lack of sufficient skill and education to follow plans and specifications and do the highest grades of work. Mound Bayou has a number of blacksmiths, engineers, surveyors, carpenters, printers and masons. The artisans are gaining fast here. "This is a distinctively Negro town and colony comprising 2,500-3,000 inhabitants, with 20,000-30,000 acres of rich land. We have three cotton gins, two of them with saw-mill attachments. There are three blacksmith shops and one printing press. These are handled exclusively by Negro labor and Negro managers. The settlement was established about 1887 and the inhabitants are chiefly cotton-growers."*

At Holly Springs many young men from the industrial schools are entering the trades; there are several carpenters and masons. There is discrimination in wages. At Grace the Negro artisans are gaining. The leading artisans include 3 carpenters, 1 engineer, 4 masons and a blacksmith. Young men are entering the trades.

41. *Missouri.* There were 150,184 Negroes in this state in 1890 and 161,234 in 1900. The census of 1890 reported these artisans:

MALE

Lumbermen, raftsmen, etc	157	Harness, saddle & trunk makers	8
Miners	915	Iron and steel workers	177
Barbers and hairdressers	909	Machinists	19
Engineers and firemen (sta.)	321	Marble and stone cutters	50
Steam railroad employees	703	Masons	231
Street railway employees	7	Millers	35
Apprentices	25	Painters	66
Bakers	13	Plasterers	262
Blacksmiths and wheelwrights	206	Printers	32
Boot and shoe makers	52	Saw & planing mill employees	233
Butchers	65	Tailors	9
Cabinet makers & upholsterers	12	Tinners and tinware makers	11
Carpenters and joiners	263	Tobacco and cigar factory operatives	222
Coopers	22		

FEMALE.

Stenographers & type writers	2	Printers	59
Telegraph & telephone operators	4	Tailoresses	294
Cotton and other textile mill operatives	106	Tobacco and cigar factory operatives	199
Dressmakers, milliners, seamstresses, etc	1,835		

There are some three thousand Negroes in the labor unions of Missouri—hod-carriers, teamsters and barbers, miners, and a few printers, carpenters and masons. In St. Louis the Negro artisan is losing; "he does not keep pace with the times in efficiency and is besides crowded out of employment by the trade unions." As to industrial training "there has been

*Report of the mayor, Mr. A. P. Hood.

a manual training department in the colored schools for more than ten years but I have not heard of any thus trained who have got positions thereby." In St. Joseph, on the other hand, there are 65 or 70 Negro artisans and they are gaining. The nine leading artisans include one paper hanger, one kalsominer, three carpenters, one painter, one mattress maker, one plasterer and one tailor. "Trade unions have to a great extend hindered the Negroes' progress" and they are barred from nearly all the unions. At Kansas City Negroes are reported by a leading trade unionist to "have done good work at bricklaying, plastering, painting, carpentry and paper hanging." Only the hod-carriers, however, are in the unions. At Joplin there are a few masons and stone cutters; at Commerce there are carpenters, blacksmiths and engineers, but the Negro is losing. The chief obstacles are "trade unions, prejudice and the lack of capital among our people."

42. *Other New England States, (N. H., Vt., R. I., and Conn.)* The states of New Hampshire, Vermont, Rhode Island and Connecticut had altogether 21,246 Negroes in 1890, and 25,806 in 1900. Over half these Negroes live in Connecticut. The census of 1890 reported the following artisans in these states:

MALE

Miners and quarrymen	7	Gold and silver workers	8
Barbers and hairdressers	159	Gunsmiths, locksmiths, bell hangers	9
Engineers and firemen (sta)	36	Hat and cap makers	12
Boatmen, canalmen, pilots and sailors	30	Iron and steel workers	44
Steam railroad employees	31	Machinists	21
Apprentices	15	Marble and stone cutters and masons	142
Bakers	9	Metal workers	16
Blacksmiths and wheelwrights	38	Painters	59
Boot and shoe makers	54	Plumbers	10
Brass workers	39	Printers	16
Butchers	31	Rubber factory operatives	8
Cabinet makers and upholsterers	18	Tailors	15
Carpenters and joiners	76	Tool and cutlery makers	4
Clock and watchmakers	2	Wood workers	15
Cotton & other textile mill op	82		

FEMALE

Cotton and other textile mill operatives	38	Paper mill operatives	2
Dressmakers, milliners, seamstresses, etc	281	Printers	1
		Tailoresses	9

There are very few Negro artisans in these states except barbers; Rhode Island has a few printers, longshoremen and masons. New Hampshire has a few in the building trades. Connecticut seems to have very few if any artisans.

43. *New York and New Jersey.* New York had 70,092 Negroes in 1890 and 99,232 in 1900. New Jersey had 47,638 and 69,844 in these years. The census of 1890 reported these artisans in New York:

MALE

Occupation	Number
Barbers and hairdressers	672
Engineers and firemen (sta.)	120
Boatmen, canalmen, pilots and sailors	240
Steam railroad employees	196
Street railway employees	16
Apprentices	20
Bakers	22
Blacksmiths and wheelwrights	51
Boot and shoe makers	39
Brickmakers, potters, etc	394
Butchers	40
Cabinet makers & upholsterers	43
Carpenters and joiners	156
Coopers	17
Cotton and other textile mill operatives	24
Iron and steel workers	49
Machinists	22
Marble and stone cutters	21
Masons	156
Painters	176
Plumbers	26
Printers	41
Saw and planing mill employees	23
Tailors	53
Tinners and tinware makers	27
Tobacco and cigar factory operatives	192
Wood workers	25

FEMALE

Occupation	Number
Stenographers and typewriters	4
Box makers (paper)	2
Cotton and other textile mill operatives	11
Dressmakers	674
Glove makers	4
Milliners	5
Printers	7
Seamstresses	215
Sewing machine operators	11
Shirt, collar and cuff makers	17
Tailoresses	17
Tobacco and cigar factory operatives	8

In New Jersey the following artisans were reported in 1890:

MALE

Occupation	Number
Miners	14
Engineers (civil & mechanical)	3
Barbers and hairdressers	257
Engineers and firemen (sta.)	61
Boatmen, canalmen, pilots and sailors	89
Steam railroad employees	102
Apprentices	14
Bakers	4
Blacksmiths and wheelwrights	20
Boot and shoe makers	56
Brick and tile makers	755
Butchers	26
Cabinet makers & upholsterers	29
Carpenters and joiners	103
Cotton and other textile mill operatives	17
Glass workers	10
Harness, saddle and trunk makers	5
Hat and cap makers	3
Iron and steel workers	61
Leather curriers, dressers, etc	19
Machinists	6
Marble and stone cutters and masons	102
Painters	49
Plumbers	15
Potters	9
Printers	14
Tailors	7
Tinners and tinware makers	8
Tobacco and cigar factory operatives	14

FEMALE

Occupation	Number
Apprentices	1
Boot and shoe makers	1
Box makers	1
Cotton and other textile mill operatives	5
Dressmakers, milliners, seamstresses, etc	238
Printers	1
Tailoresses	6
Tobacco & cigar fact'y operat'es.	3

The mass of the Negro population of New York is centered in New York City. Here the artisan has had a thorny path to travel. As late as 1836 a well-to-do Negro was refused a license as drayman and the riots of 1863 had an economic as well as a political cause. The ensuing enmity between Irish and Negroes and the absorption of the Irish into the industries kept the Negroes out. In 1890 about 10% of the working Negroes were in skilled trades as follows:*

Tobacco workers	187	Tailors	45
Sailors	132	Engineers and firemen	84
Barbers	166	Building trades	147
Painters	132	Apprentices	10
Machinists	12	Railroad employees	84
Shoe makers	12	Printers	29
Blacksmiths	13	Cabinet makers	28
Bakers	11		

Making something over a thousand in all besides some 700 dressmakers and seamstresses. Since 1890 "artisans have not perceptibly increased on account of the trade unions and the indifference of employers."

In Albany and Troy there are two tailors, one electrician, 1 printer, 1 carpenter, 1 blacksmith, 1 civil engineer, 1 mason. The Negro is not gaining here. In Rochester there are two stationary engineers. At Binghampton there are a few barbers and building laborers. At Auburn there are a few horse shoers, stationary engineers, and building laborers. A few are in the building trades in Middletown, a machinist at Hornelsville, etc.

In New Jersey there are a few more artisans but not many. From Newark we learn of a few artisans but "the trouble with the colored people here is that few of them have trades," and they "are backward about getting their boys in as apprentices." Three engineers, three masons, three lathers and one carpenter are mentioned. Trenton reports a cooper, a paper hanger, a shoe maker and a cigar maker.

44. *North Carolina.* There were 561,018 Negroes in North Carolina in 1890 and 624,469 in 1900. The census of 1890 reported these artisans:

MALE			
Lumbermen and raftsmen	810	Carriage and wagon makers	49
Miners	278	Coopers	304
Barbers and hairdressers	482	Cotton and other textile mill operatives	564
Engineers and firemen (stationary)	432	Iron and steel workers	88
Boatmen, canalmen, pilots & sailors	316	Machinists	46
Steam railroad employees	3,534	Marble & stone cutters & masons	827
Telegraph and telephone operators	3	Mechanics	74
Blacksmiths and wheelwrights	831	Millers	158
Boot and shoe makers	384	Painters	297
Brick makers, potters, etc	443	Printers	56
Butchers	144	Saw and planing mill employees	1,992
Cabinet makers & upholsterers	53	Tobacco & cigar factory operatives	2,779
Carpenters and joiners	1,789		
FEMALE.			
Cotton & other textile mill operatives	127	Tailoresses	8
Dressmakers, milliners, seamstresses	705	Tobacco & cigar factory operatives	1,462

Charlotte is a city of 18,091 inhabitants (1900), 7,151 of whom are colored; the suburbs covered by the city directory brings this total up to 25 or 30 thousand. In 1890 the city had 5,134 Negroes. A special report from this city gives the following artisans†:

*See the "Black North," a series of articles in the *New York Times*, 1901.

†Made by the kindness of Mr. H. A. Hunt, of Biddle University; the artisans were ascertained from the directories.

NEGRO ARTISANS IN CHARLOTTE, N. C.

	1885	1902
Bakers		3
Basket makers		1
Boiler makers		2
Bridge builders	1	
Blacksmiths	21	15
Brick makers		1
Cabinet makers		1
Carriage builders	1	
Carpenters	33	36
Collar makers	1	
Firemen		25
Harness makers	4	2
Lathers		1
Machinists		1
Masons (brick and stone)	20	37
Mattress makers	1	
Molders		2
Painters	6	33
Plasterers	8	16
Printers		9
Shoe makers	17	16
Tailors	1	7
Tanners	6	2
Tinners	3	3
Upholsterers		1
White washers	6	
Total	129	214

Although the artisans are more numerous than formerly still they are losing in relative importance. This is in a measure due to inefficiency, and the great growth of the South, "but more largely, perhaps, to prejudice—the prejudice incident to competition as well as race prejudice." Young men "are not entering the trades very largely as journeymen * * * I find comparatively few young men following trades learned in school, except in the art or trade of printing." The obstacles in learning trades are "the inability of colored men to have sufficient work to keep apprentices, and the unwillingness of whites to employ apprentices." The chief obstacle in working at the trade when learned is "prejudice." There is discrimination in wages, and some of the trade unions bar Negroes; other unions, like the bricklayers, have a considerable Negro membership. Directly after the war three Negroes were the leading bricklayers and plasterers, and were so acknowledged by all. To-day a Negro "is and has been for years the best bricklayer and contractor in town; he is able to follow plans and conduct a contracting business in an intelligent and profitable manner. He has built some of the best buildings in and around Charlotte—not small houses, but large ones, as, for instance: the City Hall, several churches, school buildings, etc."

The leading Negro artisans of Raleigh include 1 tinner, 1 blacksmith, 3 carpenters, 2 wood and iron workers and 5 masons. The black artisan is losing here, largely on account of indifference. Few young men enter industrial schools "with a view to making industrial pursuits a life-work."

There are no Negroes in the Raleigh unions and it is doubtful if they could get in. In Salisbury the artisan is losing also, for the older artisans are not contractors and employ no apprentices. There are, nevertheless, several good artisans; the leading ones include three tailoring establishments, 5 carpenters, 2 plasterers, 2 bricklayers, 2 shoe makers and a painter. As to young men, "my opinion is that the schools do not make good mechanics, i. e., practical mechanics. It is almost impossible to give a good mechanical and literary training in the time allotted by our manual training schools." Race prejudice and their own unreliability are the Negroes' great obstacles. Often special efforts are put forth to attract and employ white mechanics in preference to Negroes. "In some places Negroes and whites work together as artisans. In other parts of the state whites refuse to work with Negroes."*

The leading Negro artisans of Asheville are three plasterers, three brickmasons, two blacksmiths and a carpenter. The Negro is gaining here in the trades and a few young men are entering. The trade unions in most instances receive Negroes. At Goldsboro the Negro artisan "is holding his own; he is not losing." The leading artisans include 4 masons, 6 carpenters, 1 wheelwright, 2 blacksmiths and a painter. "Two young men who attended industrial schools work at their trades; one at carpentry, the other at cabinet making; two other young men who have not been away from home to any schools have good trades as masons, and are regularly employed." There is very little discrimination in wages, chiefly due to the fact that there are no unions here. In Winston-Salem the unions have Negro members.

In Hillsboro the leading artisans are two carpenters, a painter, a plasterer and two masons. These artisans "hold their own as they are the best in the little town." A few young men are entering the trades but "not as many as I could desire." The Negro is his own greatest obstacle here as there is no discrimination in wages and no unions. "The Negro artisans here are less in number than before the war. The young men seem not to care for the trades of their fathers. What few artisans we have get all the work that is to be done. They take contracts, and work colored and white hands together without friction. On all skilled work in my town a Negro has, in nine cases out of ten, been the boss. Some young men think that the trades are hard work, so they take to school teaching, hotel work, barbering, etc."†

One enterprise deserves especial mention:

"The first experiment with Negro labor in a cotton factory was made about three years ago in the city of Charleston, S. C. The outcome was unsatisfactory and the factory soon closed down. However, this test was not made under favorable circumstances. . . . .

"A more decisive test of the fitness of Negro labor for cotton mills is now being made at the Coleman cotton mill of North Carolina. The mill is owned and operated by Negroes. The site is in the Piedmont section of the state, one mile from the city

*From President W. H. Goler of Livingstone College.

†Report of Mr. L. P. Berry.

of Concord. The capitalization of the mill is $100,000, of which $66,000 has been paid in. The subscribers to the stock are scattered throughout the state and number about 350. The subscriptions vary from $25 to $1,000, and are payable in installments.

"When the mill started up in July, 1901, all of the employees were inexperienced. Mr. A. G. Smith, of Massachusetts, the superintendent, and the only white person connected with the work, had to train each employee for his or her task.

"The Coleman plant consists of 100 acres of land, one three-story brick building, 80x120, two boilers of 100 horse-power each, and a complete modern outfit of looms, spindles and other machinery necessary for spinning and weaving. The weaving capacity is 40,000 yards per week. A dozen or more very substantial tenement cottages have been erected and rented to the employees.

"The writer has visited the mill and viewed the operatives at work, and was agreeably surprised to find that only one of the operatives was inclined to go to sleep. The superintendent expressed himself as entirely satisfied with the progress of the workers, and stated that he felt confident that the enterprise would prove a financial success. Several of the operatives, he said, had been "caught napping," but, he added, that such occurrences were not uncommon even among white operatives in Massachusetts. The operatives, so far, have been very prompt in coming to work, and have shown no disposition to drop out. . . . .

"This cotton mill venture will be watched with interest, and if it succeeds, no doubt other mills will be started up with Negro help. The operatives in the Coleman mill are paid about one-half as much as the same grade of workers would receive in Massachusetts. The capitalists of the South will have a rich harvest if they can successfully operate with this cheap labor."*

45. *Ohio.* There were 87,113 Negroes in this state in 1890, and 96,901 in 1900. The census of 1890 gave the following artisans:

MALE

Miners	578	Coopers	60
Quarrymen	42	Glass workers	13
Barbers and hairdressers	1,372	Harness, saddle and trunk makers	8
Engineers and firemen (stationary)	295	Iron and steel workers	286
Steam railroad employees	355	Machinists	51
Telegraph and telephone operators	9	Marble and stone cutters & masons	280
Apprentices	28	Painters	207
Bakers	29	Plasterers	285
Blacksmiths and wheelwrights	258	Printers	19
Boot and shoe makers	97	Saw and planing mill employees	57
Brick makers, potters, etc	152	Tailors	23
Butchers	59	Tinners and tinware makers	15
Cabinet makers & upholsterers	20	Tobacco and cigar factory operatives	18
Carpenters and joiners	277	Wood workers	38
Carriage and wagon makers	23		

FEMALE.

Stenographers and typewriters	3	Paper mill operatives	1
Cotton & other textile mill operatives	8	Printers	6
Dressmakers, milliners, seamstresses	393	Tailoresses	7

"In those callings which are classed as skilled very few workmen of the dark complexion are to be found. I mean such trades as printing, cigar making, molding, machinists', etc.; while of course the number of Negro barbers is somewhat large."† Cincinnati has by far the largest Negro

*Professor Jerome Dowd, in Gunton's Magazine, Sept. 1902.

†Report of the Secretary of the State Federation of Labor.

population of the cities (14,482). Conditions here are such that Negroes are practically excluded from the unions save a few who got in in earlier years and who are usually so light in complexion as not to be easily recognized as of Negro descent. On this account Negro skilled laborers are decreasing in number, although there are many doing job work. There are some 300 Negro hod-carriers, 8 union men in the building trades and "outside of organizations Negroes working at almost every trade."

In Cleveland there are about 100 skilled artisans and they are not discriminated against to any large extent. In Oberlin, there has long been an interesting colored colony. They have among their leading artisans an excellent mason, three painters, two building contractors, and a carpenter. Compared with the past, however, the Negro is losing. "Our young men are not entering trades. Those who work at a trade have not an eye to become skilled." There is, too, considerable prejudice from the whites and the unions.* At Xenia, there are at least 40 Negro artisans. Among the leading ones are a marble cutter and letterer, two carriage makers, a stationary engineer, a boiler setter, two contracting plasterers, a carpenter, a contracting mason, four blacksmiths (two of whom are expert horse shoers, and other "the best blacksmith in the city") two tile-setters and a cigar maker. The number of artisans is decreasing because the young men do not enter the trades. One of the carriage makers, Mr. Lewis Sydes, "believes he is the first man in the United States to make the double felly in the carriage wheel. He has worked at the trade more than 50 years."**

In other localities there are a few artisans, as firemen in Mt. Vernon, engineers, bricklayers, and hod carriers in Youngstown, blast-furnace workers in Ironton, and longshoremen in Lorain.

46. *Oregon and the North West.* (*Ore., Ida., Mont., N. D., S. D., Neb., U., Wash., and Wy.*) These states had in all 5,212 Negroes in 1890, and 5,982 in 1900. There are very few artisans in this region, only one Negro carpenter being mentioned in Salt Lake City. The census of 1890 enumerated the following colored artisans—which includes Indians and Chinese—how many of the last two is uncertain:

MALE

Lumbermen and raftsmen	61	Butchers	31
Miners	2,417	Carpenters and joiners	83
Engineers (civil and mechanical)	3	Machinists	3
Barbers and hairdressers	564	Marble & stone cutters and masons	67
Boatmen, canalmen, pilots, and sailors	82	Meat, fish, fruit packers and canners	518
Engineers and firemen (stationary)	23	Painters	18
Steam railroad employees	1,183	Plasterers	86
Blacksmiths and wheelwrights	58	Printers	17
Bakers	11	Saw and planing mill men	189
Boot and shoe makers	19	Ship and boat builders	5
Brickmakers and potters	135	Tailors	250
		Tinners and tinware makers	7

FEMALE

Dressmakers, milliners, seamstresses, etc	112

*Report of Mr. Elias F. Jones. **Report of Mr. J. M. Summers.

47. *Pennsylvania and Delaware.* There were 107,576 Negroes in Pennsylvania in 1890, and 156,845 in 1900. Delaware had 28,386 and 30,697 in these years. The census of 1890 reported the following artisans in Pennsylvania for 1890:

MALE

Occupation	Number	Occupation	Number
Lumbermen, raftsmen, etc	64	Iron and steel workers	795
Miners	849	Leather curriers, dressers, finishers	68
Quarrymen	206	Machinists	29
Barbers and hairdressers	1,477	Marble and stone cutters	102
Engineers and firemen (stationary)	186	Masons	211
Steam railroad employees	526	Millers	19
Apprentices	64	Oil well employees	5
Bakers	35	Painters	57
Blacksmiths and wheelwrights	137	Plumbers	17
Boot and shoe makers	133	Printers	75
Brickmakers, potters, etc	627	Saw & planing mill employees	53
Butchers	53	Tailors	41
Cabinet makers and upholsterers	76	Tinners and tinware makers	16
Carpenters and joiners	152	Tobacco & cigar factory operatives	75
Cotton & other textile mill operat'es	77	Wood workers	51
Glass workers	19		

FEMALE.

Occupation	Number	Occupation	Number
Stenographers and typewriters	6	Dressmakers, milliners, seamstresses	983
Apprentices	12	Printers	4
Boot and shoe makers	4	Tailoresses	12
Cotton & other textile mill operatives	9	Tobacco and cigar factory operatives	5

In Delaware there were in 1890, according to the census:

MALE

Occupation	Number	Occupation	Number
Barbers and hairdressers	51	Cotton & other textile mill operatives	15
Engineers and firemen (stationary)	27	Iron and steel workers	186
Boatmen, canalmen, pilots and sailors	55	Leather curriers, dressers, tanners	75
Steam railroad employees	88	Machinists	3
Telegraph and telephone operators	1	Marble and stone cutters and masons	37
Apprentices	3	Millers	6
Bakers	1	Painters	6
Blacksmiths and wheelwrights	23	Plumbers	1
Boot and shoe makers	23	Printers	1
Brick makers	146	Saw and planing mill employees	34
Butchers	7	Ship and boat builders	28
Cabinet makers & upholsterers	4	Steam boiler makers	1
Carpenters and joiners	20	Tinners and tinware makers	3
Carriage and wagon makers	1	Wood workers	14

FEMALE.

Occupation	Number	Occupation	Number
Apprentices	2	Dressmakers, milliners, seamstresses, etc	32
Cotton and other textile mill operat'es	2		

Over a third of the total Negro population of Pennsylvania resides in Philadelphia. A detailed history of the Negro artisan in this city has been published.* The chief trades represented are barbers, cigar makers, shoemakers, engineers, masons, printers, painters, upholsterers. There are probably some two thousand Negro artisans in all. Carlisle has a few masons. At Washington there are about 50 Negroes in the tin plate and glass factories. In western Pennsylvania there are numbers of Negro miners and iron and steel workers, but no detailed report has come from this region.

*The Philadelphia Negro, Ginn & Co., 1896. See Chapters IX and XVI.

48. *South Carolina.* There were in this state 688,934 Negroes in 1890, and 782,321 in 1900. The census of 1890 reported these artisans:

MALE

Lumbermen and raftsmen	164	Butchers	274
Miners	715	Carpenters and joiners	2,730
Engineers (civil, mechanical, etc.)	26	Coopers	294
Barbers and hairdressers	380	Cotton & other textile mill operat'es	369
Engineers and firemen (stationary)	344	Machinists	42
Boatmen, canalmen, pilots, sailors	381	Marble and stone cutters	96
Steam railroad employees	3,052	Masons	793
Telegraph and telephone operators	8	Mechanics	58
Apprentices	255	Millers	108
Bakers	123	Painters	482
Blacksmiths and wheelwrights	832	Printers	57
Boot and shoe makers	353	Saw and planing mill employees	452
Brickmakers, potters, etc	286	Tailors	172

FEMALE.

Steam railroad employees	19	Cotton & other textile mill operat'es	22
Apprentices	48	Dressmakers, milliners, seamstresses	2,193
Bakers	7	Tailoresses	21

Charleston with 31,522 Negroes has always had a large number of artisans. Here, at the Vesta Cotton Mill, Negro labor was used in cotton manufacturing. The president of the mill said in 1900: "I cannot say the Negro is a success as a mill operative, lest I deceive somebody, or the statement eventually prove to be untrue. Nor am I willing to say he is a failure." The eventual giving up of the mill and its removal to Georgia was due to many reasons, of which the matter of securing competent help was only one and, it would seem, not altogether the decisive reason. It is thought that the Negro artisan is gaining in Charleston and that many young men are entering the trades. Race prejudice is still a hindrance and there are many lines of work into which a colored man cannot enter. There are 75 or 80 union masons and 12 to 25 non-union. There are several hundred carpenters, and many blacksmiths, painters, wheelwrights and plumbers. There is some discrimination in wages: masons receive $3 for a 9 hours day, and carpenters $1.75 to $2.50 for the same. In Columbia Negroes are employed in a hosiery mill and a report gives 386 skilled workingmen in all in the city. The colored artisans are gaining.*

At Anderson there are 15 carpenters, 10 masons, many blacksmiths, machinists, plumbers, 6 shoemakers, and 10 painters. The Negroes are slowly gaining. At Aiken there are 35 carpenters, 4 contracting masons and 25 journeymen under 30 years of age, 2 tailors, 4 blacksmiths, etc. The Negro is steadily gaining and forms the sole membership of the only local union—the masons. The Negro is reported to be gaining in Greenville where there are 40 carpenters, 50 masons and plasterers, 15 blacksmiths, 15 shoemakers, and 14 painters, besides tinners, plumbers, harness makers and other artisans. There is some color prejudice but young men are entering the trades. "Quite a number of young men are entering the trades and are doing well" at Chester, where again the black artisan is gaining. The leading artisans include 5 masons, 4 painters, 2 tailors, 2 carpenters, and 1 upholsterer. There are no unions here, and the whole

*Report of 3d Hampton Conference, p. 18.

growth has been since the war, as there were practically no artisans here before.*

49. *Tennessee and Arkansas.* There were 430,678 Negroes in Tennessee in 1890, and 480,243 in 1900. The census of 1890 reported the following artisans:

MALE.

Occupation	Number	Occupation	Number
Lumbermen and raftsmen	150	Harness, saddle, trunk makers	13
Miners	769	Iron and steel workers	982
Quarrymen	482	Machinists	66
Barbers and hairdressers	871	Marble and stone cutters	269
Engineers and firemen (stationary)	558	Masons	1,160
Steam railroad employees	4,039	Mechanics	48
Blacksmiths and wheelwrights	1,032	Millers	130
Boot and shoe makers	348	Painters	287
Brick makers	849	Plasterers	324
Butchers	132	Printers	43
Carpenters and joiners	1,361	Saw & planing mill employees	1,040
Coopers	111	Tinners and tinware makers	33
Cotton & other textile mill operatives	201	Wood workers	148

FEMALE.

Occupation	Number	Occupation	Number
Stenographers and typewriters	1	Dressmakers, milliners, seamstresses	915
Telegraph & telephone operators	2	Printers	2
Cotton and other textile mill operatives	48	Tailoresses	3
		Tobacco & cigar factory operatives	124

In Arkansas there were 309,117 Negroes in 1890 and 366,856 in 1900. The census of 1890 reported the following artisans:

MALE.

Occupation	Number	Occupation	Number
Lumbermen and raftsmen	94	Carriage and wagon makers	8
Miners	7	Cotton & other textile mill operatives	83
Engineers (civil, mechanical, etc.)	2	Machinists	31
Barbers and hairdressers	332	Marble & stone cutters and masons	198
Engineers and firemen (stationary)	165	Mechanics	59
Steam railroad employees	1,013	Millers	26
Telegraph and telephone operators	1	Painters	85
Blacksmiths and wheelwrights	364	Plasterers	63
Boot and shoe makers	68	Printers	17
Brickmakers, etc	269	Saw & planing mill employees	1,114
Butchers	64	Tailors	1
Carpenters and joiners	581	Wood workers	28

FEMALE.

Occupation	Number	Occupation	Number
Telegraph and telephone operators	1	Dressmakers, milliners, seamstresses, etc	266
Cotton & other textile mill operatives	5		

Memphis has already been spoken of in §19. "Jonesboro is a very small place and the Negro gets very little to do here." There are a few carpenters and masons who are kept busy. Trade schools would help our boys to learn trades, otherwise almost all of them will be common laborers.† The leading colored artisans of Clarkesville include 2 masons, 2 carpenters, 1 cabinet-maker, 1 engineer, 1 plumber, 2 printers, 1 blacksmith, and 1 cooper. "The Negro is capable of doing any skilled work but has no opportunities to develop his skillfulness." For this and other reasons, "as a rule, the Negro does not learn his trade thoroughly, that is he does not become a master workman." The demand for Negro workmen being thus curtailed there is little incentive for the young men to learn trades. Ne-

*Most of the South Carolina reports were submitted by Mr. W. W. Cooke of Claflin University.

†Report of Mr. P. L. LaCour.

groes "cannot get employment on many large contracts—the whites prefer to hire white artisans, unless they can employ colored workmen at greatly reduced wages."* Twenty years ago the Negroes of Jackson were chiefly railroad brakemen, firemen and common laborers; today the leading artisans include 7 engineers, 6 brickmasons, 5 plasterers, 5 brick-molders, 6 carpenters, 3 blacksmiths, 4 printers, 3 meat-cutters, 1 milliner, 1 upholsterer, 1 painter, 1 candy-maker, and 2 cabinet-makers. While the Negro artisans have increased however they have not kept pace with the growth of the town, and this is due mainly "to discrimination in favor of white workmen and also to the fact that young men have not entered the trades." The chief obstacles before Negroes are "Labor Unions: they do not receive Negroes as apprentices and when Negroes are employed as helpers they prevent them from receiving promotion according to merit."† At Rogersville there are about 12 artisans—4 carpenters, 2 blacksmiths, 1 paper-hanger and painter, 2 masons, 1 engineer, 1 tanner, etc. There are no unions and the black artisan is holding his own. There is little discrimination but the outlook is not encouraging because the young people do not enter and stick to the trades. "The leading merchants of our town were erecting a bank building a short time since. They wanted the work completed in a certain time. They employed colored carpenters to assist. The white carpenters complained. They dismissed them all and employed all colored. . . . .
The colored engineer referred to above stands ahead of all in the town as a plumber and electrician.

"The Negro has the ability to succeed along all industrial lines; what he needs is more faith in himself and in the opportunities before him."‡

In Columbia the Negro artisans seem "to be losing, somewhat." This is due in part to the great industrial advance of the South, in part to prejudice, and in part to the fact that "the young Negro is not patient—will not stick long enough to become master of a trade." The leading colored artisans of the city include 4 carpenters, 1 shoemaker, 2 blacksmiths, 1 wheelwright, 2 stone cutters, and 2 masons.

The Negro is gaining as an artisan in Jefferson City, although there are few artisans there. The leading brick mason "stands high with the white citizens and gets more work than he can do. The very finest jobs are generally offered him in preference to the white masons. He has been working at his trade over twenty years and owns some good property."§ In Nashville there are eight leading Negro contractors—a painter, 4 masons, 3 carpenters; there is also a prominent tailor and a leading blacksmith. "I think the whole number of skilled workmen as compared with the Negro population is less than before the war. Those mentioned above are contractors, own good homes, have other good renting property, and

*Report of Mr. R. L. Yancy.

†Report of Rev. Mr. A. R. Merry.

‡Report of Mr. W. H. Franklin.

§Report of Mr. G. N. Bowen.

are men of force and standing."* In Murfreesboro the Negro artisan "is gaining very fast," and "is in great demand." The leading artisans include 5 shoe makers, 2 masons, 4 blacksmiths, 2 engineers, 3 painters and a number of carpenters. "The young men are entering trades more now than ever" and industrial training is enabling them to take and execute contracts; this latter ability was the deficiency of the older artisans. The general condition of Negro artisans "is much better than in the times before the war, because the demand is greater, and more diversified; this sharpens the appetite for advancement and the artisan now uses his own head instead of working from dictation."† In McMinnville, also, the Negro is "gaining, not by under-bidding, but by prompt attention to business." The leading artisans are 7 masons, 4 blacksmiths, a plasterer and a carpenter. Young men are entering the trades but they are apprentices and do not come from industrial schools. There is no discrimination in wages, and there are no trade unions here. "There are more Negro artisans here now than there have been at any time before in the history of the town. Those here are well situated, owning their own homes—some of the nicest homes in town; they are good and law abiding citizens and are well thought of by both races. This town is the county-seat of Warren county and has a population of about 2,000. Negro artisans build all the bridge-piers in this and adjoining counties."‡

In Maryville the black artisans have suffered "some loss; that is, we have fewer carpenters and blacksmiths now than 20 years ago." This is chiefly due to "the neglect of parents and guardians in not impressing the importance of a knowledge of the industries upon the minds of sons and wards." On the other hand a small town like this does not demand many artisans; there are some ten masons, blacksmiths and carpenters. "Some few young men in a casual way and of necessity are entering the above named trades, but the outlook for wages is bad and our boys seem to prefer doing nothing for nothing."The difficulty with most of the local artisans is that they cannot intelligently plan their work and make specifications. "White men in the same trades use the influence of a white skin to take away trade."

"The Negro artisans of Maryville are chiefly those who learned their trades before the civil war. There are some younger men who were taught by their fathers or by the aforesaid ante-bellum men. There is no union or agreements as to hours of labor or price and every man is guided by his own judgment as to any particular piece of work. There were before the civil war about the same number of artisans as now—mostly slaves. These men now own their own homes, with but two exceptions, and from their trades derive a living, though not much more. Intelligent, up-to-date artisans could have all they could do in this section if only they could go in and assume a contract, giving bond for faithful performance

*Report of Dr. J. A. Lester.

†Report of F. G. Carney.

‡Report of Mr. A. C. Maclin.

of obligations, &c. An industrial training school for Negroes is in course of foundation."*

In Knoxville there are a good many skilled laborers; they "are gaining in the variety of trades followed, but losing when one considers the increase of population here since 1860." The leading artisans include:

Carpenters	15	Stone cutters	2
Blacksmiths	12	Printers	1
Masons	10	Tailors	1
Puddlers	9	Boiler makers	1
Dressmakers	6	Millers	1
Telegraph linemen	5	Carpet makers	1
Shoemakers	5	Contractors	1
Painters	5	Tinners	1
Plumbers	5	Furniture repairers	1
Plasterers	4	Tanners	1
Jewelers	3		

There are also numbers of iron and steel workers.

Young men are entering the trades, "or at least trying to do so," but are hindered partly by prejudice, partly by "inherent vices resulting from the former bondage of the race," and particularly by trade unions which "in but few instances" admit Negroes.† In 1900 "iron workers are being paid more for labor in consequence of the increased demand for iron and the inducements offered to local workingmen at the Carnegie Works in Pittsburg. Quite a large force from Knoxville went there in the early spring. A large iron furnace has been opened up at Bristol, Tenn., employing Negro laborers, and several smaller industries at Harriman, Tenn., employing Negro laborers exclusively."‡

Chattanooga is a center of Negro artisans and they have had an interesting industrial history. Unfortunately, however, it has been very difficult to get hold of detailed information or reports from there. The unions report a number of artisans in the building trades, and in the large establishments there are 382 skilled men reported, chiefly molders and foundry men, with some skilled saw-mill hands:

Molders,	110	Saw mill men,	20
Molders and foundry men,	52	Total,	382
Stove makers,	200		

This is a great increase over anything in the past and has been brought about by a persistent battle with the trade unions in which, so far, the Negroes are victorious.

Few detailed reports have been received from Arkansas. The state has considerable numbers of barbers, blacksmiths, brickmakers, carpenters, and masons, and many semi-skilled workmen on the railroads and in the lumber yards.

In Little Rock there are very many Negro artisans and they are "gaining all the time here." The artisans are "not from trade schools but have been apprenticed as a rule." The leading artisans include 6 carpenters, 2 masons and a blacksmith. There are, of course, many others. Their

*Report of Mr. George R. Brabham, who is the founder of the proposed school.

†Report of Mr. J. W. Manning.

‡Report of Mr. C. W. Cansler to Mr. A. F. Hilyer.

greatest obstacle is "want of capital to overcome prejudice." They can join some of the trade unions. "There were few artisans here until recent times, but now the number increases yearly."*

50. *Texas and the Southwest*, (*Tex., Ariz., N. Mex., and Nev.*) Texas had, in 1890, 488,171 Negroes and 620,722 in 1900. The census of 1890 reported the following artisans:

MALE.

Lumbermen and raftsmen,	268	Carpenters and joiners,	917
Miners,	197	Cotton and other textile mill operatives,	330
Engineers (civil, mechanical, etc.)	6	Harness, saddle, trunk makers,	7
Barbers and hairdressers,	816	Machinists,	41
Engineers and firemen (stationary),	212	Marble & stone cutters & masons,	298
Boatmen, canalmen, pilots, sailors,	45	Millers,	34
Steam railroad employees,	2,658	Painters,	133
Telegraph and telephone operators,	4	Printers,	22
Blacksmiths & wheelwrights,	537	Saw & planing mill employees,	1,881
Boot and shoe makers,	85	Tailors,	20
Brick makers,	466	Tinners and tinware makers,	19
Butchers,	174		

FEMALE.

Telegraph and telephone operators,	4	Dressmakers, milliners, seamstresses, etc.,	425
Cotton & other textile mill operatives,	9		

Arizona, New Mexico and Nevada had in all 2,786 Negroes in 1890, and 2,416 in 1900. There were reported the following artisans, including Negroes, Chinese, and Indians:

MALE.

Lumbermen and raftsmen,	45	Butchers,	12
Miners,	520	Cabinet makers & upholsterers,	9
Barbers and hairdressers,	89	Carpenters and joiners,	17
Steam railroad employees.	251	Cotton & other textile mill operatives,	6
Telegraph & telephone operatives,	1	Marble and stone cutters & masons,	10
Blacksmiths,	12	Printers,	4
Brickmakers,	15	Saw and planing mill employees,	72
Boot and shoe makers,	14	Tailors,	6

FEMALE.

Dressmakers, milliners, seamstresses, etc. 15

Texas has already been treated to considerable length in Mr. Holmes' report (§ 20). There are not many artisans in Dallas and they are losing on account of inefficiency. The city directory gives 20 carpenters, 5 blacksmiths, 4 painters, 4 printers, 3 masons, 2 engravers, 2 plasterers, a roofer, a contractor and builder, a shoe maker, a tailor, a furniture maker and a machinist. Young men are not entering the trades. The artisans "do not contract for very large jobs; they work mostly for colored people and on small jobs for whites. During and before the war most of the skilled labor was done by colored artisans."† In Navasota the number of skilled laborers is not large but "it is my opinion that the Negro is gaining constantly. . . . . . Prejudice and trade unions are the barriers that usually obstruct his path as a mechanic. There are few instances in which colored men are permitted to join the trade unions at all. They are generally barred from this privilege entirely. Sometimes discrimination in wages occurs; colored men possessing skill equal to white men, and work-

*Report of Mr. W. McIntosh.

†Report of Mr. Charles Rice.

ing with them on the same building, have, in some cases, been paid smaller wages than the whites." There are in this town 4 Negro blacksmiths, 5 carpenters, 2 painters, a wheelwright, a mason and a jeweler. "These men are doing well in their trades and securing considerable paying work both from white and colored people."*

In Georgetown also the Negroes are gaining and are at work as carpenters, blacksmiths, masons and barbers. In Ennis they are "standing still." They are barred from the unions and discriminated against in wages. In Richmond the Negro is gaining in the trades but is barred by the unions. In Bryan he is losing because of lack of properly trained men.

51. *Virginia and West Virginia.* Virginia had 635,438 Negroes in 1890, and 660,722 in 1900. The census of 1890 gave the following Negro artisans:

MALE.

Lumbermen, raftsmen, etc.,	1,091	Carpenters and joiners,	2,017
Miners,	1,700	Coopers,	403
Quarrymen,	577	Cotton & other textile mill operatives,	462
Engineers (civil and mechanical),	16	Iron and steel workers,	793
Barbers and hairdressers,	835	Machinists,	61
Engineers and firemen (stationary),	521	Marble and stone cutters,	168
Boatmen, canalmen, pilots, sailors,	812	Masons,	745
Steam railroad employees,	7,648	Millers,	212
Telegraph & telephone operators,	7	Painters,	206
Apprentices,	186	Plasterers,	524
Blacksmiths and wheelwrights,	1,554	Printers,	44
Boot and shoe makers,	849	Saw & planing mill employees,	2,541
Brickmakers, potters, etc.,	1,213	Tinners and tinware makers,	39
Butchers,	231	Tobacco & cigar factory operatives,	4,419

FEMALE.

Basket makers,	1	Printers,	6
Cotton and other textile mill operatives,	187	Tailoresses,	30
Dressmakers, seamstresses, milliners, etc.,	1,412	Tobacco and cigar factory operatives,	2,572

West Virginia had, in 1890, 32,690 Negroes, and in 1900, 43,499. The census of 1890 reported the following artisans:

MALE.

Lumbermen, raftsmen, etc,	10	Charcoal, coke and lime burners,	336
Miners,	2,016	Coopers,	20
Engineers (civil & mechanical),	3	Glass workers,	1
Barbers and hairdressers,	220	Iron and steel workers,	13
Engineers and firemen (stationary),	36	Leather curriers, dressers, tanners,	57
Boatmen, canalmen, pilots, sailors,	22	Machinists,	2
Steam railroad employees,	1,401	Marble and stone cutters,	16
Telegraph and telephone operators,	6	Masons,	60
Apprentices,	5	Millers,	4
Blacksmiths and wheelwrights,	97	Painters,	20
Boot and shoe makers,	39	Printers,	5
Brick and tile makers,	22	Saw and planing mill employees,	21
Butchers,	7	Tailors,	2
Carpenters and joiners,	51	Tobacco and cigar factory operatives,	2

FEMALE.

Cotton and other textile mill operatives,	1	Dressmakers, milliners, seamstresses,	37
		Tailoresses,	2

*Report of Mr. R. P. Neal.

Richmond is a great center for Negro skilled labor. The Third Hampton Conference reported.* "The colored people of Richmond are employed principally in all branches of the tobacco business, with the exception of cigarette making, cigar making and cheroot rolling. About 8,000 men, women and children are employed in the factories; of this number about 2,000 might be classed as skilled laborers. Perhaps 2,000 more are employed in the iron works." The census of 1890 reported 1,345 tobacco workers, 293 skilled iron and steel workers, besides 139 blacksmiths, 123 shoe makers, 150 carpenters and 165 plasterers. The Allen & Ginter branch of the American Tobacco Co. employ 18 tobacco packers and porters at an average weekly wage of $6.53 and 208 stemmers and machine hands at $4.09. The T. C. Williams Company employ Negro labor almost exclusively; "our experience with this labor has been very satisfactory." The P. Whitlock branch of the American Tobacco Co. have these Negro employees:

167 leaf tobacco	strippers,	$3.50–$4.00	per week.
42 " "	bookers,	5.00	" "
22 helpers,		5.00	" "

"We have been working Negroes in the above capacities for a number of years, having found them very efficient in this class of work." The Richmond Stemmery of the American Tobacco Co. employs 1,000 Negroes at an average of $4.50. "For the class of work for which we employ them there is no other help in the world so good." The Continental Tobacco Co. employs "at times from six to seven hundred Negro employees and we consider this class of labor quite satisfactory."† The Hampton conference thought the skilled Negro laborer losing in this city but a report of 1902 says: "I think he is gaining on the whole, inasmuch as his skilled labor is of a higher order. They are to-day doing some of the high grade work in this city." As to efficiency the report says: "Colored workmen, as a rule, are not efficient here. The exclusion from labor organizations, the general unwillingness of white workmen to work with Negroes, and the consequent loss of hope of employment furnishes the explanation of slow progress." Industrial training "is doing something for the race, but the many skilled laborers of Richmond received their trades by the old method of apprenticeship. The fact is the industrial school is yet an experiment." Many young men are entering the trades. There is discrimination in wages "but this is the price Negroes pay if they get any employment at all from some employers." Nearly all the unions exclude Negroes, but they have unions of their own in the tobacco industry and among longshoremen. "During the last 20 years the number of shoe makers, blacksmiths, carpenters and plasterers have increased. . . . . Many of these artisans have more work than they can do."‡ The directory for 1902 gives the following Negro artisans:

Carpenters,	59	Printers,	9
Blacksmiths,	55	Iron workers,	13
Plasterers.	63	Upholsterers,	5

*In July 1899; printed report, page 19.

†From personal letters to Mr. A. F. Hilyer, 1900.

‡Report of Mr. J. R. L. Diggs.

Shoe makers,	84	Painters,	11
Dressmakers,	24	Candy makers,	5
Coopers,	25	Bakers,	9
Millers,	1	Umbrella maker,	1
Glazier,	1	Dyers,	4
Masons,	18	Plumbers,	2
Engineers,	4	Regalia maker,	1
Butchers,	14	Cabinet makers,	2
Pavers,	2	Broom makers,	5
Photographers,	6	Contractors,	4
Decorators,	2	Tinner,	1
Cigar makers,	1	Wheelwright,	1
Tailors,	9	Machinist,	1
Carriage makers,	1		

There are manifest omissions in this list—as in the case of iron workers, carpenters, etc—but it illustrates the diversity of trades.

At Danville the Negro artisan is said to be gaining in spite of the fact that "very few young men are entering the trades; the most of them want to be dudes." There are 19 masons, 21 blacksmiths, 11 plasterers and 4 painters. There is some discrimination in wages and most of the unions are closed to Negroes.

Some interesting news came from Lynchburg in 1900:

"The bricklayers especially are experiencing a decided improvement in their work. Several years ago colored bricklayers were excluded entirely from all work on the principal streets of the city, and their opportunities generally to follow their trade were very limited in this community.

"A change has gradually taken place in the last year or two which has brought them well to the front. No colored mechanic was employed to lay pressed brick in this city several years ago. He was thought to be utterly incapable to do high grade work of that kind. But now colored bricklayers are seen constructing churches and business houses on the principal streets of the city, requiring the best skilled labor necessary to do such work. The first Presbyterian church (white) constructed in this city recently at a cost of $35,000 of pressed brick was started by white mechanics. After they had carried the walls up some distance, they struck for more wages. The contractor, who was white, declined to make any advance. The white mechanics quit. Colored mechanics were employed and they finished the brick work. It may be said that they built the church. It is one of the handsomest church structures in this city or section.

"One of the largest as well as most difficult buildings ever constructed in this locality is the addition made to the cotton mill here within the last year. It was built by Negroes and the great difficulty of putting the machinery in place was all supervised by a colored mechanic with entire satisfaction to all concerned.

"In asking this very efficient mechanic a few days ago about the outlook, he remarked the situation is growing brighter every day. It is simply a question of *capacity* and *reliability*. Said he to me, 'I am about to be offered the largest job I ever had to build one of the largest structures in the state.'

"The colored mechanics have been asked to join the white trades union with the distinct understanding that the white mechanics would not work with them. This request was declined with thanks.

"The lesson of the year in this city is, that colored mechanics ought to fit themselves thoroughly to do the highest grade of work in their line, so that when white mechanics strike they may be able to take their places without causing the work to suffer in the least."†

†Report of Mr. Geo. E. Stephens.

In Manchester the Negro mechanic appears to be losing. There are among the leading artisans 1 dyer, 7 shoemakers. 7 blacksmiths, 2 engineers, 5 plasterers, 2 painters, a carpenter, a printer and a tinner. The unwillingness of young men to enter the trades and the opposition of trades unions are the chief hindrances. There is some discrimination in wages but not as much as in some places. "Frequently white and colored artisans work on the same job."* Newport News has about 100 skilled Negro workmen and the Shipbuilding and Dry Dock Company are receiving Negro mechanics and apprentices. They are not admitted to the unions. Norfolk has "many competent and reliable colored mechanics."†

In West Virginia a report of 1900 says:‡

"There are about 8,000 or 10,000 colored miners in the Flat-top coal fields and about the same number of white miners.

"These colored miners are admitted on the same terms with white miners to the United Order of Mine Workers. About half of the firemen on the Pocahontas division are colored, half the trainmen, and 90% of the yard men. There is a gang of 20 colored men who do common labor about the round house.

"None but the miners are admitted to the labor unions. While the other colored men get the same as white men for like work in the divisions mentioned, they are debarred from the unions because they are colored, and are plainly told so."

At Bluefield the artisans are gaining; there are a number of railway firemen, masons and blacksmiths. Trade unions are a hindrance to Negro workmen and the lack of responsible contractors able to give bonds.

"There were not more than 600 Negroes in this section previous to the war and but two skilled laborers. Immediately after the war both these left the section, leaving the section without any until 1883-85, when Negroes having various trades came, brought by the opening of the coal mines of this region, in which several thousand Negroes find employment to-day. In the building of this town Negroes were employed equally with the whites and entrusted with the same kind of work, being made foremen on buildings or given the more finished parts of the work to do. I have been assured by their employers that they gave satisfaction."§

At Parkersburg the black artisan is gaining but there are not many mechanics there.

52. *Summary of Local Conditions.* The statistics given are far from complete and of varying value; the opinions reflect different personalities and different opportunities of knowing. On the whole, however, there is evident throughout the nation a period of change among colored artisans. For many years after the war the Negro became less and less important as an artisan than before the conflict. In some communities this retrogression still continues. It is due in part to loss of skill but primarily to the great industrial advancement of the South. In many communities this industrial revolution has awakened and inspired the black man; he has entered into the competition, the young men are beginning to turn their at-

*Report of Rev. D. Webster Davis.

†Report of 3rd Hampton Conference, p. 19.

‡From Mr. Hamilton Hatter.

§Report of Mr. R. R. Sims.

tention toward trades and the economic emancipation of the Negro seems approaching in these particular communities. In the light of these two counter movements it is interesting to compare communities by tabulating the cases where the artisans are reported as gaining or losing. We must, of course, remember that such reports are based on opinions and that the personal equation must be largely allowed for:*

NEGRO ARTISANS REPORTED TO BE "GAINING" IN NUMBER AND EFFICIENCY.

State	Town	Total Pop.	Negro Pop.	Remarks
Ala.	Anniston.	9,695	3,669	
	Birmingham.	38,415	16,575	
	Montgomery.	30,346	17,229	Absolutely if not relatively.
	Tuskegee.	2,170		
Ark.	Little Rock.	38,307	14,694	"All the time."
D. C.	Washington.	278,718	86,702	
Fla.	Jacksonville.	28,429	16,236	
Ga.	Atlanta.	89,872	35,727	
	Marshallville.	879		
	Milledgeville.	4,219	2,063	
	Washington.	3,300	2,163	
Ill.	Chicago.	1,698,575	30,150	"Slowly."
Ind.	Indianapolis.	169,164	15,931	
	Mt. Vernon.	5,132	892	
I. T.	Ardmore.	5,681	1,158	
Kan.	Atchison.	15,722	2,508	
Ky.	Danville.	4,285	1,913	
	Georgetown.	3,823	1,677	"I think."
	Paducah.	19,446	5,814	
La.	Baton Rouge.	11,269	6,596	
	New Orleans.	287,104	77,714	"At least holding his own."
Miss.	Ebenezer.	170		"May be."
	Gloster.	1,661		"Not satisfactorily."
	Grace.			
	Holly Springs.	2,815	1,559	
	Mound Bayou.	287	287	"Assuredly."
	Woodville.	1,043		
Mo.	Jefferson City.	9,664	1,822	
	St. Joseph.	102,979	6,269	"Slightly."
Pa.	Carlisle.	9,626	1,148	
	Pittsburg.	321,616	17,040	
S. C.	Charleston.	55,807	31,522	
	Columbia.	21,108	9,858	
Tenn.	Chattanooga.	1,980		
	Knoxville.	3,909	2,248	Absolutely not relatively.
	McMinnville.	30,154	13,122	"Very fast."
	Murfreesboro.	32,637	7,359	
Tex.	Georgetown.	2,790	608	
	Houston.	44,633	14,608	
	Navasota.	3,857	2,105	"Constantly."
	Richmond.			
Va.	Danville.	16,520	6,515	
	Newport News.	19,635	6,798	
	Richmond.	85,050	32,230	
W. Va.	Bluefield.	4,644	754	
	Parkersburg.	11,703	783	

*The population given is for 1900.

NEGRO ARTISANS REPORTED TO BE "LOSING" IN NUMBERS OR EFFICIENCY.

State	Town	Total Pop.	Negro Pop.	Remarks
Ga.	Albany.	4,606	2,903	
	Greensboro.	1,511		
Ky.	Lebanon Junction.	509		
Miss.	Westside.			"Beginning to do better."
Md.	Baltimore.	508,957	72,258	
Mo.	Commerce.	588		
	St. Louis.	575,238	35,516	
N. Y.	Troy and Albany.	154,802	1,578	? (contradicted).
N. C.	Charlotte.	18,091	7,151	Relatively to growth.
	Raleigh.	13,646	5,721	
	Salisbury.	6,277	2,408	"On the whole."
O.	Oberlin.	4,082	641	
	Xenia.	8,696	1,988	
	Cincinnati.	325,902	14,482	
Tenn.	Columbia.	6,052	2,716	Somewhat.
	Jackson.	14,511	6,108	Proportionately.
	Maryville.			
	Memphis.	102,320	49,910	
	Nashville.	80,865	30,044	"I think."
Tex.	Bryan.	3,589	1,515	
	Dallas.	42,638	9,035	
Va.	Manchester.	9,715	3,338	

NEGRO ARTISANS REPORTED TO BE "HOLDING THEIR OWN" AND NEITHER GAINING NOR LOSING.

State	Town	Total Pop.	Negro Pop.	Remarks
Fla.	Pensacola.	17,747	8,561	
	St. Augustine.	4,272	1,735	
	Tampa.	15,839	4,382	
Ga.	Savannah.	54,244	28,090	
	Augusta.	39,441	18,487	Relatively, not absolutely.
Ky.	Louisville.	204,731	39,139	
Mass.	Boston.	560,892	11,591	
N. Y.	New York.	3,437,202	60,666	
N. C.	Goldsboro.	5,877	2,520	
Pa.	Philadelphia.	1,293,697	62,613	
Tenn.	Jonesboro.	854		
	Rogersville.	1,386		
Tex.	Ennis.	4,919	1,057	"Standing still."

In the villages and smaller towns of the South where there has been some industrial awakening the Negro artisan has advanced; in others he is standing still or losing his place in the trades; in the larger Southern cities he has in some cases gained, in others lost. Much of this loss, however, is apparent and relative rather than absolute: when, for instance, Augusta, Ga., was a small town the Negroes did all the skilled work; now that it is a growing manufacturing centre the Negroes do only a part of the skilled work; nevertheless there are probably more skilled Negro artisans in Augusta today than formerly, and they are following more diversified trades. This view is further borne out by the fact that a count of the Negro artisan ten or twenty years since by the defective, but nevertheless valuable testimony of the directories, proves in most cases that there is a larger number of artisans now than formerly. There is good ground for assuming that in many cities like St. Louis, Mo., Charlotte, N. C., Baltimore, Md., and Nashville, Tenn., relative retrogression on the part of the Negro artisan compared with the growth of the community, is nevertheless absolute advance in numbers and skill so far as the Negro is concerned. This is not true in all cases but it certainly is in many. In the great Northern centres of industry, on the other hand, the Negro had no foothold in the past and is gaining none at present save in some western communities. His great hindrance here, as at the South, is lack of skill and general training, but outside of that it is manifest that the black mechanic is meeting strong resistance on the part of organized labor; that in both South and North the trade union opposes black labor wherever it can and admits it to fellowship only as a last resort.

53. *The Negro and Organized Labor.* It would be interesting to know if Crispus Attucks, the Negro who fell as the first martyr in the Revolution, was a member of that roistering band of rope walk hands whose rashness precipitated the Boston Massacre. If so, then the Negro's connection with organized labor, like his connection with all other movements in the history of the nation, dates back to early times. There appeared, too, in early times that same opposition to Negro workingmen with which we are so familiar today.* This opposition came chiefly from the border states where the free Negro mechanics came in contact with white mechanics. On the other hand in the actual organizations of workingmen which began in the North nothing is usually heard of the Negro problem except as the labor movement avowedly made common cause with the abolition movement. The Evans brothers, who came from England as labor agitators about 1825, put among their twelve demands: "10th. Abolition of chattel slavery and of wages slavery."† From 1840 to 1850 labor reformers were, in many cases, earnest abolitionists; as one of them said in 1847:

"In my opinion the great question of labor, when it shall come up, will be found paramount to all others, and the operatives of New England, peasant of Ireland and laborers of South America will not be lost sight of in sympathy for the Southern slave."‡

"Indeed, the anti-slavery agitation and the organization of the mechanics of the United States kept pace with each other; both were revolutionary in their character and although the agitators differed in methods, the ends in view were the same, viz. the freedom of the man who worked."||

Along with this movement went many labor disturbances which had economic causes, especially the series of riots in Philadelphia from 1829 until after the war, when the Negroes suffered greatly at the hands of white workingmen."§ The civil war with its attendant evils bore heavily on the laboring classes, and led to wide-spread agitation and various attempts at organization.

"In New York City, especially, the draft was felt to be unjust by laborers because the wealthy could buy exemption for $300. A feeling of disloyalty to union and bitter-

*Cf. pp. 15, 16.

†Ely; labor movement, p. 42.

‡McNeill: Labor movement, pp. 111, 113.

||Powderly: Thirty years of labor, p. 51.

§The Philadelphia Negro, ch. IV.

ness toward the Negro arose. A meeting was called in Tammany Hall and Greeley addressed them. Longshoremen and railroad employees struck at times and assaulted non-unionists. In New York Negroes took the places of longshoremen and were assaulted."*

The struggle culminated in the three days' riot which became a sort of local war of extermination against Negroes.

There had been before the war a number of trade unions—the Caulkers of Boston (1724), the Ship-wrights of New York (1803), the Carpenters of New York (1806), the New York Typographical Society (1817), and others. There had also been attempts to unite trades and workingmen in general organizations as the Workingmen's Convention (1830), in New York, the General Trades Union of New York City, (1833 or earlier), the National Trades Union (1835) and others. In all these movements the Negro had practically no part and was either tacitly or in plain words excluded from all participation. The trade unions next began to expand from local to national bodies. The journeymen printers met in 1850 and formed a national union in 1852; the iron molders united in 1859, the machinists the same year, and the iron workers the year before. During and soon after the war the railway unions began to form and the cigar makers and masons formed their organizations; nearly all of these excluded the Negro from membership.

After the war attempts to unite all workingmen and to federate the trade unions were renewed and following the influence of the Emancipation Proclamation a more liberal tone was adopted toward black men. On Aug. 19, 1866, the National Labor Union said in its declaration:

"In this hour of the dark distress of labor, we call upon all laborers of what ever nationality, creed or color, skilled or unskilled, trades unionist and those now out of union to join hands with us and each other to the end that poverty and all its attendant evils shall be abolished forever."†

On Aug. 19, 1867, the National Labor Congress met at Chicago, Illinois. There were present 200 delegates from the states of North Carolina, Kentucky, Maryland and Missouri. The president, Z. C. Whatley, in his report said among other things:

"The emancipation of the slaves has placed us in a new position, and the question now arises, What labor position shall they now occupy? They will begin to learn and to think for themselves, and they will soon resort to mechanical pursuits and thus come in contact with white labor. It is necessary that they should not undermine it, therefore the best thing that they can do is to form trades unions, and thus work in harmony with the whites."‡

It was not, however, until the organization of the Knights of Labor that workingmen began effective co-operation. The Knights of Labor was founded in Philadelphia in 1869 and held its first national convention in 1876. It was for a long time a secret organization, but it is said that from the first it recognized no distinctions of "race, creed or color."‖

---

*McNeill, p. 126.
†McNeill, p. 162.
‡McNeill, p. 136.
‖Powderly, p. 429.

Nevertheless admission must in all cases be subject to a vote of the local assembly where the candidate applied, and at first it required but three black balls to reject an applicant. This must have kept Northern Negroes out pretty effectively in most cases. On the other hand the shadow of black competition began to loom in the horizon. Most people expected it very soon and the Negro exodus of 1879 gave widespread alarm to labor leaders in the North. Evidence of labor movements in the South too gradually appeared and in 1880 the Negroes of New Orleans struck for a dollar a day but were suppressed by the militia.

Such considerations led many trade unions, notably the iron and steel workers and the cigar makers, early in the eighties, to remove "white" from their membership restrictions and leave admittance open to Negroes at least in theory. The Knights of Labor also began proselyting in the South and by 1885 were able to report from Virginia:

"The Negroes are with us heart and soul, and have organized seven assemblies in this city (Richmond) and one in Manchester with a large membership."*

So, too, the Brotherhood of Carpenters and Joiners said about 1886 that they had Negro unions as far South as New Orleans and Galveston:

"In the Southern States the colored men working at the trades have taken hold of the organization with avidity, and the result is the Brotherhood embraces 14 unions of colored carpenters in the South."†

Even the anarchists of this time (1883) declared for "equal rights for all without distinction to sex or race."‡ By 1886, the year "of the great uprising of labor," the labor leaders declared that "the color line had been broken, and black and white were found working together in the same cause."‖ That very year, however, at the Richmond meeting of the Knights of Labor, ominous clouds arose along the color line. District Assembly 49 of New York had brought along a Negro delegate, Mr. F. J. Ferrell, and he was the source of much trouble in the matter of hotels and theatres and in a question of introducing to the convention Governor Fitzhugh Lee. Mr. Powderly had to appeal to the chief of police for protection, the press of the nation was aroused and the Grand Master Workman issued a defense of his position in the Richmond *Dispatch*:

"You stand face to face with a stern living reality—a responsibility which cannot be avoided or shirked. The Negro question is as prominent today as it ever was. The first proposition that stares us in the face is this: The Negro is free; he is here and he is here to stay. He is a citizen and must learn to manage his own affairs. His labor and that of the white man will be thrown upon the market side by side, and no human eye can detect a difference between the article manufactured by the black mechanics and that manufactured by the white mechanics. Both claim an equal share of the protection afforded to American labor, and both mechanics must sink their differences or fall a prey to the slave labor now being imported to this country. * * *

"Will it be explained to me whether the black man should continue to work for starvation wages? With so many able-bodied colored men in the South who do not

---

*Ely, p. 83.

†McNeill, p. 171.

‡Manifesto o International Working People's Association, anarchists blacks: Powderly, p.693.

‖McNeill, p. 360.

know enough to ask for living wages it is not hard to guess that while this race continues to increase in number and ignorance, prosperity will not even knock at the door, much less enter the home of the Southern laborer." * * * * * *

"In the field of labor and American citizenship we recognize no line of race, creed, politics or color."*

This was high ground for a labor leader to take—too high, in fact, for the constituency he led, since the history of the labor movement from 1886 to 1902, so far as the Negro is concerned, has been a gradual receding from the righteous declarations of earlier years.

The Knights of Labor, after a brilliant career, having probably at one time over half a million members, began to decline owing to internal dissentions and today have perhaps 50,000-100,000 members.† Coincident with the decline of the Knights of Labor came a larger and more successful movement—the American Federation of Labor which has now nearly a million members. This organization was started in 1881 at a meeting of disaffected members of the Knights of Labor and others. From the beginning this movement represented the particularistic trade union idea as against the all inclusive centralizing tendencies of the Knights. And although the central administration has grown in power and influence in recent years, it is still primarily a federation of mutually independent and autonomous trade-unions, among which it strives to foster co-operation and mutual peace. The declared policy of such a body on the race question is of less importance than in the case of the Knights of Labor, since it is more in the nature of advice than law to the different unions. The attitude of the Federation has been summed up as follows:

"It has always been regarded as one of the cardinal principles of the Federation that 'the working people must unite and organize, irrespective of creed, color, sex, nationality or politics.' The Federation formerly refused to admit any union which, in its written constitution, excluded Negroes from membership. It was this that kept out the International Association of Machinists for several years, till it eliminated the word 'white' from its qualifications for membership.‡ It was said at one time that the color line was the chief obstacle in an affiliation of the Brotherhood of Locomotive Firemen with the Federation. The Federation seems, however, to have modified the strictness of the rule. The Railroad Telegraphers and Trackmen have both been welcomed and both restrict their membership to whites.

"In a considerable degree the color line has been actually wiped out in the affiliated organizations. Great Unions controlled by Northern men have insisted in Southern cities on absolute social equality for their colored members. Many local unions receive whites and blacks on equal terms. Where the number of Negroes is large, however, national unions usually organize their white and their colored members into separate locals. In 1898 the Atlanta Federation of Trades declined to enter the peace jubilee parade because colored delegates were excluded.

"The convention of 1897 adopted a resolution condemning a reported statement of Booker T. Washington that the trades unions were placing obstacles in the way of

---

*A Richmond lady wrote inviting Mr. Powderly to replace her black coachman "as you are so much in sympathy with the Negro."

Powderly, pp. 651-62.

Public Opinion, II p. 1.

†Report of Industrial Commission, Vol. XVII, p. XIX.

‡As a matter of fact it practically excludes Negroes still.

the material advancement of the Negro, and reaffirming the declaration of the Federation that it welcomes to its ranks all labor without regard to creed, color, sex, race or nationality. One delegate from the South declared, however, that the white people of the South would not submit to the employment of the Negro in the mills, and that the federal labor union of which he was a member did not admit Negroes. President Gompers said that a union affiliated with the Federation had no right to debar the Negro from membership.

"With increasing experience in the effort to organize the wage earners of the South, the leaders have become convinced that for local purposes separate organizations of the colored people must be permitted. President Gompers said in his report to the convention of 1900, that here and there a local had refused to accept membership on account of color. In such cases where there were enough colored workers in one calling, an effort had been made to form a separate colored union, and a trades council composed of representatives of the colored and the white. This had generally been acquiesced in. In some parts of the South, however, a more serious difficulty had arisen. Central bodies chartered by the Federation had refused to receive delegates from local unions of Negroes. The Federation had not been able to insist that they be received, because such insistence would have meant the disruption of the central bodies. President Gompers suggested that separate central bodies composed of Negroes be established where it might seem practicable and necessary. The convention accordingly amended the constitution to permit the executive council to charter central labor unions, as well as local trade and federal unions, composed exclusively of colored members."*

The attitude of the American Federation of Labor may be summed up as having passed through the following stages:

1. "*The working people must unite and organize irrespective of creed, color, sex, nationality or politics.*"

This was an early declaration but was not embodied in the constitution. It was reaffirmed in 1897, after opposition. Bodies confining membership to whites were barred from affiliation.

2. "*Separate charters may be issued to Central Labor Unions, Local Unions or Federal Labor Unions composed exclusively of colored members.*"

This was adopted by the convention of 1902 and recognizes the legality of excluding Negroes from local unions, city central labor bodies, &c.

3. *A National Union which excludes Negroes expressly by constitutional provision may affiliate with the A. F. L.*

No official announcement of this change of policy has been made, but the fact is well known in the case of the Railway Trackmen, Telegraphers, and others.

4. *A National Union already affiliated with the A. F. L. may amend its laws so as to exclude Negroes.*

This was done by the Stationary Engineers† at their Boston convention in 1902, and an (unsuccessful ?) attempt in the same line was made by the Molders at their convention the same year. The A. F. L. has taken no public action in these cases.‡

*Report of Edgerton & Durand in Report of Industrial Commission, Vol. 17, pp. 36-7.

†"The Stationary Engineers are organized under the International Union of Steam Engineers." Frank Morrison, Sec. A. F. L., Dec. 22, 1902. The Steam Engineers are affiliated with the A.F.L.

‡The above statement has been submitted to the President of the American Federation of Labor for criticism. Up to the time of printing this page no reply has been received. If one is received later it will be printed as an appendix.

This is a record of struggle to maintain high and just ideals and of retrogression; the broader minded labor leaders, like Samuel Gompers, have had to contend with narrow prejudice and selfish greed; it is a struggle parallel with that of the Negro for political and civil rights, and just as black Americans in the struggle upward have met temporary defeat in their aspirations for civil and political rights so, too, they have met rebuff in their search for economic freedom. At the same time there are today probably a larger number of effective Negro members in the trade unions than ever before, there is evidence of renewed inspiration toward mechanical trades and a better comprehension of the labor movement. On the other hand the industrial upbuilding of the South has brought to the front a number of white mechanics, who from birth have regarded Negroes as inferiors and can with the greatest difficulty be brought to regard them as brothers in this battle for better conditions of labor. Such are the forces now arrayed in silent conflict.

If we carefully examine the various trade unions now in existence, we may roughly divide them as follows:

1. Those with a considerable Negro membership.
2. Those with few Negro members.
3. Those with no Negro members.

The first two of these classes may be divided into those who receive Negroes freely, those to whom Negroes never apply, and those who receive Negro workmen only after pressure.

54. *Unions with a Considerable Negro Membership.** These unions are as follows:

Trade Unions	Negro Membership 1890	Negro Membership 1900	Total Membership 1901
Journeymen Barbers' International Union	200	800	8,672
International Brick, Tile and Terra-Cotta Workers' Alliance.	50	200	1,500
International Broom-makers' Union.			380
United Brotherhood of Carpenters and Joiners		1,000	20,000
Carriage and Wagon Workers' International Union.	240	500	2,025
Cigar-makers' International Union.			33,954
Coopers' International Union.		200	4,481
International Brotherhood of Stationary Firemen.	0	2,700	3,600
International Longshoremen's Association.	1,500	6,000	20,000
United Mine Workers of America.		20,000	224,000
Brotherhood of Painters, Decorators and Paper-hangers of America.	33	169	28,000
International Seamen's Union.			8,161
Tobacco Workers' International Union.	1,500	1,000	6,170
Brotherhood of Operative Plasterers.			7,000
Bricklayers' and Masons' Union.			39,000

These unions represent the trades in which the Negro on emerging from slavery possessed the most skill, i. e., the building trades, work in tobacco, and work requiring muscle and endurance. Most of these unions deny any

*The figures as to Negro membership are reported to us by the unions. The figures as to total membership are minimum estimates made by the A. F. L. and based on actual fees paid. See Report of Industrial Commission.

color-discrimination, although the secretary of the carpenters merely says, "None that I know of;" the carriage and wagon workers: "None that has been reported;" the coopers: "If any, it was many years ago;" and the painters' secretary: "I do not know." The carpenters and coopers both admit that local unions could refuse to receive Negroes, and the carpenters and plasterers are not certain that the travelling card of a Negro union man would be recognized by all local unions.

The following note in the barbers' official journal throws light on the situation in that craft:

"At a previous convention of our International Union a resolution was passed, calling upon our General Organizer to make a special effort to organize our colored craftsmen in the South. To-day we have, at a fair estimate, about eight or nine hundred colored members. My experience with them, both as General Secretary-Treasurer and President of a local, has shown that when they become members they at once become earnest and faithful workers. I find, however, that during the past term an unusual amount of friction has taken place in the South and that some of our white members, who still have the southern objection to a colored man, have sought to bring about class division. It is, of course, known to all of us, that the labor movement does not recognize class, creed, or color; that the black man with a white heart and a true trade union spirit is just as acceptable to us as a white member. Hundreds of letters have reached me asking if the colored man could not be kept out of the union. In every case I have answered that if he is a competent barber our laws say that he must be accepted. If below the so-called Mason and Dixon line where the color line is still drawn, they have the right to form them into separate unions, if above that line they can join any local.

"A question of the color line, and one which must be acted on in some way by this convention, is the trouble now existing in Little Rock, Ark. Bro. Pinard was in that city in February of last year and organized a union of colored craftsmen. No white union could be formed as they would not attend a meeting. In October following, however, a white union was formed. From that time on there has been trouble. The whites want to control the situation and want our colored local to adopt their laws. The colored local, however, was organized first and refused. This has brought on a heated correspondence and when the photo of delegates was asked for, the delegate from the white union stated distinctly that his photo must not appear near any colored man, as he was a white man and must not be placed near any burly Negro. In a number of places he refers to them as black demons. I know nothing definite as to their trouble, as it is a question of law and as such comes under the jurisdiction of the General President, but I felt that as No. 197 is a union in good standing in the International they were entitled to protection."

The trouble is not confined to the South; in Northern cities barbers are sometimes refused admittance into unions, and one secretary in Pennsylvania writes:

"We have to recognize them to hold our prices and short hours, but we find it very hard to get along with them."

The Negro membership seems, however, to be increasing rapidly and members are reported in nearly every state.

The secretary of the brick-makers writes:

"We have had a number of strikes where the colored man was imported to take the place of any man, therefore, there is more or less prejudice against them but we hope that will be removed in time."

They have but few of the large number of colored brick-makers.

The secretary of the broom-makers writes:

"I am informed that some organizations refuse membership to the Negro. I consider it a serious mistake, as white labor cannot expect the Negro to refrain from taking their place unless we will assist him in bettering his condition."

Nine-tenths of the black membership of the carpenters is in the South and mostly organized in separate unions from the whites. In the North there are very few in the unions; there are a few in the West. In great cities like Washington, Baltimore, Cincinnati, Philadelphia, New York and even Boston it is almost impossible for a Negro to be admitted to the unions, and there is no appeal from the decision.

The cigar-makers' is one of the few unions that allows its locals little discretion as to membership:

"Our constitution makes it obligatory on the part of local unions to accept journeymen cigar makers as members. Any journeyman cigar maker who has served three years at the trade can come in, and by paying his initiation fee in installments, if he wants to, he is regarded as having been initiated. It requires no vote; the constitution makes it mandatory."

Colored cigar makers can be found in small numbers in nearly all Northern cities and in large numbers in the South. Florida alone reports 2,000.

The secretary of the coopers' writes:

"We have local branches composed entirely of colored coopers at Egan, Ga., Norfolk and Lynchburg, Va. At New Orleans, Hawkinsville, Ga., and other places they work together in the same local union."

Practically no Negroes have been admitted to Northern unions—Trenton, N. J., alone reporting a single union Negro.

The stationary firemen in 1899 requested the St. Louis union to stop color discrimination and they have organized a number of Negro locals, especially in the mining regions. They assert that Negroes are received in all locals and this would seem to be so in most cases.

Among the longshoremen, who may be classed as semi-skilled artisans, the Negro element is very strong. From the great lakes a secretary reports:

"We have many colored members in our association, and some of them are among our leading officials of our local branches. In one of our locals that I can call to mind there are over 300 members, of which five are colored; of these two hold the office of President and Secretary; so you can see that nothing but good feeling prevails among our members as regards the colored race, and when you consider that our people average fifty cents per hour when at work, you can readily imagine that our people are not half-starved and illiterate."

From the gulf another writes:

"In New Orleans we have been the means of unity of action among the longshoremen generally of that port, both in regards to work, wages and meeting in hall together. I believe that we are the only craft in that city who have succeeded in wiping out the colored question. Our members meet jointly in the same hall and are the highest paid workmen in New Orleans."

Still the color question arises here and there:

"In 1899 a color line difficulty arose among the longshoremen of Newport News, Va. The local unions there of longshoremen were composed entirely of colored men. White men refused to join them. The colored men were finally persuaded to consent to the issue of a separate charter for the white men."

The membership of Negroes is very large; Florida alone reports 800; Detroit, Mich., 60, and large numbers in Virginia, Louisiana and Texas.

The United Mine Workers receive Negroes into the same unions with whites, both North and South; Secretary Pearce testified before the Industrial Commission:

"As far as we are concerned as miners, the colored men are with us in the mines. They work side by side with us. They are members of our organization; can receive as much consideration from the officials of the organization as any other members, no matter what color. We treat them that way. They are in the mines, many of them good men. There is only one particular objection, and that is they are used to a great extent in being taken from one place to another to break a strike, as we call it, in such cases as we have here now at Pana, where this trouble is going on, and that trouble they had at Virden, Ill."

In the Alabama mines, 50% of the miners are black, still the whites are said to

"Recognize—as a matter of necessity they were forced to recognize—the identity of interest. I suppose among miners, the same as other white men in the South, there are the same class differences, but they have been forced down, so that they must raise the colored man up or they go down, and they have consequently mixed together in their organization. There are cases where a colored man will be the officer of the local union—president of a local union."

The state president of the Federation, however, reports considerable dissatisfaction on the part of the whites at the recognition of Negroes. Negro union miners are reported in Pennsylvania, West Virginia, Alabama, Illinois, Iowa, Kansas, Kentucky and Missouri. There are also a few members of the Northern Mineral Mine Workers Progressive Union, a kindred organization operating in Michigan.

The secretary of the painters' union writes:

"The only difficulty we find with Negroes is that there is a disposition on their part to work cheaper than the white man. This is due largely to want of education and the influence of men of their own race who are opposed to the Trades Union movement. The Trades Union movement is the only movement that will ever settle the Negro question in America, and men who are interested in the advancement of the Negroes should thoroughly investigate the whole question of Trades Unionism, as it relates to the Negro and the working people in general."

There would seem to be other difficulties, however, as there are almost no colored union painters in the North—one or two being reported in Portland, Me., Cincinnati, O., and Trenton, N. J. They seem to be pretty effectually barred out of the Northern unions, and in the South they are formed usually, if not always, into separate unions. Florida reports a considerable number, but there are not many reported elsewhere.

The secretary of the seamen writes:

"We are exerting every effort to get the Southern Negroes into the union at present, and if we can once convince them that they will have an opportunity for employment equal to the white man I believe that we can succeed. We have nearly all the

Portuguese Negroes in the union at present. And they get the same wages as the white men, and the same opportunity for employment. The Negro seaman is now becoming a menace to the white seaman since the ship owner is endeavoring to use him against the union to break down wages, and they take the pains to impress on their minds that if they join the union and demand the same wages as the white men they will not be given employment. The Negro seaman being somewhat more illiterate than his white brother believes this, rather than believe us. We may in time be able to convince them that this is not so, but at present it is an uphill fight. The most of the colored sailing out of New York are union men and we have increased their pay from $16 and $18 to $25 and $30. Our worst ports are Philadelphia, Baltimore and Norfolk."

The following quotation from the testimony of the secretary of the tobacco workers is characteristic of the labor union attitude:

"Probably one of our greatest obstacles will be the colored labor, for it is largely employed in the manufacture of tobacco in the South. It is pretty difficult to educate them to the necessity of organization for the protection of their interests. In the South I suppose 75% in the tobacco business are colored, although there are a number of white people it seems, going in from the country to work in the factories, as I have been told. A number of manufacturers told me they did employ and would employ one wherever they could, either male or female. . . . . . .

"There was one colored tobacco workers union organized in Winston but the white men resisted the organization and I do not think it succeeded. I do not think there is any colored organization in the state now."*

Opposition on the part of Southern white workmen, and the eagerness of union organizers to replace Negro by white laborers explains the difficulty of extending the union movement and the justifiably suspicious attitude of Negroes toward it. The tobacco workers' constitution especially prohibits color distinctions, but separate locals are organized. The colored union men are chiefly in Kentucky, Virginia and the Carolinas.

The plasterers have a good number of Negro members. In Memphis, Birmingham, Atlanta, Richmond, Danville, Savannah and New Orleans they are said to outnumber the whites, and in the South there are some "in most, if not in all, of our locals." They are scarce in the North, however, 2 being reported in Pennsylvania, 1 in Massachusetts, and a score or more in Illinois. The Southern unions are often mixed.

The masons and bricklayers also have a large Negro membership in the South and often in mixed unions. Considerable numbers are reported in Texas, Tennessee, Virginia, Louisiana and South Carolina; there are some 200 in Florida, and at least that number in Georgia, and probably in Alabama. In the North, however, it is very difficult for Negroes to enter the unions. The First General Vice-President of the National Building Trades Council testified before the Industrial Commission that "we do not permit" Negroes to join our organization in the city of Washington—"we do not admit colored men to our organization." He said, however, that the national organization "does not prohibit colored men from becoming members"† and that there were members in some other cities. A Negro bricklayer and plasterer of St. Mary's, Ga., who has long worked

*Report Industrial Commission, Vol. 7, pp. 405, 497; Vol. 17, p. 320.

†Report of Industrial Commission, Vol. 7, pp. 162–3.

as foreman, and can read and write, has travelled over a large part of the country. Although he had his union travelling card he was refused work and recognition in Tampa, Fla., Norfolk, Va., Washington, D. C., Baltimore, Md., and New York City. He was allowed to work in Boston and Chicago and most other Southern towns. In Cincinnati, a report says:

"We have some colored bricklayers here but those that work on buildings with union men and who belong to the unions are men so fair in complexion as not to be noticed, among sun-burned and brick dust covered white men, as colored men. I have a distinct recollection of an experience I had with a black bricklayer who came to this city in 1893, from Chicago. He was a member of a union there and worked with white men in that city. He came to Cincinnati with a band of white bricklayers who vouched for him. They were given, by the local union here, union cards and immediately got work. He, the black man, was kept dancing attendance on the master of the local union and delayed upon one pretext and other until he was driven from the city without being permitted to follow his trade because the local union did not give him his card. I was remodeling a building of ours and I gave him work as a plasterer. The union hod carrier, an Irishman, refused to carry mortar for him because he did not have a card from the local plasterers' union as a plasterer. He was compelled to work as a scab to get money enough to get out of town."*

The Knights of Labor claim 6,000 Negro members at present, and 8,000 in 1890, a decrease of 25 per cent. This report came too late for insertion in the table.

To sum up we may make the following list in the order of increasing hostility toward the Negro:

Miners—Welcome Negroes in nearly all casses.
Longshoremen—Welcome Negroes in nearly all cases.
Cigar-makers—Admit practically all applicants.
Barbers—Admit many, but restrain Negroes when possible.
Seamen—Admit many, but prefer whites.
Firemen—Admit many, but prefer whites.
Tobacco Workers—Admit many, but prefer whites.
Carriage and Wagon Workers—Admit some, but do not seek Negroes.
Brick-makers— " " " " " " "
Coopers— " " " " " " "
Broom-makers—
Plasterers—Admit freely in South and a few in North.
Carpenters—Admit many in South, almost none in North.
Masons— " " " " " " "
Painters—Admit a few in South, almost none in North.

The evidence on which the above is based cannot all be given here; it is, however, pretty conclusive: there are, for instance, numbers of competent Negro painters, carpenters and masons—yet who has seen one at work in a Northern city? There are numbers of brick-makers, wheelwrights and coopers, but few have been brought into the unions and in the North few can get in. The seamen, firemen and tobacco workers have many Negroes, but Negroes fear to join them lest, by demanding union wages, their white fellow-workmen will hasten to supplant them. This has virtually been admitted by labor leaders and others. A South Carolina employer says that among bricklayers of equal skill Negroes receive \$1.75 and whites \$2.50 a day and "the object of the white men in organizing the Negroes is to get them to demand the same wages that the whites de-

*Report of Mr. Geo. H. Jackson.

mand." Messrs. Garrett and Houston, President and Secretary of the Georgia Federation, confirm this, as do many others, and the Secretary of the Southern Industrial Convention adds: "There is discrimination even in the union. The white members try to get employment for each other and to crowd out the colored members." The same thing occurs in the North; now and then a Negro is admitted to a union but even then he stands less chance of getting work than a white man.*

55. *Unions with Few Negro Members:* The following national unions report a few Negro members:

Trade Unions	Negro Membership	Total Membership†
Journeymen Bakers and Confectioners' International Union	"Several."	6,271
International Brotherhood of Blacksmiths	"Very few."	4,700
National Association of Blast Furnace Workers and Smelters of America	100 or more.	
Boot and Shoe Workers' Union	A few.	8,037
National Union of United Brewery Workers	12.	25,000
Amalgamated Society of Carpenters and Joiners‡	A few.	2,500
National Society of Coal Hoisting Engineers	4.	950
Amalgamated Society of Engineers	"Several."	1,779
International Union of Steam Engineers	A few—1 local.	4,409
United Garment Workers of America	10.	15,000
Granite Cutters National Union	5.	6,500
United Hatters of America	Very few.	7,500
International Union of Horse Shoers of United States and Canada	?	2,100
Hotel and Restaurant Employees' International Alliance and Bartenders' International League of America	100.	10,962
Amalgamated Association of Iron, Steel and Tin Workers	"Practically none."	8,000
Shirt, Waist and Laundry Workers' International Union	2 locals.	3,066
Tube Workers' International Union	"Some."	
Amalgamated Meat Cutters and Butcher Workmen of North America	A few.	4,500
International Association of Allied Metal Mechanics	?	2,400
American Federation of Musicians	A few—1 local.	8,100
Jonrneymen Tailors' Union of America	10.	9,000
National Alliance of Theatrical Stage Employees	10.	3,000
International Typographical Union	A few.	38,991
Watch-case Engravers' International Association	1.	285
Wood, Wire and Metal Lathers' International Union	25–50 ?	
Amalgamated Wood workers' International Union of America	?	14,500
Amalgamated Association of Street Railway Employees	5–10.	4,000

*Possibly the hod-carriers ought to be mentioned under this division as semi-skilled laborers. They have a predominating Negro membership in all parts of the country, but have no national association. The local bodies are usually associated with the various city central labor bodies. The teamsters have a national body and many Negro members.

†Based mainly on actual paid membership tax Cf. Report Industrial Commission: Vol. 17.

‡Not the same as the Brotherhood of Carpenters and Joiners, but a smaller independent body allied with English unions as well as with the A. F. L.

The small Negro membership in these unions arises from two causes: the lack of Negro mechanics in these lines, and color discrimination. Probably the first is the more important in the case of boot and shoe makers, brewers, granite cutters, hatters, metal workers, watch-case engravers and metal lathers. In these cases the real discrimination is in keeping Negroes from learning the trades. In the case of most of the other unions, however, especially blacksmiths, blast-furnace workers, engineers, horse-shoers, hotel employees, iron and steel workers, musicians, street railway employees and printers, the chief cause of the small number of Negroes in the unions is color discrimination. Without doubt incompetency plays some part here, too, but it is doubtful if it is the leading cause. The granite cutters say that "employers do not care to employ Negro apprentices, hence the few Negro journeymen." The steam engineers say through their secretary:

"The Trade Union movement is based upon the broadest lines and recognizes that every wage worker ought to be within its ranks. There is, of course, an unfortunate feature, one that will take time and education to remove, and that is the biased opinion held in regard to the Negro. Our organization grants charters to Negroes when same is requested and there are a sufficient number of them to support a self-sustaining local. We have some difficulty with the accepting of a card when presented by a Negro but headquarters has always taken action in the matter and endeavored to have the card recognized."

The prejudiced element prevailed, however, at the last meeting in Boston, 1902, of the Stationary Engineers (an organization formed under the Steam Engineers,) and it was voted to have the word "white" placed before the word "engineers" in one of the articles of their constitution. The motion was made by a Mr. Grant of New Orleans, and was the cause of a most passionate debate. The vote was carried by a large majority, but not until there had been many strong speeches, the Southerners of course taking the affirmative and the Northerners opposing. Mr. Grant said that if the association granted "the Negro this social equality he did not deserve," it would lose all standing in the South, and that the Negro belonged in Africa. Mr. Optenberg of Wisconsin said if he voted to shut out the Negro he would be ashamed to look any Grand Army man in the face. Mr. Babbitt of Worcester said he knew colored engineers who deserved respect and he would stand for the colored man. But when Mr. C. Eli Howarth of Fall River declared that there were men present whom he would rather discard than the Negro, he was hissed for a full minute, and the Southerners had their way.

The secretary of the iron and steel workers thinks it is "only a question of time when it will be necessary to accord the Negro the same privileges as are extended to the white brethren." In the recent strike of steel employees against the Steel Trust the color line was broken for the first time and Negroes invited into the union. Few, if any, seem to have entered.

The hotel employees and bartenders have spent $525 "in a futile effort to organize colored locals," no Negro being allowed in a white local. "The main objection from our membership against Negroes appears to come from locals in the southern part of the country." The printers usually exclude Negroes; there are a few individual exceptions here and there, but not many. The secretary of the Atlanta Federation of Trades when asked if the printers there barred Negroes said: "I cannot answer that; we have no colored typographical men in the South that I know of." There are from 50 to 100 black printers in Georgia alone.

The metal lathers report a few members in Birmingham, Savannah, Asheville, Augusta, Memphis, Nashville and Jacksonville, but none in the North. Three colored shoemakers are reported. There was a local in New Orleans which barred Negroes but this is now defunct. The meat handlers have colored members in Kansas City and Boston. In the latter city they took part in the strike of the freight handlers of last summer. In one local a Negro has held office, and the last convention had several Negro delegates. The book binders say: "Some of our people refuse to recognize Negroes as mechanics," but there are no actual discriminating statutes.

When asked how many Negro applicants had been refused admission to the unions, the Amalgamated carpenters, musicians, blacksmiths, street railway employees and brewers returned no answer; the engineers, granite cutters and glass workers were evasive, saying that they were without official data or did not know. Most of the others answered, "None." Many acknowledged that local unions could refuse to recognize a travelling card held by a Negro, although several said the action was "illegal."

56. *Unions with no Negro membership.* The following unions report that they have no colored members:

Trade Union	Negro Members	Total M'mb'rship*
Brotherhood of Boilermakers and Iron Shipbuilders	"Not wanted."	7,078
International Brotherhood of Bookbinders	"No record."	3,730
International Association of Car Workers	"None."	
Chainmakers' National Union of the U. S. A.	"None."	465
Elastic Goring Weavers' Amalgamated Association	"None in trade."	250
International Brotherhood of Electrical Workers	"Not allowed."	7,000
International Ladies' Garment Workers' Union	"None in trade."	2,000
American Flint Glass Workers' Union	"Never had any."	
Glass Bottle Blowers' Association	"None in trade."	1,400
Amalgamated Glass Workers' International Association	"No applications."	278
International Jewelry Workers' Union of A.	"None in trade."	1,000
Amalgamated Lace Curtain Operatives	"Quest'n undecided."	
United Brotherhood of Leather Workers on Horse Goods	"None."	3,402
International Association of Machinists	"Not admitted."	30,000
Metal Polishers, Buffers, Platers, Brass and Composition Metal Workers' International Union	"None."	6,000
International Brotherhood of Oil and Gas Well Workers	"None."	670
United Brotherhood of Paper makers	"None."	1,000
Pattern-makers League of North America	"None."	2.403
Piano and Organ Workers International Union of America	"None in trade."	
United Association of Journeymen Plumbers, Gasfitters, Steamfitters, and Steamfitters' Helpers	"None."	8,000
National Association of Operative Potters	"None."	2,450
International Printing Pressmen and Assistants' Union	"No record."	9,745
Order of Railway Telegraphers and Brotherhood of Commercial Telegraphers	Barred by constit't'n	8,000
Brotherhood of Railway Trackmen	" " "	4,500
National Steel and Copper Plate Printers' Union	"None known."	700
International Stereotypers and Electrotypers Union	'Question not settled'	
Stove Mounters, Steel Range Workers, and Pattern Fitters and Filers International Union of North America	"No legislation."	1,269
United Textile Workers of America	"No applications."	3,435
Ceramic, Mozaic and Encaustic Tile Layers and Helpers' International Union	" "	357
Trunk & Bag Workers International Union	"None."	234
Upholsterers International Union of N. A.	"	1,400
The American Wire Weavers Protective Association	"Would not work with Negro."	226
International Wood-carvers' Association	"No applicants."	
Grand International Brotherhood of Locomotive Engineers	Barred by constitut'n	37,000
Brotherhood of Locomotive Firemen	" " "	39,000
Brotherhood of Railway Car-men	" " "	
The Switchmen's Union of North America		15,000
Brotherhood of Railway Trainmen	Barred by constitut'n	15,000
Order of Railroad Conductors	Would not be ad'tted	25,800
The Stone Cutters Association	Don't admit Negroes	·10,000
Special Order Clothing-makers Union	"None."	
D. A. 300, K. of L. (window glass workers)	"None."	
Custom Clothing Makers' Union	"None."	

*Based mainly on actual paid membership tax. Cf. Report Industrial Commission, Vol. 17.

These unions fall into three main groups: those who say that they admit Negroes but have no Negro members; these include the goring weavers, trunk workers, tile layers, leather workers, metal workers, plumbers, plate printers, car workers, paper workers, oil well workers, ladies' garment workers, special order clothing workers, chair makers, upholsterers and piano workers. Their explanation is that no Negroes work at these trades and they consequently have no applications. This is true except in the case of plumbers and upholsterers. The plumbers have a semi-secret organization and there can be no doubt that they practically never admit a Negro, although one Negro member is reported in Flint, Mich. The organizer says that most Negroes are incompetent.

"Such Negroes as have shown a greater ability than others have usually found their way into a small business and are patronized by the Negro residents of our Southern cities. There is no general law in our organization to exclude Negroes but as before stated none have ever joined and to the best of my knowledge but one has ever made application to us."

A prominent official of the chain makers reports that they had 6 Negro members in 1901, but that they refused to strike which "naturally would cause hard feelings." The general secretary of the metal workers thinks "there would be no difficulty in initiating a colored metal worker into one of our local unions," but adds "I am speaking from a personal standpoint on this question. There is no doubt but what we have some members who are prejudiced against the Negro."

The second class of unions is those which are undecided or non-committal on the Negro question. These are the various glass workers, the potters, stove-mounters, jewelry workers, wood carvers, textile workers, stereotypers and electrotypers, printing pressmen, metal polishers, steam fitters and lace curtain operatives. As no Negroes work at most of these trades the question of their admission has not been raised or decided. The textile workers are exceptions and have very clearly drawn the color line, North and South, although they do not acknowledge it. The Negroes working at the trade have never been allowed to join the union, and the attempt to introduce Negro mill labor in Atlanta a few years ago so strengthened the Textile Union in the South that "it is doubtful whether in the future a Southern cotton mill can employ any Negro labor unless it is ready to employ all Negro labor."* There appear to be one or two printing pressmen in Rhode Island and Illinois.

The last class of unions includes those who openly bar the Negro. These are the great railway unions—the engineers, firemen, telegraphers, car men, switchmen, train men, track men, and conductors; and the stone cutters, machinists, electrical workers, boiler makers, and wire weavers. The editor of the organ of the engineers attributes the exclusion of the Negro to the prejudices of Southern engineers, but thinks that most of their fellows agree with them. Mr. E. E. Clark, Grand Chief Conductor and member of the Coal Strike Arbitration Commission, writes:

**Outlook*, Vol. 56, p. 980.

"I think wherever any opposition to the colored race on the part of organized labor is manifested, it can generally be traced to the fact that colored men are always willing to work for wages which white men cannot, and should not be asked, to work for."

The Grand Master of the Trainmen says:

"The Brotherhood has no plans for the organization of colored men employed in railway occupations. Some ideas have lately been proposed along these lines, but as yet they have not met with any general favor among our membership."

Mr. John T. Wilson, president of the trackmen, was once addressing some Negroes in St. Louis on the advantages of unionism. They reminded him of the attitude of his union and he replied that

"I was employed to execute laws, not to make them, and if they could see themselves as I saw them, they would not be surprised at my inability to annihilate race prejudices."

And he added that

"Concerted action on the part of practical and intelligent Negroes and white men of character who really desire to see the conditions of the down trodden masses improved without regard to race, would eventually cause the white and Negro workmen to co-operate in industrial organization for their mutual advancement."

The Negro locomotive firemen are still active competitors of the white, although forced to take lower wages and do menial work.* The Commissioner of Labor of North Carolina testified before the industrial commission that

"The truth of it is, a great many engineers like Negro firemen best. They had Negroes at first and are now only working white men in; the white men are taking the place of Negroes. . . . . A great many of the old engineers prefer Negro firemen. They treat them differently—make them wait on them. The white man does not do that."

The Grand Secretary of the Boiler-makers says:

"There is not one man in this order that would present the application of a Negro for membership. This without laws forbidding him. Hence we have none. Being a Southern man myself, having lived 30 years in New Orleans, I know that no Negro has worked at boiler making since the war."

The secretary of the wire weavers says:

"Our laws, up to a few years ago, provided that only white males were eligible, but it at present makes no distinction, but at the same time I am satisfied that our men would not work with a Negro. We work partners and coming in such contact with one another no white man would take a Negro for a partner. And I am frank enough to say that I don't think any of the men would allow a Negro to start at the trade."

The International Association of Machinists was organized in 1888:

"Almost alone among national labor organizations, excepting the railroad brotherhoods, it put a clause in its constitution excluding colored men. It desired to join the American Federation of Labor, but the Federation refused at that time to admit unions whose constitutions recognized distinctions of color. . . . .

"At the Federation convention of 1892 the president of the Association of Machinists appeared before a committee of the Federation, expressed satisfaction with the action of the executive council, and stated that the next convention of the Machinsts' Association would eliminate the color line from its constitution. It was not until 1895 that affiliation with the Federation was finally effected."†

---

*Cf. p. 115.

†Report Industrial Commission, Vol. 17, p. 217.

Notwithstanding this the secretary of the Washington lodge writes us in 1899 "the Negro is not admitted to the International Association of Machinists," while the secretary of the National Union refused to answer questions as to the eligibility of black men. A labor leader when asked by the Industrial Commission if he had ever worked with a Negro machinist, answered:

"No, sir; I never worked in a shop with a Negro as a machinist."

"Would you not?" "No, sir; I would not."

The president of Turner Brass Works tells how the machinists in his establishment objected to a colored workman, but the Negro "was so good natured and did his work so well" that he was permitted to stay—but not to join the union.

"Right there is my objection, and right there is my reason for declining to treat locally with unions, because the men out of the union should have as good a right to employment as the men in the union. We do not ask them if they are Methodists or Democrats, or whether they are Masons or union men. We ask them, 'Can you do this work!' "*

There may possibly be one or two Negroes in the machinists' union in Boston.

The secretary of the electrical workers reports:

"I will state that we have no Negroes in our organization. We received an application from Jacksonville, Fla., but it was thrown down by our locals. We are in favor of the colored men organizing, but we believe that they should have locals of their own, and not mixed with the whites."

In the Jacksonville case it is said that the local was granted a charter; then it was learned that they were colored and the charter was revoked. There are one or two Negro members in Massachusetts and New Jersey.

The reasons adduced for discrimination against Negroes vary:

"Unfit for the business."—Telegraphers.

"Not the equals of white men."—Boiler-makers.

"Color."—Electricians, Locomotive Firemen.

"Race prejudice among the rank and file of our members."—Trainmen.

When asked if these objections would disappear in time, the answers were:

"No."—Locomotive Firemen.

"Eventually; co-operation will come."—Trainmen.

"We hope so."—Electricians.

"Not until prejudice in the South disappears."—Engineers.

"Time makes and works its own changes."—Boiler-makers.

"Think not."—Telegraphers.

Finally the Railway Educational Association writes:

"Usually the railroad service is open from the top to the bottom for promotion to those who enter it, but your race seems to be discriminated against and barred from promotion. I understand that you are working on the idea that education is the power that must advance your race, and finally break down opposition to the progress of its members. In this you are surely right, although the time for the realization of your hopes may be more distant than you expect."

*Report of Industrial Commission Vol. 8, p. 38.

There are a number of unions from whom repeated inquiries secured no information, as, for instance, the bridge workers, core makers, table knife grinders, iron molders, paving cutters, tin plate workers, marble workers, lithographers and sheet metal workers. The addresses of others were not found in time, as the powder workers, brick makers, spinners, box makers, marine engineers and firemen, and stogie makers. Most of these, however, have none or very few Negroes, except possibly the core makers and molders, in which trades many Negroes are employed. In the last Toronto meeting of the molders, 1902, its is said that:

"A warm discussion was precipitated in the iron molders convention this morning by a delegate from the South touching the admission of Negroes to the Iron Molders' Union. The delegate thought they should be excluded, but those from the Northern States, ably assisted by the Canadian members, championed the Negro. They thought there should be no difference made. They objected to the making of a race question."*

Repeated letters to the secretary of the molders' as to the result of this proposal and the general attitude of the molders, have elicited only this response:

"You will have to kindly excuse me from giving such matters any more of my time as I am very busy with my office work!"

57. *Local option in the choice of members.* The general attitude of the Federation of Labor, and even of the National Unions, has little more than a moral effect in the admission of Negroes to trade unions. The present constitution of the Knights of Labor admits members "at the option of each local assembly."† The real power of admission in nearly all cases rests with the local assemblies, by whose vote any person may be refused, and in a large number of cases a small minority of any local may absolutely bar a person to whom they object. The object of this is to keep out persons of bad character or sometimes incompetent workmen. In practice, however, it gives the local or a few of its members a monopoly of the labor market and a chance to exercise, consciously or unconsciously, their prejudices against foreigners, or Irishmen, or Jews, or Negroes.

The following unions require a majority vote for admission to the locals:

Boot and Shoe Workers.
Amalgamated Carpenters.
Bottle Blowers.
Glass Workers.
Wood Workers.
Coopers.
Stogie-makers.
Amalgamated Engineers.
Metal Polishers.
Stove Mounters.
Bakers.
Barbers.
Steam Engineers.
Coal Hoisting Engineers.

The wood workers, coal hoisting engineers, and coopers, require an examining committee in addition.

The following require a two-thirds vote for admission to the locals:

Brotherhood of Carpenters.
Painters.
Tile Layers.
Flint Glass Workers.
Iron and Steel Workers.
Sheet Metal Workers.
Pattern-makers.
Tin Plate Workers.
Broom-makers.

*Toronto Star, July 9, 1902.

†Report Industrial Commission, Vol. 17, p. 18.

Nearly all these require also the favorable report of an examining committee. Among the iron and steel workers and tin plate workers two black balls can make a second election necessary.

These unions require more than a two-thirds vote for admission:

Electrical Workers, two-thirds vote, *plus* one, and examination.
Molders, " " " " "
Core-makers, " " " " "
Boiler-makers, three black balls reject.
Blacksmiths, " " " " two require second election.
Street Railway Employees, three-fourths' vote.
Leather Workers, (horse goods), three black balls reject.

The Typographical Union and printing pressmen and many others leave all questions of admission to the local unions absolutely, except that an appeal lies to the National Union. In nearly all cases save that of the cigar-makers the adverse vote of a local practically bars the applicant. It is here, and not, usually, in the constitutions of the National bodies, that the color line is drawn ruthlessly in the North.

The colloquy between the Industrial Commission and the First General Vice President of the Building Trades Council brought this out with startling clearness:

Question.—"It seems to be true here that the local organization has the power to draw the color line absolutely, without regard to the qualifications of the applicant. To what extent does that power generally go with local organizations? Is it absolute? Could it extend to a Roman nose, gray eyes, wart on the chin, or must it rest upon some reason? What is the law about it?

Answer—Such a condition might be possible, but not at all probable.

Q.—You mean that all those things rest absolutely upon the will of the local organization?

A.—Why, yes; they rest upon the will of the majority."*

In like manner the methods regulating apprenticeship militate against Negroes in nearly all the trades. Many unions, like the hatters, trunk makers, printers, stone cutters, glass workers, and others, limit the number of apprentices according to the journeymen at work. Very often, as in the case of the hatters, the union prescribes the terms of apprenticeship and oversees the details. In the case of the coal hoisting engineers, elastic goring weavers, and some others, the consent of the local must be obtained before any particular apprentice is admitted. In other cases there are age limits, and there is very general demand among the unions for still more rigid regulation and the use of articles of indenture. Strong unions go so far as to refuse to recognize a workman who has not served his apprenticeship in a union shop or begun it between the ages of 17 and 18. The tin plate union especially enjoins its members from teaching their trade to any unskilled workingmen about the mills. The black boy who gets a chance to learn a trade under such circumstances would indeed be a curiosity.

---

*Report of Industrial Commission, Vol. VII, pp. 162, 163.

58. *Strikes against Negro workmen.* It is impossible to get accurate statistics on the number of cases where white workmen have refused to work with black men. Usually such strikes, especially in the North, are concealed under the refusal to work with non-union men.* Strikes for this cause have occurred in 2,751 establishments in this country in the last 20 years, and nearly 70% of them have been successful. It is thus possible in some trades for three men absolutely to bar any Negro who wishes to pursue this calling.

There are a number of cases where the object of getting rid of Negro workingmen has been openly avowed. These, by causes, are as follows:†

STRIKES FROM JAN. 1, 1881, to DEC. 31, 1900.

	Total	Succeeded	Failed
Against employing colored girls	1		1
" " " men	23	5	18
" " " " and for increased wages	1		1
" " " foreman	1	1	
" working with Negroes	7	1	6
For discharge of Negro employees	16	5	11
" " of foreman and vs. colored laborers doing journeymen's work	1		1
Total	50	12	38

INDUSTRIES IN WHICH STRIKES AGAINST NEGRO LABOR HAVE OCCURRED.

	No	Succeeded	Failed
Agricultural Implements	1		1
Brick	1		1
Building Trades	4		4
Clothing	1		1
Coal and Coke	6	3	3
Cotton Goods	3	2	1
Domestic Service	2		2
Glass	2	1	1
Leather and Leather Goods	1	1	
Machines and Machinery	2		2
Metals and Metallic Goods	3		3
Public Ways Construction	2		2
Stone Quarrying and Cutting	1	1	
Transportation	18	3	15
Wooden Goods	1		1
Miscellaneous	1		1
Total	49	11	38

*"From the data in my possession it is not possible to secure any information as to the number of strikes against non-union men which were in reality against Negroes."—Carroll D. Wright, Commissioner of Labor, Dec. 22, 1902.

†From the Reports of the U. S. Bureau of Labor. A slight discrepancy in the totals will be noticed. This is unexplained.

STRIKES BY YEARS.

Year	Cause	Establishments	Succeeded	Failed
1882	Against employment of colored men..........	2		2
1883	" " " " "	2	1	1
1885	For discharge of colored employees............	1	1	
	Against employment of colored men..........	1		1
1887	Against working with colored men.............	1		1
1888	For discharge of colored employees............	5		5
	Against employment of colored men and for increased wages..............................	1		1
1889	Against working with colored men.............	2		2
	" " " " "			
	For discharge of colored employees............	1		1
	Against working under colored foreman.......	1	1	
1890	Against working with colored men.............	1		
1891	" " " " "	1		1
1892	" " " " "	1		1
1894	For discharge of colored employees............	2	1	1
	Against employing colored men...............	12		1
1897	For discharge of colored employees	1	1	12
1898	Against employing colored men...............	1	1	
1899	Against certain rules and for discharge of colored head-waiter..........................	1		1
1899	For discharge of colored employees...........	4	1	3
1900	Against employment of colored girls..........	1		1
	" " " " men..........	5	3	2
	Total..................................	47	10	37

Detailed information as to all of these strikes is unfortunately not available for the last ten years; for the first ten years 1.458 men were engaged in such strikes, involving 21 establishments and entailing a pecuniary loss to employers and employed of $215,945. If the strikes of the last ten years were similar in character we may say that in the last 20 years 3,000 white workingmen have fought against the employment of other workingmen for the sole reason that they were black at a cost of nearly half a million dollars. And that moreover this probably is only a small part of the strikes against colored men, since usually the strike is technically against "non-union labor."

The greatest strike of which we have record before 1891 is that which took place in a steel works in Pittsburg in 1890. The Iron and Steel Workers Union ordered out 400 of the 500 employees because Negroes were employed. The strike lasted over eight months and failed. The wage loss was $15,000, toward which labor unions contributed $8,000. The employers lost $25,090 and eventually 300 new hands were hired in place of the strikers.

Of the 25 strikes, 1894 (July 1) to 1900 (Dec. 31), the Department of Labor has kindly furnished details as to seven, and also details as to 15 strikes in which Negro workmen struck against color discrimination:

Locality.	Occupation.	Cause or object.	Ordered by labor organizations.	No. of establishments involved.	Establishments: Closed.	Establishments: Not closed.	Duration of strike days.	Succeeded?	Empl'yes: Wage Loss.	Empl'yes: Assistance.	Employers' Loss.
									$	$	$
1898 Selma, Ala.	Carders, cotton.	Against employment of colored men.	No.	1	—	1	1	Yes	9	—	—
1895 Ocala, Fla.	Employees, cigar factory.	To compel teacher to admit colored children to school in buildi'g own'd by employer, or for his discharge....	No.	5	5	—	3	Yes	1,750	—	1000
1900 Pensacola, Fla.	Lumber handlers	Against alleged discrimination against colored employees.	Yes	10	—	10	7	Yes	4,395	—	—
1896 Atlanta, Ga.	Machinists.	Against colored laborers doing machinists' work..........	No.	1	—	1	14	No.	512	—	300
1897 Atlanta, Ga.	Carders, cotton.	For discharge of colored employees..	No.	1	1	—	5	Yes	3,332	—	7000
1899 Barnesville, Ga.	Cutters & knitt'rs cotton factory.	For discharge of colored employees..	No.	1	1	—	5	No.	221	—	1000
1895 Missouri City, Mo.	Miners, coal.	For discharge of colored weighman..	No.	1	1	—	2	Yes	250	—	—
1899 Bridgeton, N. J.	Snappers-up, glass.	For discharge of colored watchman..	No.	1	—	1	1	No.	365	—	100
1899 Haverstraw, N. Y.	Burners, laborers & molders, brick.	For discharge of colored employees..	No.	1	1	—	10	No.	1,000	—	150

59. *Summary of the Attitude of Organized Labor.* Putting the strength of organized labor in the United States at the conservative estimate of 1,200,000, we may say:

Unions with 500,000 members, include 40,000 Negroes.
" " 200,000 " " 1,000 "
" " 500,000 " " No Negroes.

The rule of admission of Negroes to unions throughout the country is the sheer necessity of guarding work and wages. In those trades where large numbers of Negroes are skilled they find easy admittance in the parts of the country where their competition is felt. In all other trades they are barred from the unions, save in exceptional cases, either by open or silent color discrimination. There are exceptions to this rule. There are cases where the whites have shown a real feeling of brotherhood; there are cases where the blacks, through incompetence and carelessness, have forfeited their right to the advantages of organization. But on the whole a careful, unprejudiced survey of the facts leads one to believe that the above statement is approximately true all over the land.

It is fair, on such a vital point, however, to let the white labor leaders speak for themselves and the opinions of a few are here appended.

60. *Views of Labor Leaders*—(By C. C. Houston, Secretary of the Georgia Federation of Labor, Samuel Gompers, President of the American Federation of Labor, and others).

"A labor union is primarily a business institution and very little sentimentalism enters into its make-up. It is for the collective bargaining, conciliation and arbitration of labor. It is to the working man what the Chamber of Commerce is to the business man. It differs from a commercial trust in that it is not a close corporation, but its influences for good are world-wide, and its membership is restricted only to those qualified to perform the work of any special calling in a workmanlike manner. It gives greater liberty and independence of action to the workman and insures not only a higher standard of wages but a higher standard of living.

"Dr. George E. McNeill, author of a volume entitled 'The Labor Movement,' says: 'There is no such thing as liberty of contract between a single wage-worker and an employer. It first becomes possible through the efforts of trade unions. The union is to the laborer what a republican form of government is to the citizen—it gives him freedom. Unions have first made labor problems a matter of interest to the people generally, and have increased respect for labor. They have brought back self-respect and have a strong educational influence. Drunkenness and other bad habits are frowned upon by labor unions.'

"Were it not for the labor unions the working people of this and other civilized countries would be in little better condition than were the chattel slaves of this section before the civil war, and this is the only power that can resist the great and growing combination of capital. There are in the United States today over 2,000,000 skilled working men and women enrolled in the ranks of the various labor organizations. The system comprises local, state and national unions. Each local union is a self-governing body, and is to the national body what a single state is to the United States. Each local union has complete trade autonomy, and regulates its own internal affairs. These local unions range in membership from seven to over six thousand, the last being "Big Six" typographical union of New York City, the largest local labor organization in the world.

"The older trade unions, which have practically complete control of their trade membership, such as the printers, stone cutters, tailors, engineers, conductors and cigar makers, have comparatively few strikes and it is only the newer organizations that are usually forced to resort to strikes to gain recognition of demands for wage scales and regulation of hours. In the case of the older trade unions they have local and sometimes national agreements with associations of employers as to wages and hours of labor. Through the efforts of trade unions few skilled workmen now work over ten hours, while in a great majority of instances eight and nine hours constitute a day's labor at a greater wage scale than formerly prevailed for ten and eleven hours.

"In this general trade union movement the Negro artisan has been a beneficiary in proportion to his membership. It is only during the past ten years that the colored workingman has become in any great measure a factor in organized labor affairs, for there are very few unions among unskilled laborers.

"With the possible exception of the railway orders, none of the trade unions of this country, North or South, exclude the Negro, and his connection with the labor movement is becoming more apparent every year, and he is fast finding out that it is to his individual and collective interest to become affiliated with the organization of his craft. In this the white artisan is lending encouragement and assisting the Negro, giving him a seat, with voice and vote, in the labor councils, local, state and national. The feeling that formerly prevailed among the Negro skilled artisans that the white laborer's sympathy for him was for a selfish purpose is being rapidly dispelled by the mutually beneficial results of organization."—C. C. Houston.

The President of the American Federation of Labor writes:

"It has been and is now our endeavor to organize the colored workers whenever and wherever possible. We recognize the necessity of this if it is hoped to secure the best possible conditions for the workers of every class in our country." Later, on reading §53, he replied: "I should say that your statement is neither fair nor accurate. After careful perusal of the summing up of the attitude of the A. F. of L. toward colored workmen, I should say that you are inclined, not only to be pessimistic upon the subject, but you are even unwilling to give credit where credit is due."—Samuel Gompers.*

The following opinions are from various states:

VIRGINIA.—"One of the greatest drawbacks to the labor movement in the South is the ignorant prejudice against the Negro on the part of the whites in trades unions."

MASSACHUSETTS.—"I always considered a Negro as good as a white man, in any labor union, provided they live up to the obligations."

KANSAS.—"Unions do not bar Negroes by their laws but do not solicit them. If they would apply they would be rejected."

IOWA.—"There are only a few Negroes here but they are not discriminated against according to my knowledge except in the Federation where a Negro can not act as a delegate legally."

FLORIDA.—"The Negroes in this city have no need to complain, as the white men work, smoke, eat and drink together with them, meet in Central Union and hold office together. I organized and installed the Central Union, as General Secretary, and I am a Negro, and have held the same for two elections and was elected by the whites, who are in majority. I have presided over the same body, but do not visit their

*On pp. 157 and 165, it is stated that the Stationary Engineers who met in Boston and passed a law excluding Negroes from membership were connected with the Union of Steam Engineers and affiliated with the A. F. L. Mr. Gompers does not deny this and Secretary Morrison writes as though this were true, (cf. p. 157 note). Nevertheless, it is possible that this body of Stationary Engineers is not connected with the A. F. L., but is a separate organization. Prolonged cor respondence has not been able to settle this point.

daughters and have no wish. The white painters do in a way draw a line, but not openly; the boiler makers also, but none others."

Illinois.—"We have but one Negro in this town and don't need him."

Iowa.—"The Negro in the world is fast learning to overcome superstition, race prejudice, etc. . . . . He is 90% a better citizen than the semi-civilized pack of humanity that is being imported into this country by capitalists from Asia Minor and Syria."

Massachusetts.—"I have met Negroes in the printing trade who were rapid compositors and good union men."

Illinois.—"There is only one union here but what the Negro stands on a level with whites, and they would take them in when they apply; but the Negro knows better than to apply."

Indiana.—"It is my opinion that if a Negro proves himself a mechanic and a man, and holds up trades rules, he has a right to work and make an honest living, the same as any one else; but don't understand by this that I am in favor of this class of people in general, for I am not."

Pennsylvania.—"The working people do not believe in distinctions of races at all."

Washington.—"I want to say under this head that the Negroes as a race are bigoted and should not, in my opinion, be allowed to associate with whites on an equal basis. Although they do not follow my line of business, I have had enough experience with them to convince me that any time they are treated as equals by whites they go too far and apparently consider themselves entitled to more consideration than a native born white American citizen."

Pennsylvania.—"I have known cases here where colored men were refused admittance to a trades union, the reason being that there are so many of them who are unreliable; which is due to a great extent to their want of education, and this but points more forcibly to the need of the 8 hour day for the colored workman, and their organization into some body which will awaken them to the greater possibilities of elevation, both material and intellectual, offered them by trades unionism."

Ohio.—"I am of the opinion that the Negro in common labor pursuits is far ahead of the whites, and many in trade occupations. One Negro friend of mine holds a very responsible position with this union—has been presiding officer since its organization three years ago, and the organization has about 200 members, white and black."

Indiana.—"We have had no test here in regard to admitting Negroes to our local unions. How they would be received is hard to tell at present.

Texas.—"Color discrimination must disappear, if the trade union movement succeeds."

Texas.—The Negro question is the one draw back to the success of the labor movement today, especially is this true in the South. The Negro has always been the stumbling block in the way of success in many cases; this, however, is not the fault of the Negro, but until the white men realize that it is with the organization and assistance of the Negro, that they can and must win, the labor movement will not be as successful as we hope for. I believe that if the Negro was organized thoroughly, then the solution of the labor problem would be found. They are laborers, in a larger percentage, than their white brothers; they are the ones used to whip the white men into line when striking for their rights or demanding recognition from their employers, whereas, if they were organized, no inducement could be made to cause them to falter in their duty to mankind."

Michigan.—"In my opinion it is only a question of time—the evolution which will bring with it the higher civilization—when a colored man will be recognized and entitled to all the rights and privileges now enjoyed by the whites, and by such enjoyment proving the claim that it is civilization and education that makes the man."

61. *The Employer, the Artisan, and the Right of Suffrage.* A few quotations throw an interesting side light on the suffrage question in the South and its relation to the Negro. The last Southern Industrial Convention at Chattanooga said:

"We recommend that every possible means shall be used to educate the public sentiment of the South to regard the Negro as a factor in the upbuilding of the South, and that as such we should use all possible means to make him as efficient as possible, and pledge him the fullest guaranty of earning a living in every honest field of honest endeavor, and protection in his God-given right of self-support."

A prominent Southern man said before the Industrial Commission:

"I believe that in the Negro labor of the South lies the panacea for the wrongs frequently committed by organized labor,and a reserve force from which can be supplied any needed number of workers when the time shall come when they shall be needed."

Most workingmen in the South laugh at such threats because they are certain the Negro cannot become a formidable competitor in skilled labor. A writer in the Molder's Journal makes considerable fun of the exaggerated predictions as to the Negro molder and writes him down as a "dismal failure." Another writer, however, takes him to task and asserts that the writer

"Will not woo us into a sense of fancied security and induce us to look upon the Negro problem in our trade as one that will solve itself by the Negro's demonstrating his incapacity and being ignominiously dismissed from the foundry.

"That is very flattering to our vanity, but it is contrary to facts. I believe I am well within the mark when I say that in the last twenty years Negro molders have increased 500 per cent., and that excluding the Negro pipe molders, whom I do not class as skillful mechanics, I know of two foundries, at least, where the molding is done entirely by Negroes—three if we include the Ross-Mehan annex in Chattanooga. There is the one at the foot of Lookout Mountain, and another in Rome, Ga. A few years ago a mere handful of Negroes worked at molding in Chattanooga, today there are over two hundred; and I am convinced that the question of what shall be done with the Negro molder is one which, in the very near future, will demand more of our attention if we would maintain for ourselves fair wages and conditions in the South."*

On the other hand a white speaker in the 10th Barbers' Convention said:

"Is the disfranchisement of the Negro the first step toward making history repeat itself? I for one will not believe it, as I have too much confidence in American manhood to think that they will allow it. Those of you who live in the South may feel, you may even say it is right, and then I will say to you, If it is right to deny the right of franchise to any American citizen, though his color or nationality be what it may, then it may be your turn tomorrow, because those who seek to disfranchise the Negro today will seek to extend their power by disfranchising you tomorrow. Our protection for tomorrow calls on us to protest in favor of the disfranchised Negro of today."

Here, then, are the four great forces: the Northern laborer, the Southern laborer, the Negro and the employer. The Southern laborer and the employer have united to disfranchise the Negro and make color a caste; the Northern laborer is striving to make the whites unite with the Negroes and maintain wages; the employer threatens that if they do raise labor troubles he will employ Negroes. The Northern laborer sees here the

*Cf. Chattanooga Tradesman, Nov. 1, 1901.

danger of a disfranchised, degraded and yet skilled competitor, and raises the note of warning. Is not this a drama worth the watching?

62. *The Employment of Skilled Negroes in the South.* The Chattanooga *Tradesman* made, in 1889 and 1891, inquiries into the status of Negro labor in the South. The employers questioned in 1889, employed 7,000 Negroes of whom possibly 2,000 were skilled or semi-skilled. "The general tenor of the replies indicated perfect satisfaction with Negro labor." In 1891 replies were received from the employers of 7,395 Negroes of whom 978 were skilled and many semi-skilled and the editor concluded that "the Negro, as a free laborer, as a medium skilled and common worker, is by no means a 'failure;' that he is really a remarkable success."*

In 1901, a third joint investigation into Negro skilled labor was made by the *Tradesman* and the Sociological Department of Atlanta University.** It was not an exhaustive inquiry and there is no way of knowing what proportion of the employers of skilled Negro laborers were reached. In 1891, twelve per cent. of the Negroes employed by those written to were skilled or semi-skilled; in 1901, twenty per cent.; 344 firms answered in 1901, employing 35,481 men, of whom 16,145 were Negroes, and 2,652 of these were skilled or semi-skilled workmen. Negroes were employed at given occupations as follows in the various establishments:

KINDS OF EMPLOYMENT FOLLOWED BY NEGROES, BY ESTABLISHMENTS.†

Shipping clerk.	1	Plasterers,	1
Saw sharpening,	5	Edgers,	14
Pan shoving,	3	Setters in planing mill,	9
Farmers,	2	Trimmers,	2
Engineers,	23	Teamsters,	1
Sawyers.	20	Graders,	4
Wood workers,	2	Lumber inspectors,	2
Pressmen,	29	Cupola tenders,	6
Meal cooks,	40	Stove mounters,	1
Linters,	17	Molders,	14
Handlers Cotton Seed Products,	1	Log cutters.	1
Handlers of Machines,	26	Watchmen,	1
Firemen,	45	Planers,	5
Huller men,	4	Raftsmen,	1
Grinders,	3	R. R. engineers,	2
Cake millers,	5	Wood turners,	2
Ginners,	14	Boiler makers,	2
Pipe fitters,	2	Furnace men,	3
Mill wrighters,	1	Core makers,	5
Pump men,	4	Electric linemen,	1
General oil mill men,	5	Painters,	3
Stockers,	1	Stone cutters,	1
Truckers,	1	Inspectors of castings,	1
Sackers,	1	Drillers,	1
Ice plant men,	1	General saw mill workers,	1
Cake formers,	3	Barrel makers,	1
Oilers,	4	Stave makers,	1
Machine repairers,	1	Plow polishers,	1
Strippers,	2	Stove tenders,	1
Foremen,	4	Pattern makers,	1
Blacksmiths,	14	Iron pourers,	1
Blocksmen,	5	Riveters and drillers,	1

*Yet Hoffman in his "Race Traits and Tendencies" twists these same figures into proof of the Negro's economic retrogression. **See schedule on p. 12.

†This table means, e. g., that 23 establishments employed Negroes as engineers and not that there were necessarily only 23 engineers.

(Kinds of Employment Followed by Negroes, by Establishments—*Continued.*)

Carpenters,	11	Sash door makers,	1
Mechanics,	2	Hanging sash doors,	1
Brick makers and setters,	6	Shingle packing,	1
Brick layers,	5	Section foreman on R. R.,	1

The reports according to kinds of business and number of skilled laborers employed are as follows:

REPORTS ACCORDING TO BUSINESS AND STATE.

	Tennessee.	Georgia.	Florida.	Alabama.	Mississippi.	Louisiana.	Texas.	Arkansas.	North Carolina.	South Carolina.	Virginia.	West Virginia.	Kentucky.	Unknown.	Total.
Founders and Machinists	9	9	4	3	3	1	4		3	4	3	1	1	1	46
Cotton Seed Products	4	8		12	12	8	26	5	9	10				2	96
Saw and Planing Mills	3			14	5	1	4	6	2		1		2		38
Lumber	7			7	1	8	1	8	6	2			2	1	43
Wagon Manufacture	1	2		1		1			1		1		2		9
Iron Works	4	1		6			2			1	3				17
Plow Manufacture	2	1									3		1		7
Stave Manufacture						1				1	1				3
Brick Manufacture	2	3			2		1	1	2		1				12
Stove Manufacture	1	1		1							2				5
Sugar Manufacture						2									2
Shingle Manufacture				2				1	1						4
Wood Working	2								1		2				5
Contractors and Builders		1						1					1		3
Hardwood Work	1							1							2
Manufacture of Pumps & Porch Col'ns	1														1
Manufacture of Handles				1											1
Sash, Doors, Blinds, etc	1			1	1		1	1	6	1			1		13
Furniture Manufacture					1						1	1	1		4
Ginning and Delinting				4	1										5
Steel and Galvanized Sheets													1		1
Farming and Merchandise							1								1
Refrigerator and Gin Manufacture	1							1							2
Soil Pipe and Fittings	1			1											2
Fruit Packing		1													1
Manufacture of Coffins and Caskets									1						1
Wood Textile Mill Supplies										1					1
Spoke Manufacture	2				1										3
Box Manufacture						1		1			1				3
Ship Building											3				3
Manufacture of Sad Irons and Hollow-ware	1														1
Brick and Lumber Builders' Supplies				1											1
Boiler Works			1		1										2
Tin Manufacture									1						1
Dishes, Fruit Packing and Veneering											1				1
House Finishing and Manufacturing						1									1
Furnace Manufacturing and Erecting	1														1
Mill Building	1														1
Manufacture of Farm Implements					1								1		2
Saw Manufacturing		1													1

NUMBER OF SKILLED LABORERS EMPLOYED, (NOT INCLUDING ABOUT 400 SEMI-SKILLED).

	Tennessee.	Georgia.	Florida.	Alabama.	Mississippi	Louisiana	Texas.	Arkansas.	N. Carolina.	S. Carolina.	Virginia.	W. Virginia	Kentucky.	Unknown.	Total.
Founders and Machinists..	137	34	8	1			3		5	5				2	195
Cotton Seed Products........	75	38		46	57	63	234	37	49	39				7	645
Saw and Planing Mills......				33	20		18	56	50		8				185
Lumber	26			11	6	33		70	21	13			2	1	183
Wagon Manufacture.........		14		20					4						38
Iron Works.....................	45			75							10				130
Plow Manufacture............	225	1													226
Stave Manufacture...........						5									15
Brick Manufacture..........	91	21			17		1		8		30				168
Stove Manufacture............											1				1
Sugar Manufacture...........						10									10
Shingle Manufacture.........				7					7						14
Wood Working................											3				3
Contractors and Builders..									3						3
Hardwood Work..............	1							14							15
Manufacture of Pumps and Porch Columns.............	1														1
Manufacture of Handles...															
Sash, Doors, Blinds, etc.....							1		1						2
Furniture Manufacture.....															
Ginning and Delinting......				4	7										11
Steel & Galvanized Sheets.															
Farming & Merchandise....															
Refrigerator Manufacture; Gin Manufacture............								8							8
Soil Pipe & Fittings..........															
Fruit Packing..................															
Manf. of Coffins & Caskets.															
Wood Textile Mill Supplies															
Spoke Manufacture..........	12				1										13
Box Manufacture............						2		5							7
Ship Building..................											151				151
Manufacture of Sad Irons and Hollowware........															
Brick & Lumber Builders' Supplies........................				13											13
Boiler Works..................					10										10
Tin Manufacture..............															
Dishes, Fruit Packing and Veneering..................											175				175
House Finishing & Manf'g						1									1
Furnace Manf. & Erecting.															
Mill Building..................															
Manf. of Farm Implements															
Saw Manufacturing..........															
Total	613	108	8	210	118	114	257	190	148	57	378		2	10	2213

It is difficult to get a statement of the wages paid in tabular form. The following table gives the *maximum* wages per day paid skilled Negro laborers in various industries:

MAXIMUM WAGES, PER DAY, PAID ANY SKILLED NEGRO LABORER, ACCORDING TO ESTABLISHMENTS AND KINDS OF BUSINESS.

	Under $1.	$1.00–$1.17.	$1.25–$1.45.	$1.50.	$1.60.	$1.65.	$1.66⅔.	$1.75.	$1.80.	$1.83⅓.	$2.00.	$2.25.	$2.50	$2.72.	$3.00 & over.	Totals.
Contractors and Builders				1											1	2
Founders and Machinists	1	3	2	1			1	2			4		2	1	2	19
Stove Manufacturing								1					1			2
Lumber Manufacturing	1	2	5	2		1		2			3	1	7		2	26
Wagon Manufacturing			1	3								1	1			6
Woodworking			1								1					2
Ginning and Delinting	1	1											1			3
Boiler Works													1			1
Iron Works			1	1				1			3		2		1	9
Stave Manufacturing													2			2
Brick Manufacturing		1	1	1	1					1	1	1				7
Saw and Planing Mills	2	2	3	2				5			2	1	1		4	22
Plow Manufacturing		1									1					2
Gin & Refrigerator Manufacturing								1								1
Furniture Manufacturing		1														1
Sash, Doors, Blinds, etc				1		1					1					3
Mfg. Wood Pumps & Porch Columns															1	1
Hardwood Works			1	1												2
House Finishing and Manufacturing							1									1
Steel and Galvanized Sheets											1					1
Brick and Lumber Builders' Supplies											1					1
Spoke Manufacturing		1	1	1												3
Box Manufacturing											2					2
Sugar Manufacturing																2
Ship Building			1										1		1	1
Cotton Seed Products	3	17	3	10	1			8	1		17	3	4	1	1	69
Total	8	29	20	24	2	2	2	20	1	1	37	7	23	2	13	191

Condensing we have this table of maximum wages:

Under $1	— 8	establishments.
$1 -$1.49	— 49	"
1.50- 1.99	— 52	"
2.00- 2.99	— 69	"
3.00 or more	— 13	"
Total	191	"

The answers to the various questions were as follows:

A. *How do Negroes compare in efficiency with white workmen?*

Answers.	Establishments Answering.	Negroes Employed—Skilled.	Negroes Employed—Semi-Skilled.
"Far inferior."	17	96	38
"Not as good."	28	135	55
"Poor average, some as good."	23	260	57
"Better" for "this work" or "at same wages" or "than available whites."	42	382	89
"As good."	43	456	145
"Better."	19	665	80
No answer	4	79	
Cannot say	3	34	
"Cannot compare, employ no whites."	9	49	7

Some of the comments were:

"No good, but the white help is mighty poor, too."

"Not reliable—lack judgment."

"Haven't as good hands for skilled work."

"Would give perfect satisfaction if they were steady."

"Prompt, willing and steady, but lack judgment."

"Not as quick to learn, but stick closer to work."

"More easily controlled."

"As good or better."

"Perfect satisfaction."

B. *Are Negro Workmen Improving in Efficiency?*

Answers.	Establishments Answering	Negroes Employed. Skilled	Semi-Skilled.
"Yes."	64	1,261	114
"To some extent."	47	415	136
"Cannot tell."	13	137	10
"No."	46	252	101
Unanswered	26	198	119

C. *How much education have your Negro workmen received?*

Answers	Establishments Ans.	Negroes Employed. Skilled	Semi-Skilled.
"None."	16	173	14
"Very little."	68	1,125	99
"Majority can read and write."	33	302	141
"All can read and write."	27	204	68
"Common school training."	16	115	45
"Good education."	2	10	4
"All they can stand."	1	1	
Unanswered	33	283	109

Taking those who report that their workman can read and write, or have received more training than this, we find that they answer as follows to this question:

D. *What effect has this education had?*

Answers.	Establishments	Employing Negroes. Skilled	Semi-Skilled
'Bad effect."	16	73	66
"No effect."	9	134	22
"A little learning is a dangerous thing."	4	30	57
"Little effect."	4	7	13
"Cannot say."	5	41	
"Helps some, hinders others."	5	31	
"Would help if industrial."	1	40	
"Good effect."	28	257	89

Some comments follow:

"Think they feel more responsibility than the ignorant ones—want more and are more willing to work to get what they want."

"Somewhat improved by it."

"The education has had a good effect on them and I had rather employ these Negroes with education than if they had no education."

"Educating a Negro makes him worthless as a laborer. He gets saucy and thinks he is as good as a white man. Uneducated Negroes give no trouble. Educating a Negro makes him mean and indolent. You find more criminals in educated Negroes than in uneducated."

"Makes them better citizens by giving them means to employ their minds. The bad Negro, as a rule, is the most ignorant."

"There is some more indolence and disposition to loaf among Negroes who have a smattering of education, although there are exceptions. We would much prefer to have a man who can at least read, write and figure a little than one entirely ignorant, provided he is a steady worker."

"Enables them to undertake more. It is questionable whether education tends to modify or decrease their humility towards white men, probably it does. They are still, on the whole, inferior to the white man."

"Can't say, except in our opinion it follows as a matter of course that the more a man learns, the more he is worth."

"Has done but little good, owing to lack of sense to start with."

"We believe educating the Negro is having the effect of taking them from the farms, going to the towns and cities hunting public works at better pay. This is but natural and we believe in the end will prove beneficial."

"We can't but feel that education improves them, our experience, though, has been that those who have some knowledge of books are profligate. This may be due to bad selection on our part."

"What kind? We guess you mean training. A Negro can not be educated. We only want a Negro with educated hands and bodies. Some darkies can learn to read and write a little—and just then they are ready and ripe for the penitentiary or for Hades."

"From our observation the result is not good from an industrial standpoint. Our opinion being that the trouble is that the little education they have received has been literary instead of industrial."

"It has detracted from his usefulness in positions where he is the most useful, such as hard manual labor, without fitting him to take a better position in the ranks of skilled labor."

"We have but few positions where education of itself would be of much value. Coupled with other good qualities it would have value. Our colored people are generally self-respecting and we believe better because of their steady employment, but they seem to lack in thrift, frugality and in saving their wages."

"We believe that education would have a good effect if with it there was some systemized effort to make them property owners, and to build up a healthy interest in their particular community. This does not seem to be the trend of affairs, and until present conditions change, as they will, perhaps sooner than any of us think now, we do not look for much radical improvement."

"We have heard a good deal about education spoiling the colored man as a laborer; our experience here, however, convinces us that the better he is educated the better he is able to compete with the white man in giving close attention to the business that employers require of him, thereby giving better satisfaction and better work. It is true in many cases that an education seems to spoil the colored man, but we think he would be spoiled anyway, just the same as among white men many times, the highly educated seem to feel themselves above doing manual labor."

E. *Shall you continue to employ skilled Negro labor?*

Yes.	140 establishments.	1,950 skilled.	293 semi-skilled.
No.	16 "	30 "	44 "
Prefer white labor.	5 "	29 "	25 "
Shall employ semi-skilled.	3 "		28 "
Only as laborers.	1 "		5 "
Can't say.	1 "		1 "
As they drop out we shall fill their places with whites.	1 "	1 "	1 "
Unanswered.	29 "	207 "	79 "

Some general comments on Negro workmen follow:

"Yes, they understand my way of having work done and are willing workers when treated right. I never allow them imposed upon by any one and have no strikes; they are the best judges of human nature on earth."

"The most satisfactory sawyer, shop man (blacksmithing and wood working), green yard fireman, train track fireman, logging engine fireman, log-trippers, cant hook man, night watchman, edger man, trimmer man, or teamsters, and men grading lumber in saw mill, are all Negroes."

"Best laborers we can get. We believe the Negro the best laborer in the South."

"Are more tractable, steadier and can be depended upon in their particular places. In an emergency whites have better judgment. On the whole we prefer Negroes where it is possible to use them."

"The work they do is well done and for furnace work equally as efficient as that of white men and indeed I prefer them."

"Some are just as good as any or most white men, while a greater number are just as poor as the white trash."

"After living in the South for twenty years and employing from one to twenty Negroes all the time will say from any standard there are no skilled workmen with black skins, and I have employed the best to be found in Montgomery, as carpenters, bricklayers, engineers, firemen and machine operators."

"We find that many of our most thrifty and intelligent Negroes are drifting North and securing employment in the large industries about Pittsburg, and many of them making good records for efficiency."

"We have just this day begun the employment of Negro molders for our stove foundry. We have been employing white molders for the past fifteen years but as nearly all the foundries in this city are employing Negro molders and seem well satisfied with the result, we decided to do so also. We believe we will make a success of the venture, but will not be able to answer your questions until we have had them at work for awhile."

"We consider them a necessity in our business because white labor is not obtainable. Considering the condition of their ancestry and the conditions in which they themselves live I think they are doing very well indeed. Future generations will doubtless see the race in a better condition and more intelligent, making better citizens."

"In this line they are much superior to white labor. White men would not stand the heat and grease. We don't want white labor. They are too prone to strike. Give them the earth and they would strike for the moon. White men *could* be more efficient than Negroes, but they *wont.*"

"Do the same work and obey better, more profit, less trouble."

"Some of them display excellent judgment, while others are stupid. They don't expect as much as white men, and do, if anything, more faithful work than the white labor."

"The younger class are more given to loafing and light work. When given places as foremen, or semi-responsible, they are usually very exacting."

"A Negro is a Negro with us and is made to keep his place."

"The white workmen do not like to work side by side with the Negro workmen. However, they treat them politely, and there is the kindliest feeling between whites and blacks here."

63. *The Negro Inventor.* It was a Massachusetts lawyer who said in response to an inquiry from the United States Patent office: "I never knew a Negro to invent anything but lies." Nevertheless, the Patent Office was able in 1900 to report a partial list of 357 patents issued to Negro inventors. They were issued as follows:

Before 1875	21	1890–95	90
1875–80	15	1895–1901	126
1880–85	31	Year unknown	1
1885–90	73	Total	357

The inventions may be classified as follows:

Domestic appliances,	101	Building apparatus,	4
Transportation,	10	Games,	6
Agricultural implements.	15	Textile and paper-making apparatus,	18
Horse and vehicle appliances,	32	Mercantile appliances,	5
Telegraph, telephone, and electrical apparatus,	27	Photography,	2
Medical and surgical apparatus and appliances,	4	Fire escapes and fire extinguishers,	4
Boot, shoes, and shoe working apparatus,	12	Musical instruments,	3
Railroad appliances,	60	Books and printing and writing devices,	7
Machinery & mechanical devices,	35	Miscellaneous,	3
		Total,	357

The inventors according to number of inventions are:

Inventor.	Inventions.
1	27
1	22
1	16
1	10
1	8
1	7
3	5
4	4
14	3
28	2
138	1
193	357

The most prolific inventors are Mr. Granville T. Words, of New York, with 27 electrical devices, many of which are in use all over the country, and one of which is the well-known transmitter used by the Bell Telephone Co.;

and Mr. Elijah McCoy, of Detroit, with 22 inventions (and another in collaboration) who is the pioneer in the matter of machinery lubricators, and whose inventions are used on nearly every railroad in the country. With such a record the mechanical genius of the Negro can hardly be doubted.

64. *Summary.* We have studied in considerable detail the history of the Negro artisan, the industrial schools, the condition of Negro mechanics throughout the country, the attitude of organized labor toward the Negro, the opinions of employers, and Negro inventions. On the whole the survey has been encouraging, although there is much to deplore and criticise. Our conclusions may be summed up as follows:

1. Slavery trained artisans, but they were for the most part careless and inefficient. Only in exceptional cases were they first-class mechanics.

2. Industrial schools are needed. They are costly and, as yet, not well organized or very efficient, but they have given the Negro an ideal of manual toil and helped to a better understanding between whites and Negroes in the South. Eventually they may be expected to send out effective artisans, as they have already begun to do.

3. There are a large number of Negro mechanics all over the land, but especially in the South. Some of these are progressive, efficient workmen. More are careless, slovenly and ill-trained. There are signs of lethargy among these artisans and work is slipping from them in some places; in others they are awakening and seizing the opportunities of the new industrial south.

4. The labor unions, with 1,200,000 members, have less than 40,000 Negroes, mostly in a few unions, and largely semi-skilled laborers like miners. Some labor leaders have striven against color prejudice, but it exists and keeps the mass of Negroes out of many trades. This leads to complicated problems, both industrial, political and social.

5. Employers on the whole are satisfied with Negro skilled labor and many of them favor education as tending to increase the efficiency of Negroes. Others think it will spoil the docility and tractableness of Negro labor. The employment of Negro skilled labor is slowly increasing.

6. The Negro evinces considerable mechanical ingenuity.

On the whole this study of a phase of the vast economic development of the Negro race in America but emphasizes the primal and emphatic need of intelligence. The situation is critical and developing swiftly. Deftly guided with the larger wisdom of men and deeper benevolence of great hearts, an outcome of good to all cannot be doubted. Muddled by half trained men and guided by selfish and sordid interests and all the evils of industrial history may easily be repeated in the South. "*Wisdom*" then "*is the principal thing; therefore, get wisdom, and with all thy getting, get understanding.*"

FINIS.

INDEX.

LaVergne, TN USA
06 September 2010

196062LV00004B/37/A